THE OTHER SIDE OF THE HAND OF GOD

THE OTHER SIDE OF THE HAND OF GOD

INSIDE THE MOST NOTORIOUS MATCH IN WORLD CUP HISTORY

ASIF BURHAN

First published by Pitch Publishing, 2026

1

Pitch Publishing
9 Donnington Park, 85 Birdham Road
Chichester, West Sussex, PO20 7AJ
www.pitchpublishing.co.uk
info@pitchpublishing.co.uk

Set in Warnock Pro 11.5/16pt

Typeset by Pitch Publishing

Cover design by Olner Design

Printed and bound in Great Britain by TJ Books, Padstow

The authorised representative in the EEA is
Easy Access System Europe OÜ, Mustamäe tee 50, 10621 Tallinn, Estonia gpsr.requests@easproject.com

A CIP catalogue record for this book is available from the British Library

ISBN 978-1-83680-520-5

Papers used by Pitch Publishing are from well-managed forests and other responsible sources

Contents

To Stewart Lester Rowe (1950–2024)

Acknowledgements

For all those who supported me on my journey from being a boy who could only dream of being at World Cups to a man who went to one final as a fan, then went from being an unpaid blogger on the game who worked his way up to be an accredited journalist at another World Cup Final.

To my beautiful wife Nicola for encouraging me to go for it when I said I wanted to write a book. Thanks for putting up with me over the past two years whenever I was distant, moody or seemingly forever preoccupied with events from the last century on a foreign field rather than enjoying our wonderful life together in the present.

To my agent Jonathan Harris for persevering with this project despite numerous setbacks, and to the people at Pitch Publishing for giving my obsession with a single game of football a platform in print.

Finally, to the late Diego Armando Maradona, who captivated me as a boy and still inspires me as an adult. In 2017, I fulfilled one ambition of watching you play – and score a goal – in a FIFA Legends match, and now I realise another. I hope this book does justice to your legacy. May you rest in peace.

Introduction

–Diego Maradona

It is a testimony to the magnitude of the 1986 World Cup quarter-final between Argentina and England that, due to one event in this match, the phrase 'Hand of God' has passed into popular parlance, not to signify divine intervention, but as a handball in a game of football.

For everything that he subsequently achieved in the game, and everything he became as perhaps the ultimate icon of devotion in the world's number-one sport, when Diego Maradona passed away in November 2020, the majority of English newspapers led with the image of him punching a ball past Peter Shilton. Leading French sports paper *L'Équipe* simply said, with a nod to the phrase, 'Le Dieu est mort' (God is dead).

On a BBC *Match of the Day* Podcast in 2022, Gary Lineker described the match as the most famous football game ever played. His consolation goal in the final stages turned him into England's first Golden Boot winner at the FIFA World Cup, and ultimately one of the most venerated personalities in the game, one of the many footnotes from a match that changed lives.

Many of the arguments used to justify the introduction of Video Assistant Referees ahead of the 2018 World Cup revolved around the prevention of a goal such as Maradona scored six minutes into the second half ever again being decisive in a game of such importance. Some even argue that the use of VAR may have even denied us Maradona's 'Goal of the Century' four minutes later, Glenn Hoddle having been taken out by a late challenge from Óscar Ruggeri seconds before Héctor Enrique provided the 'assist' for Maradona's never-to-be-forgotten slalom into immortality.

Would the sport have been any richer for those interventions? Beneath the hype and controversy, this was, by and large, a poor game of football, going nowhere fast until Maradona broke the monotony with his out-of-the-box thinking. At the Estadio Azteca on 22 June 1986, he proved himself to be the ultimate game-changer, even if it meant breaking the rules of fair play.

After the halcyon perception of the previous World Cup in Mexico 16 years earlier as being won by a Brazilian team encapsulating everything beautiful in the game, some may regard Maradona's handball as symbolic of the dark cynicism pervading the game at the top level, the definition of winning at all costs. Certainly, that might have been the case had Maradona's first goal stood alone, as a cheating act committed by an average footballer forever defined by a single moment of infamy.

However, Maradona was anything but an average footballer. He was never destined to be. Four minutes later, he demonstrated it conclusively. No other goal as his second of the match that afternoon has reached such heights, inspired such adoration, meant so much for so many people. Not for nothing is it known as the 'Goal of the Century'. It took less than a week for the owners of the Estadio Azteca to commemorate it – Maradona himself unveiling a plaque in honour of the goal ahead of the 1986 World Cup Final the following weekend. It still sits alongside another one marking the 'match of the century' between Italy and West Germany at the same venue in 1970.

The 'Goal of the Century' plaque would have remained even had Argentina lost to West Germany in the World Cup Final. Like Johan Cruyff in 1974, whether or not Maradona won the trophy seemed almost secondary to the awe he had already engendered among the people who saw him play. The fact that Maradona did lift the World

Cup cemented his place in the pantheon at the age of 25 and gilded everything else he may or may not achieve later in his career.

He had already been recognised as the world's greatest player for at least four years. He had already become the first player in history to attract two world record transfer fees for his 1982 move to FC Barcelona and his subsequent transfer to SS Napoli in 1984.

After Mexico, he would inspire the southern Italian side to their first and second Serie A titles as well as the 1989 UEFA Cup, monumental achievements for a historically underachieving club. In 1990, he led a poor Argentina to another World Cup Final, and another four years on, until he failed a drug test, his return to the national side, at the age of 33, galvanised a team who had struggled to qualify, transforming them into the most captivating side to watch during the first week of the 1994 finals.

With or without the 1986 World Cup, Diego Maradona was a great footballer. Yet those four minutes against England on 22 June 1986 elevated him to a stratosphere beyond his sport, a place few footballers ever occupy and somewhere perhaps no one except him ever has.

On 4 May 2022, I visited the Sotheby's Auction House on New Bond Street in London. Beyond the reception, a café was a hive of activity during a spring afternoon as people from all walks of life milled about. Opposite the café was a square room patrolled by a single security guard. Occasionally someone leaving the café would peer momentarily into this darkly lit area, wondering what was inside. Most people realised that a football shirt was on sale but few hung around for long.

The auction for the shirt ended at four o'clock that afternoon. It was to be conducted online so there was no need for any potential bidders to be at Sotheby's in person or even in the country. The opening bid for this two-week auction had held steady for several days and satisfied the reserve price placed on it by the seller. Like an eBay auction, the price could be viewed in real time on the Sotheby's website.

INTRODUCTION

In the last few minutes, more bids began to be placed and I sat opposite the reception desk refreshing my tablet, desperate not to miss the final few moments of the auction. In front of me, three officials from the auction house were doing likewise on their desktop computer as the seconds to four o'clock counted down. The figure began to leap dramatically until it settled once and for all on a number that would make history … £7,142,500![1]

Over seven million pounds for an unwashed piece of blue polyester bought from a Mexican market store with a wonky, unofficial national team crest not even sewn on all the way around, and worn threads visible around the midriff.

It instantly became the most valuable match-worn shirt in world history. Eighteen months later, Lionel Messi auctioned six of the shirts he wore during Argentina's 2022 World Cup triumph at Sotheby's in New York, including the one from probably the most epic World Cup Final ever played. Together they sold for $7.8 million, around £1 million less than this one.

Why? This one was Maradona's. This was the shirt he wore when he scored both the most controversial and most celebrated goals in the history of the World Cup. And it was against England, the country Argentina wanted to defeat more than any other.

Having now won the World Cup, it is undeniable that Lionel Messi's achievements on the pitch have surpassed Diego Maradona's.

Moving towards his sixth World Cup tournament at the age of 39, Messi has also been greater for far, far longer. Yet, Messi's achievements were on the pitch, the legend of Maradona went beyond the field he played on. In the words of Maradona himself, 'Messi may or may not be greater than I was. Now I scored two goals against England, goals that honoured the boys who fell in the Malvinas [Falkland Islands] and their families. I gave them some

---

1   https://www.sothebys.com/en/buy/auction/2022/the-hand-of-god/diego-maradona-the-hand-of-god-goal-of-the-century?locale=en

consolation, and no one else – and I mean no one – is going to be able to do that.

'What happened that day was unique. Beyond words. You can't write it.'

Nevertheless, here I go anyway …

The Colossus of
Santa Úrsula

Just over a month before the start of the 1966 World Cup, the FIFA President Sir Stanley Rous visited the Mexico City suburb of Santa Úrsula, 16 kilometres south of the capital. He was there to witness the inauguration of a new stadium.

Built on the site of a lava plain created by the eruption nearly 2,000 years earlier of the nearby Xitle volcano, the stadium was the brainchild of Emilio Azcárraga Milmo. Azcárraga was the man who would eventually take over his father's business, Televisa (TElevision Via SAtellite), which bankrolled and exclusively broadcast the 1986 World Cup around the world.

Pedro Ramírez Vázquez won an architectural competition to design the new stadium. His proposal had the advantage of having a fully cantilevered roof, with no supports holding it up from the inside, which was the case at Wembley Stadium, fully enclosed for the first time ahead of the 1966 World Cup.

Vázquez's initial blueprint meant for the stadium to have rectangular sides parallel to the playing surface but subsequently this was altered. The ground would be more of an oval, with each of the four sides slightly curved but, without an athletics track, the first rows of seating would still be close to the pitch. This so-called 'quadric plan', unobstructed by pillars, allowed for the best possible view from every single seat in the stadium.

And it would have many. The new ground opened with a capacity for 107,494 spectators, making it the largest purpose-built, all-seater football stadium in the world, The opening match between Necaxa and Torino on 29 May 1966 finished in a 2-2 draw.

In a competition run by the Mexican postal service, suggestions for a name of this new stadium were sent in, with the most popular winning out. The one contained in most entries was a name paying homage to the country's ancient civilisation, the Estadio Azteca.

Ahead of the 1986 World Cup, the capacity was enlarged and the stadium hosted nine matches, including the third of the four quarter-finals at the 13th edition of the tournament. Despite hosting two World Cup finals, it is this match that is immortalised outside the entrance of the stadium.

On a black metal plaque in gold lettering beneath the logo of the 'Mexico '86' World Cup are inscribed the following words: 'The Estadio Azteca pays tribute to Diego Maradona for his extraordinary goal scored in the Argentina-England match with which they advanced to the semi-finals – 22 June 1986.'

In 2026, the Estadio Azteca in Mexico City will become the first stadium in the world to stage matches in three World Cup finals when Mexico, after staging the tournaments in 1970 and 1986, co-host the 23rd edition of the world's greatest competition alongside Canada and the United States. This time, it will not be centre stage. Once the largest all-seater stadium in the world, the requirement of individual bucket seats and the need to have more hospitality areas have reduced its once colossal 120,000 capacity to a proposed 87,523.

In 1986, the Estadio Azteca became the first stadium in history to stage the final in two World Cup tournaments. It was a feat unmatched until 2014 when the Estádio Maracanã in Rio de Janeiro, completely renovated since its first World Cup in 1950, became the second.

Aside from four matches involving the hosts Brazil back in 1950, the Azteca has also played host to the only six-figure crowds in the tournament's history, as 13 of its 19 World Cup matches have attracted attendances of over 100,000.

The quarter-final between Argentina and England was watched by an official attendance of 114,580, the seventh-largest crowd at any World Cup. It is the biggest by far to witness England play in the tournament, almost 20,000 more than those who were at Wembley to see them win the 1966 World Cup. The 1986 World Cup quarter-final recorded the highest-ever attendance for a match not involving the host nation outside the final.

Those six-figure crowds always seemed magical to me growing up in a pre-Premier League age when a crowd of over 40,000 in the First Division was a novelty, reserved for a local derby or a game played over the Christmas period.

The official film of the 1970 FIFA World Cup, *The World at Their Feet*, features a small boy practising his skills entranced by the prospect of world-class footballers playing at the Estadio Azteca. He seemed to speak for me when he dreamed that 'if I could get to the Azteca Stadium, just see the Azteca ...'

I had watched matches at the old Wembley Stadium, sitting among crowds of 75,000 upwards, but that was still 40,000 (the population of a reasonably sized town) less than the Azteca attendances. Wembley was the self-styled 'Home of Football' and seemed vast, so how grand must the Azteca be? I had to find out for myself.

The perfectionist in me was never going to be happy travelling over 5,000 miles to watch a game at a half-full Azteca. For years, I pored over the crowd figures of Mexico's international games in *World Soccer* magazine. With World Cup qualifying often a formality for *El Tri*, there was little interest in most of their competitive matches, except one.

Whenever their ever-improving neighbours from across their northern border were in town, the encounter took on an added significance beyond mere World Cup qualifying. Historically, the Mexicans always defeated the United States, who did not qualify for a World Cup finals for 40 years between 1950 and 1990. Then in 1994, the United States hosted the World Cup and eventually established their first professional league since the end of the NASL (North American Soccer League). Before long, a strange thing started to happen, the United States started to beat Mexico on a regular basis, at least when they played at home.

From the turn of the century, the United States defeated Mexico ten times in 15 matches, including their first-ever meeting at the World Cup finals in 2002. The United States also won their home qualifier for the 2010 tournament, strategically played in Columbus, Ohio, a city with a low Mexican population, minimising the numbers who might turn up to support the away team.

However, at the Azteca, Mexico remained unbeatable against the United States. Nine previous meetings had brought eight wins and one solitary goalless draw. Yet, the United States, fresh from stunning the world that summer by ending Spain's 35-match unbeaten record at the FIFA Confederations Cup, were opponents to be taken seriously and talked optimistically about ending the Azteca curse.

It was August 2009. I flew from London to Mexico City via Paris. It was my first experience of high altitude. Like a madman, after checking into my hotel, I immediately ventured to an even higher plain, to the neighbouring city of Toluca, another World Cup venue in both 1970 and 1986. At 2,680 metres (8,790 feet) above sea level, Toluca is the highest-ever venue to stage a World Cup finals match. I was there for more than historical curiosity. That afternoon, their high-flying local club side CD Toluca were playing an Apertura league match against Pumas UNAM at the Estadio Nemesio Díez, known to everyone as the Bombonera (the chocolate box).

What strikes you most about watching football in Mexico is how authentic the experience is. You would be hard-pressed to find a country more passionate about the beautiful game. Outside the stadium, as well as the usual concession stands, stalls of people selling football cards peppered the exterior of the ground.

The Bombonera, which hosted seven matches in 1970 and 1986, including Mexico's first-ever World Cup quarter-final, against Italy, is quintessentially English. Four steep, asymmetric rectangular stands come down within spitting distance of the touchline and are hemmed in by rows of suburban housing. Stanchions impeded the view in every direction and chicken wire separated the players from the baying fans. Although it has since been renovated, in 2009 it still looked every inch the stadium in which Julio César Romero and Enzo Scifo first cut a swathe during the group stage of the 1986 finals.

Toluca won 3-0 and went on to finish top of the regular season standings but this match was just an appetiser for the main course at the Estadio Azteca four days later. After the obligatory visit to the pyramids of the Sun and Moon at Teotihuacán, I visited the modern-day temple to the gods of football.

Now, a train line runs directly to the Estadio Azteca, but in 1986 it fell short, requiring fans to complete the remaining 6km south from Tasqueña metro station down the Calzada de Tlalpan thoroughfare by taxi or rickety minibus.

The new Estadio Azteca station now sits on the opposite side of the Tlalpan to the stadium. To cross the highway, one must traverse the road on a pedestrian bridge carrying you over the highway and offering the visitor their first elevated view of the famous monolith over the top of the adjacent buildings.

The exterior is in the brutalist architectural style, with exposed vertical concrete struts criss-crossed with shallow ramps circling the structure. The stadium was built to withstand the frequent seismic activity that is a constant threat to every building in the area. One such earthquake, measuring 8.0 on the Richter Scale, devastated the city eight months before the 1986 World Cup but left the Azteca relatively unscathed.

Walking around the concourse, I came across the iconic *El Sol Rojo* (Red Sun) monument designed by renowned American sculptor Alexander Calder ahead of the 1968 Summer Olympic Games. The three-legged steel structure is, at 25.7 metres high, the largest sculpture created by Calder. A giant red disc sitting on a stark three-dimensional black tripod has been stylised into the logo of the stadium, appearing on all of its ticketing and merchandise.

Calder's monument, for decades a meeting point for fans all over the world, had been restored earlier that year by American Express, whose emblem now sits around the circular base. However, in 1986, the original *El Sol Rojo* was used to frame any exterior shot of the Azteca, its indescribable shape as unfathomable to television viewers as the spider shadow on the centre of the pitch.

After purchasing my ticket to the match from a scalper on the concourse at a little over face value, I paid to experience the obligatory stadium tour. Having just missed the only English-language slot of the day, I joined a group of about 15 other Hispanic fans on the Spanish-speaking tour.

We visited the bowels of the stadium first. The subterranean changing rooms where Maradona had led his team-mates in a medley of terrace chants moments after defeating England seemed familiar to me. As did the ramp leading up towards the pitch and the heat of the midday sun illuminating the grass. To the side of the field, a lawnmower was parked having just trimmed the pitch, its fresh clippings still in the grass catcher. I hung back to pocket some of the hallowed turf, which I smuggled back to England but have long since misplaced.

The female tour guide took us on to the pitch – something that would never be allowed in a major stadium in Europe – into the penalty area closest to the tunnel. This happened to be the one. The one where Maradona had scored his two goals against England. As the tour guide spoke in Spanish, I stood away, attempting to locate the spot from which Maradona had jumped to punch the ball past Peter Shilton. Sensing why I was there, she suddenly looked at me and said in English, 'And this was the goal where the "Hand of God" was scored.'

Two days later, I returned on the suburban train to Estadio Azteca, but this time with a lot more people. Crossing the narrow pedestrian bridge was now a slow process and the walk to the stadium was an assault to the senses. The nasal sounds of plastic horns being blown, a year before anyone in Europe or South America became familiar with African vuvuzelas; the sight of lurid green shirts on Mexican fans in the technicolour summer sunshine that was, just south of the Tropic of Cancer, already burning through my clothes.

Having bought my ticket from unofficial sources, my fear was that I had somehow been duped into purchasing a fake and my once-in-a-lifetime opportunity to watch a game in the Azteca would be denied me, and I instead would end up facing a police interrogation in a language I did not comprehend. Luckily my ticket was accepted, its stub removed and I was through on to the stadium esplanade made so familiar to me by endlessly watching archive footage of the 1970 and 1986 FIFA World Cups in Mexico.

Hawkers displayed their wares on the ground, with most fans eager to purchase square pieces of cushioning decorated with an infinite number of designs and club crests.

Once I had found my entrance gate, I began the long, long climb to the top. During the tour, we had been taken to the top by a lift but that was not an option now. The stadium's exterior was encased by a series of gently sloping ramps that wound their way to the top of the bowl.

Sitting halfway up the vast upper tier, the stadium seemed to have changed little from 23 years earlier. The sinuous curves of the stands instantly recognisable to the boy who had been endlessly fascinated by every picture he could find in books and magazines on the 1986 World Cup.

The seemingly fluorescent green grass, more vivid under the light of a fierce Mexican sun. The digital scoreboard, repeatedly featured in 'Hero' during Argentina's matches was still operational with its 1980s dot matrix display relaying information along the bottom of the second tier. The square goal nets that became so familiar to viewers of the 1986 World Cup were still there, now black instead of white. Looking down on them, they seemed to be as far from the goal line as the edge of the six-yard box in the opposite direction.

There were some notable differences. In addition to the installation of red plastic seats in the lower tier, two giant video screens had been installed underneath the thick rim of the grey concrete roof, which had reduced the overall capacity from 115,000 to 105,000. On the upper concourse, where I had purchased one of the cheap seats, there were no actual seats as such. The steps of the bowl were dissected by small right-angled pieces of metal screwed into the concrete to act as seat dividers.

Each place had a number but no one paid much effort to find the number designated on their ticket. The majority of the locals brought a cheap foam cushion in with them to give their backside a reprieve from sitting on the naked concrete. Others used the free newspapers or other leaflets they had been given by traders outside the ground.

The first roars bellowed around the bowl as the fans recited the traditional football chant first popularised during the 1986 World Cup following its use in a Carta Blanca beer commercial: 'Chiquitibum a la bim bom ba, chiquitibum a la bim bom ba, a la bio, a la bao, a la bim bom ba, México, México, rah rah rah.'

A mid-afternoon heat haze gave the in-person matchday view from the stand a similar fuzzy quality to the transatlantic satellite coverage on analogue television in 1986. The first sight of the gringos from the north elicits ear-splitting whistles. The playing of the 'Star-Spangled Banner' national anthem is met with a similar shrill response.

As the Mexican national anthem is played, every single man and woman, young and old, performed the *saludo a la bandera* (salute to the flag), holding their right arm, palm down, straight across their chest. The hymn, a call to all patriots to fight for their homeland, infuses the crowd with a fervour that never subsides during the entirety of the game.

The match was everything that I had hoped it would be. The United States took an early lead after Landon Donovan's clever pass released Charlie Davis to score with a smart finish. As he celebrated by using the corner flag as a microphone, Mexican plastic horns were hurled at him.

The threat of an historic first defeat on home soil to the neighbours from the north merely whipped the hysteria up several notches. It took just ten minutes for Mexico to equalise, Israel Castro striking home a fulminating shot from outside the area that crashed in off the underside of the crossbar. It would be Castro's only-ever goal in international football.

Mexico came out all guns blazing in the second half, attacking the end at which I was sat, seemingly several thousand feet above the action. All the power of the Azteca came at me in the second half as *El Tri* unleashed wave upon wave of attack towards the goal Tim Howard was defending.

The intensity built and built until the 82nd minute, when the new star of Mexican football, Andrés Guardado, surged past Donovan on the right and cut the ball back for substitute striker Miguel Sabah. He controlled the ball and set himself before thrashing the ball over Howard into the roof of the square net.

The result sent the locals home satisfied that they had maintained their supremacy over their northern rivals, even though the United States would qualify as group winners, one point ahead of Mexico.

The crowd figure was as large as I had hoped for – 104,499. It is the first, and probably only, six-figure football attendance I will ever be part of and made me feel like I had lived my own authentic 'Mexico '86' experience. The Chiquitibum chants echoed through the concrete skeleton of this historic monolith on the way down the ramps and beyond.

The Un-Level Playing Field

Gary Lineker believes the biggest advantage that the footballers now have over their predecessors is the playing surface. 'If there's one thing I'm envious about in the modern game that's it, because I'd never miss. In those days we used to have to watch and wait to see which bobble it would hit, but now it's just like a carpet.'

No football stadium in the world has hosted more matches at the World Cup finals than the Estadio Azteca in Mexico City. Ahead of the 2026 World Cup, when it will stage another five games, a new hybrid pitch is being installed that will combine natural grass with advanced ventilation, drainage and air-injection systems.

None of those were available during the last century, the overused grass surface forced to withstand extremes of climate enclosed within its steep concrete bowl. As recently as November 2018, an American football game between the Kansas City Chiefs and Los Angeles Rams had to be moved away from the Azteca with less than a week's notice because the pitch did not meet NFL (National Football League) standards for playability and consistency.

Speaking to Sotheby's in 2022, Glenn Hoddle described the Estadio Azteca as 'the best stadium I've ever played in … but the pitch wasn't the best, the pitch was awful'.[2] In 1970, it had staged

---

2   https://www.youtube.com/watch?si=WeJBpV_o-a-6uQnr&v=S7if41rfOUw&feature=youtu.be

ten of the 32 games at the three-week tournament. Sixteen years on, in a now 52-game competition, it was the venue for nine matches. The quarter-final would be the seventh of those within 23 days.

After finishing second in Group F, England were spared having to stay and play another game in the furnace of Monterrey, their first-round venue – which was the dubious prize for the group winners, Morocco. They instead travelled 700 kilometres south, and 1,750 metres up, to the slightly cooler but more elevated and more populous Mexican capital.

Nine of the England starting line-up against Argentina had played at the stadium the previous summer during the preparatory Copa Ciudad de Mexico tournament in Mexico City, narrowly losing twice to Italy and Mexico before defeating an ill-prepared West Germany side 3-0 in a third standalone match.

In contrast, none of the Argentinian starting line-up had ever played at the Azteca. Two preparatory matches away to Mexico in 1984 and 1985 had been staged in Monterrey and Puebla and both ended in score draws. Argentina had last played in the stadium in 1975, and three previous matches there for the national team had brought two defeats and a draw.

In fact, going into the 1986 World Cup, the senior Argentina team had never previously won a match on Mexican soil and, amazingly, have not played in the country at all in the four decades since the tournament. Nevertheless, at the 13th World Cup finals, they had recorded three wins out of four so far, the first two of those in Mexico City's other showpiece stadium, the Olimpico '68.

Three years earlier, Argentina had competed at the FIFA World Youth Championship – now the U20 World Cup – in Mexico. There, they played three games at the Azteca, winning the first two against China and Poland before losing 1-0 to Brazil in the final played in front of a staggering 110,000 spectators. However, from that squad, only goalkeeper Luis Islas returned in 1986 – he was named among the five substitutes for every Argentina match at the tournament.

The first two quarter-finals of the 1986 World Cup played on Saturday, 21 June Guadalajara and Monterrey had ended in the elimination of the favourites, Brazil, and the hosts, Mexico. Not only did this deprive the end of the tournament of the two best-supported teams at the finals, it left Argentina as the only non-European nation still competing at the World Cup.

The 1986 World Cup was the sixth tournament played in the Americas. Each of the previous five had produced a South American winner – first Uruguay in 1930 and 1950, Brazil in 1962 and 1970, then Argentina themselves in 1978 – as well as, at least, another semi-finalist from the continent. This had created a belief that European teams, with their hard-running, pressing style could never win a World Cup in the Americas, a myth that ultimately persevered for another 28 years until Germany won the 2014 tournament in Brazil.

Of the 24 nations that had begun the 1986 World Cup finals, only four were from South America and some had looked to their continent's most recent champions Uruguay as the potential winner of this World Cup. However, after a controversial progression through the group phase in which they achieved as many red cards as goals, they were the first South American side to be eliminated, by Argentina in the Round of 16.

Two days later, Paraguay, playing in their first World Cup since 1958, followed them. Led by the reigning South American Footballer of the Year, Julio César Romero – Maradona had not won the prize since 1980 – they had impressed in the group phase by defeating Iraq and coming from behind to hold both hosts Mexico and Belgium to entertaining score draws.

After failing to capitalise on early defensive errors, Paraguay were ultimately outclassed by an improving England team in Mexico City. Writing in the *Daily Mirror* the following day, Harry Harris suggested that 'if England can contain Maradona as effectively as they closed down Romero anything is possible'. Romero – while conceding that England deserved to defeat his own nation – felt differently, claiming that 'against Argentina, who have better technique, individual talent, strength and speed, England will surely fail'.

There was still Brazil, the winners of the last World Cup in Mexico in 1970, playing, as then, in their home-from-home, the Estadio Jalisco in Guadalajara. They went into their quarter-final against European champions France having not conceded a single goal and winning each of their previous three games by increasing margins.

Yet it was France who went through in the tournament's first penalty shoot-out after a titanic encounter, a match for the ages. Brazil's wait for a fourth World Cup would go into a third decade, and now South America's unbroken hold on every World Cup played on the western side of the Atlantic rested on Diego Maradona's Argentina.

The previous World Cup in Spain had ended with an all-European semi-final line-up for the first time since 1966. If Argentina failed against England, with Belgium and Spain still to play in the remaining quarter-final, there would be four European semi-finalists for the second tournament in succession. To date, this has still never occurred after 22 tournaments spanning a century.

The way the draw panned out, England knew they would play all their remaining games at the 115,000-capacity Estadio Azteca as long as they remained in the 1986 World Cup. The squad had nicknamed the ground 'Palladium'. Yet, any advantage they might have gained from their previous experiences at the stadium was negated by the condition of the pitch.

Two days before the Round of 16 match against Paraguay, the England players were forced to wait an hour before being allowed to train in the stadium, which had just hosted the first knockout game between Mexico and Bulgaria the previous afternoon. After hundreds of divots were hurriedly replaced, the players spent much of their time slipping and sliding on a pitch with a loose top layer.

'It was a terrible surface,' recalls Alvin Martin, who was to play his only World Cup finals match against Paraguay. 'It looked okay from the cameras, it looked lovely and green and a plush pitch, but it wasn't. We found out when we trained on it for the first time. There were potholes everywhere.'

Goalkeeper Chris Woods told me he recalls many of the players being captivated by the public address system, designed in the shape of a traditional Mexican piñata, which hung suspended from cables over the centre circle. 'We were trying to smash balls up at it at the end of training. We couldn't get near it!'

Amazingly, the pre-match press conference took place on the Azteca pitch the day before the game. Describing the top layer of the pitch as a rug on top of a hard polished wooden floor, journalist Patrick Barclay remembers his main concern was not Bobby Robson's words but retaining his balance on the loose surface.

Not established in the soil, the long grass moved under the players' feet, which made any change of direction at speed very difficult. The England squad believed that the poor state of the playing surface would hinder any player attempting to dribble on it.

Torrential rainfall that evening, which blighted the Round of 16 match between Argentina and Uruguay in nearby Puebla, seemed to have helped the Azteca grass re-establish itself. Ahead of the Paraguay game, Peter Beardsley said 'the pitch is in good condition. We're quite surprised really, when we came Monday, it wasn't the best but I think the drop of rain has done it good.'

Nevertheless, speaking on ITV, the Manchester United manager Ron Atkinson derided the playing surface. 'For a big match, it's arguably the worst underfoot conditions I've ever seen. It's making control and passing hard. Once or twice, players have tried to lay the ball off, it just got stuck in the grass.'

The suspended Ray Wilkins, who was eligible to return to action against Argentina, also hoped something could be done to improve the playing surface ahead of the quarter-final on Sunday. 'The pitch isn't very good. In actual fact it was diabolical on Monday and it was quite good today.'

The following Saturday, ahead of the quarter-final against Argentina, the England players did not even get a chance to test the surface. They intended to train early in the morning to allow the players to return to their hotel before noon in order to watch the eagerly anticipated opening quarter-final between Brazil and France. They arrived to find the dressing rooms locked and they were then denied the opportunity to train on a pitch that was once more being repaired. Despite angry calls to FIFA, whose own regulations stipulated that each team have 45 minutes to train on the surface, the head groundsman only permitted the players to walk across it in their trainers and without a ball. Bobby Robson concluded that 'the pitch was lousy, worse than ever'.

Gary Stevens of Tottenham Hotspur, who played the last half an hour against Paraguay admitted, 'The pitch was terrible, it was long. It was a very coarse grass. There were big divots that hadn't been properly filled. It was a shocking surface, absolutely shocking.'

The state of the pitch in the enclosed stadium had been an issue for all the teams who had played there. England captain Peter Shilton admitted he had voiced his concerns to the Football Association. 'It's a bumpy pitch, not what you would choose. There are problems and I have asked our officials to speak to the FIFA people to see if anything could be done about it. One goalmouth is particularly bad.

'I think they have tried to do their best, but putting in new pieces of turf is the worst thing they could do because it doesn't have time to grow in. It really needs a heavy roll but what we have asked is that at least it is left alone until the game to settle down.'

Martin explained the scene that the England players encountered the day before the World Cup quarter-final. 'There were groundsmen all over the pitch with little buckets and trowels filling in holes and then they were spraying them green.'

Where there was established turf, that was not ideal either. Gary Stevens of Everton recalled that 'the grass was really quite long, and they kept it long for the quarter-final as well. I always preferred a zippier pitch.'

The England squad were told they could train on the surface if they waited until after Argentina had their session at 11am. Still unable to enter the dressing rooms, an irate Robson warned that he would lodge a protest if England's opponents were allowed to train on the pitch and they were not. In the event, neither team trained at the stadium ahead of the game. Suggestions from stadium officials that the players could practise on the pitch itself if they wore flat shoes were deemed unacceptable by Bobby Robson. 'That was no good to us. It would not have served our purpose so I took the lads to a private training ground where we could do more serious preparations.'

A nonplussed Gary Lineker explained the situation to ITV the night before the game. 'It's not very good, it's very bobbly. It tends to give way. They seem to fill divots after the game with a different sort of turf. It's a bit difficult. We tried to train on it today to see what it was like but they wouldn't let us. We had to go and train somewhere else. I don't know whether it's improved too much.

'There was a storm yesterday, and they said it was a bit too wet. They didn't want it cut up or anything. They didn't tell us until we got there which was the worst thing. We had another three-quarters of an hour drive to another training ground.'

In his official report submitted to FIFA after the game, the DFB President Hermann Neuberger, described the state of the pitch as 'strained', adding that he thought the Mexican Organising Committee should be urged to take more care of the surface. The German was perhaps thinking ahead, as a week later his national team would be playing on it during the World Cup Final.

In his 'Other Observations' on the match, Neuberger made no mention of the disputed first goal but once more referred to the field of play, making a suggestion for the head of the World Cup Organising Committee, Guillermo Cañedo. Neuberger said that there was a need for better (underlined) equipment to be used on the pitch with an effort made to shorten the length of the grass on a daily basis, adding that particular attention was needed to be shown in the two penalty areas.

Unable to train at the Azteca, the England squad hurriedly made alternative arrangements to practise at the city's Estadio Azulgrana (now Estadio Ciudad de los Deportes), then the home of Atlante FC. Assured someone would be waiting to let them in, they arrived to find the gates bolted. It took the intervention of their police escort to find them a trained locksmith to let them into the stadium. Even after all that, the players found the dressing rooms were still locked. The increasingly irritated players had no option but to make their way into the stands and climb down on to the pitch, sunken well below street level. A frustrated Robson lost his temper at the media's proximity to his session shouting, 'Hey, buzz off, go on.'

Surrounded by the world's press, the England squad stripped in the open and trained for less than half an hour before answering questions on the pitch and then returning back to their hotel in time to watch the second half of Brazil v France, having missed the game's only two goals.

BBC v ITV

As during the previous World Cup four years earlier in Spain, the BBC and ITV had agreed before the tournament to employ 'sensible sharing' of the 52 matches at the 1986 finals. Between them, the channels had spent £10 million to provide armchair viewers back home with 150 hours of programming live from Mexico but many feared the saturation coverage would turn the audience off. Therefore, games were alternated between the two to give the British public something else to watch.

The BBC had already broadcast England's games against Portugal and Poland in the group stage, with ITV showing the match against Morocco in between. ITV therefore believed they had 'a gentleman's agreement' to exclusively televise England's next game, the Round of 16 clash with Paraguay. It dated back to the so-called Tesler-Scott agreement between the two corporations in 1979.

The BBC did not see it that way, arguing the deal only covered the group stage matches, and chose to broadcast the game as well, which kicked-off at 7pm on a Wednesday. In order to make room in the scheduling, the BBC opted to postpone its weekly episode of hit US soap *Dallas*, which elicited hundreds of protests from angry viewers.

The Independent Broadcasters Association (IBA), the regulatory body for commercial television, said the simultaneous transmission was 'against the public interest and contrary to the spirit of the understanding between the UK broadcasters which the BBC had previously accepted'. BBC Director General Alasdair Milne pointed out that of the nine games involving the British teams in the group stage – England, Scotland and Northern Ireland – ITV had broadcast live coverage of five against the four screened by the BBC.

The match against Paraguay was remarkably the first and only time during the tournament that the BBC had broadcast a live match in its entirety during prime time on a weekday evening in preference to its flagship talk show. During the group stage they had given priority to *Wogan*, habitually going out on Mondays, Wednesdays and Fridays at 7pm.

Only at 7.40pm did the BBC go to live coverage of three first-round matches – Argentina v South Korea, West Germany v Uruguay, and Brazil v Algeria – in time for the second half only. For the majority of the knockout stages, the BBC had elected to broadcast the late match on weekday evenings, kicking off at 11pm.

After the two channels went head to head for the Paraguay match, there was never any chance the BBC were going to concede to ITV in televising the more marketable quarter-final against Argentina on the weekend.

Fully aware that the majority of the television audience would choose the BBC in any head to head, thereby affecting the reach of their advertising, ITV had offered the BBC two potential solutions. Either they could toss a coin for the rights to exclusive coverage of the quarter-finals or they would concede to the BBC in showing the Argentina match in return for gaining exclusive rights to England's potential semi-final the following Wednesday.

The BBC, and their new managing director Michael Grade, rejected both options. Grade, the former head of ITV, said, 'There is nothing new in our position and I didn't make the decision in isolation from more senior executives. We are simply doing what the BBC always says it should do – cover events of major national interest.'

On the Friday morning, ITV executives called a meeting with their BBC counterparts, who refused to back down. Andy Allen, a spokesman for the ITV networks said, 'We regret the BBC's decision to elbow an agreement that has worked well since 1979. It seems ironical [sic] that the man who was behind the alternation agreement in 1979 – Michael Grade, who was director of programmes for LWT and is now head of programmes for BBC TV – is the man who has broken this agreement.'

Speaking to the *Sunday Times*, an unnamed ITV executive was quoted as saying that 'we have always been rivals, but friendly ones. After this, we won't talk to the BBC unless we have a squad of lawyers to check the small print.'

In the *London Evening Standard*, BBC Managing Director Bill Cotton wrote a column explaining 'why ITV are being such bad sports'. He argued that 'over the years the BBC has made a far greater investment in the coverage of sport than ITV. We support dozens of sports which ITV ignores. We covered each of the last four Olympics. ITV turned up for one. If ITV cared so much for the sporting public, why did they drop *World of Sport* from Saturday afternoons? The truth is that ITV only takes a real interest in the big events which look like bankers with the audience.'

Along a similar vein, the *Sunday Times* ran a similar justification written by Milne on the day of the game, entitled 'Why we had to do it'. He insisted that 'our commitment to sport overall is clearly more comprehensive than the ITV companies. For the climax of England's World Cup challenge, as for the Royal Weddings, General Elections and the great occasions of state, the BBC has an obligation to give of its best and to offer the nation uninterrupted coverage of events.'

However, not everyone was in favour of watching England's fortunes play out live from Mexico City across two networks. In 1986, there were only four television channels on offer to the vast majority of the British public.

The games in Mexico were remarkably the first knockout matches played by England at a major tournament since the last World Cup in the country. On that occasion, 16 years previously, BBC television had broadcast the world champions' defence of their trophy as it ended in quarter-final defeat to West Germany in León. Following that competition, England failed to qualify for the final stages of four successive major tournaments (two European Championships and two World Cups), only ending that ignominious run by reaching the 1980 European Championships in Italy. There they went out in the group stage, and two years later at the 1982 World Cup, the second phase involved another group stage in which the BBC and ITV once more shared the two England matches between them – the BBC showing the first game against West Germany with ITV broadcasting the ultimately decisive second match against Spain, after which England were eliminated.

Another failure to qualify for the European Championships in 1984 meant that only now in 1986 were the BBC and ITV facing a situation where England were playing a winner-takes-all knockout tie at a major tournament.

The Argentina match would therefore be shown live on both BBC1 and ITV, with the commercial station getting a head start by beginning their broadcast five minutes earlier at 6.40pm, following an episode of the aptly named Jimmy Tarbuck show *Winner Takes All*. Brian Moore fronted coverage, accompanied by the soon-to-be-classic theme tune intro of 'Aztec Gold'. The song, written by Rod Argent and Peter Van Hooke, and released as a single under the name Silsoe, remained in the public consciousness for years to come as the theme tune of ITV's *Big Match* and, later still, on the opening credits of Saturday lunchtime staple, *Saint and Greavsie*.

With Brian Moore unwilling to travel to Mexico for the duration of the World Cup, Martin Tyler would once more commentate on the match for ITV. The 40-year-old had taken the microphone for all of England's games so far at the tournament and would be joined by the recently appointed Tottenham Hotspur manager David Pleat.

Moore was supposed to have gone out for the final week of the 1982 World Cup but changed his mind following England's exit. Left with four commentators to cover the four remaining matches in Spain – Gerry Harrison, John Helm, Gerald Sindstadt and Tyler

– ITV surprisingly allocated the final to the junior member of the quartet, something Tyler himself admits was 'a bit of a punt'.

On the BBC was John Motson, another 36-year-old commentating on his first World Cup Final in 1982, the pair born just two months apart in the summer the Second World War ended. Tyler acquitted himself well. He memorably described Marco Tardelli's iconic celebration for the second goal as 'expressing what it's like to score in a World Cup Final'.

However, this time Tyler knew in advance he would not get another opportunity to commentate on a World Cup Final for ITV. He revealed to me: 'I was told in about January 1986 that Brian would be going out, so I wouldn't do the final whatever the situation was. On the day of the final, I was given the choice of going to the game as an observer, just as a reward for my efforts, or sitting in the studio back in Mexico City in the International Broadcast Centre in case the line [to England] went down.' Tyler made the professional choice. 'I had broadcast the last final for ITV and, had the line gone down, I would have been able to do it again. But it didn't.'

It remains the only World Cup Final Tyler has missed since 1982 up to and including the 2022 final in Qatar. 'It wasn't easy, I'll be honest with you,' he told me. 'No disrespect to Brian, who was a wonderful broadcaster and a very great help to me. It was difficult because four years earlier I was the one holding the microphone, but I was well ahead of schedule in doing that. So it sort of balanced out. That was one I sat out by choice, but sometimes you have to be a sub, and sometimes the sub doesn't get on.'

Following an English league season that began with a complete television blackout due to the perceived undervaluing of broadcast rights by the BBC and ITV, the World Cup suddenly offered an avalanche of live games in a single month.

For someone like Tyler, commentating on a live match was the ultimate test in his profession. 'I grew up on recorded highlights working for ITV, which was one of the reasons when I was struggling to get some sort of consistency interlinking it into commercial breaks working for Sky many, many years later, I started to say "and it's live!" Because for me "and it's live" still means something.

'BBC and ITV were big rivals, all the way through my time, from when I joined in 1973. I've never worked for the BBC, so I was always a team player for ITV, and I guess for Sky as well. Not that I've anything against the BBC, but they've always been the rivals in my mind, and, you know, I want my team to win!'

On the BBC, Motson and Barry Davies had shared two England games each in 1986. Motson was in situ in Mexico City, having described the Round of 16 match between England and Paraguay at the Estadio Azteca four days before the quarter-final.

At the previous World Cup, Motson had commentated on both of England's matches shown live on the BBC but now, ahead of his country's biggest game since 1970, he was summoned to the Maria Isabel hotel in Mexico City by BBC Head of Sports and Events Jonathan Martin. There he was informed that Davies would commentate on the quarter-final. Motson was instead sent to Guadalajara and voiced what became a modern-day classic between Brazil and France. The next day, he travelled to Puebla to commentate on the Belgium v Spain quarter-final, watching the England match alongside the Manchester United manager Ron Atkinson, who was working as a co-commentator on the later match for ITV.

The 47-year-old Davies, who had commentated on England's group stage matches against Morocco and Poland, would be accompanied by Jimmy Hill at the Estadio Azteca. Speaking to me, Davies does not know to this day why he was selected ahead of Motson. 'I don't think there was any particular arrangement. If there was, I wasn't told about it.'

What is certain, is that Davies's World Cup was to end that weekend, regardless of the result of the match. The multitalented commentator was due to fly home to be in London for the start of the Wimbledon Championships, which began the next morning. He told me that might have been a factor in the BBC's choice. 'It was lucky for me, but I think, over the years, I was entitled to some luck!'

Davies admitted to me that there were no conversations shared between the two rivals for the BBC microphone. 'When we're doing different matches in different parts of a foreign country, I didn't see much of John. People tended to rather exaggerate the contest between the two of us. I know I was very happy to be given this particular game because it was always going to be a good match.'

Reflecting on his commentary that day in the *Daily Telegraph*, Davies was honest about his own performance. 'From the 51st minute to the 55th, I was a total disaster. I said something quite stupid about the first goal, that it might be offside. I couldn't understand what England were appealing about. Except how could it be offside when the ball arrived in the air between the goalkeeper and Maradona?

'I was still thinking about it when Maradona received it [for the second goal] in the centre circle, facing the other way. Plus, Jimmy Hill was still complaining beside me about the fact that he had needed to get up so early for the farce of a midday kick-off.'

Unlike the minimum hour-long prelude to any England tournament match in the 21st century, BBC1 gave themselves only 15 minutes' build-up ahead of the 7pm kick-off (UK time). Their 'Aztec Lightning' opening title sequence signalled the start of *World Cup Grandstand*, hosted by Des Lynam beginning at 6.45pm, immediately after the ten-minute evening news with Jan Leeming.

Both channels' coverage was due to end at 9pm, with the BBC's quiz show *Mastermind* and ITV's United States' cop show, *Dempsey and Makepeace* at risk of delay if the quarter-final went to extra time.

For those unwilling to spend their Sunday watching sport, the alternatives were few. As the BBC1 coverage from Mexico City began, BBC2 were winding down their five-hour *Sunday Grandstand* show, which had featured county cricket between Northants and Yorkshire, and show jumping from Hickstead.

BBC2 then showed the short-lived American sitcom *Foley Square*, which was followed by *The World About Us*, featuring a rail journey across Canada. Channel 4 offered a repeat of their documentary series in which viewers went on *A Journey with Tom Vernon*, this time travelling to North Yorkshire to profile the 'Spirit of Whitby'.

According to a nationwide survey, 93 per cent of viewers across the country believed that one of the country's two flagship channels should have offered an alternative to the World Cup in the prime-time slot on Sunday evening. However, there was surprise that the viewing figures for the World Cup were being significantly bolstered by female fans. Chris Horsley, the media director for an advertising agency, said, 'There is very little evidence of women turning away from football. If anything, the housewife is chasing her husband's viewing patterns. Even when there's a housewife programme on the other side, women are staying with the World Cup.'

In an age where live football on television was still a novelty, Pat Ryan, a spokesman for London's pub landlords, believed that the accessibility of the game in people's homes was fatally affecting business in the nation's public houses: 'Customers are staying away to watch the World Cup. The Argentina match will be another nail in the coffin for many pubs.'

However, Crossley's Bar, situated in the Dean Clough complex in Halifax, tried to make the most of the situation by advertising that they would be showing the match on their 'big screen'. At a time when the average price of a beer in the UK was 82p, Crossley's was offering all pints sold during the match between 7pm and 9pm at a knockdown price of 60p.

Ultimately, 15.35 million watched the BBC coverage, the highest single-channel viewing figures of the World Cup. A further 8.3 million tuned into ITV, creating a combined audience of 23.7 million. The split between the two channels was 64:36 in favour of the BBC.

The Argentina v England match attracted the highest viewing figures for the World Cup. An estimated 22.3 million watched the final played on the following Sunday evening, with 11.7 million choosing the BBC coverage and 10.6 million opting for ITV, a 52:48 split. The match attracted far fewer viewers than the audience for the year's top-rated programme, the Christmas Day edition of *Eastenders*.

According to the Broadcasters' Audience Research Board (BARB), 30.15 million viewers were glued to their sets as Dirty Den served his wife Ange with divorce papers on the steps of the Queen Vic pub.

The World Cup did not even provide the biggest television single-channel audience for a sporting event in 1986, as 18.3 million had tuned into BBC1 to watch the World Featherweight Championship title fight between Barry McGuigan and Denilo Cabrera in February.

On the disputed Falkland Islands, pubs and clubs on Port Stanley stayed open throughout the afternoon so the inhabitants could show their support for England. At the time there was no live television broadcast on the islands. A spokesman for the Ministry of Defence admitted, 'Unfortunately there is no way the match can be relayed live by British TV to the Falklands.' The only way by which the 3,500 troops still stationed on the Falklands could watch the game would be to point their aerials in the direction of Patagonia in the hope of picking up the Argentinian transmission. The now defunct charity, the Services Sound and Vision Corporation (SSVC) had been set up in 1982 to keep British armed forces abroad entertained. They had made arrangements to transmit the live radio commentary almost 8,000 miles by satellite.

For all those unable to access a television, BBC Radio 2 would be broadcasting live commentary from the Estadio Azteca. The England manager at the previous World Cup, Ron Greenwood, provided analysis alongside the legendary broadcasting pair of Bryon Butler and Welshman Peter Jones, both covering their fifth World Cup finals. As was the norm on radio at the time, the pair would split each half of the action between them.

Butler, from Somerset, was handed the first half of each 45-minute period and therefore was on the mic for both of Maradona's goals. His commentary was immortalised on the official 1986 FIFA World Cup film, and for those in the English-speaking world his words have become synonymous with arguably the two most famous goals in World Cup history.

The now famous pitch-level footage of the game was released a year later when the official film of the 13th FIFA World Cup, *Hero*, was released in the summer of 1987. Produced by Worldmark, it was written and directed by Tony Maylam, who had worked with producer Drummond Challis on the 1979 British spy thriller, *The Riddle of the Sands*. Two weeks before the tournament began, Maylam and Challis arrived in Mexico with a crew of 36 and a plane full of equipment. For the four weeks of the finals, their film crews travelled over 15,000 miles and shot 250,000 feet of film from which 86 minutes of action was distilled.

Challis had been part of the production team four years earlier for the official 1982 World Cup film, *G'olé*, which had told the story of that championship in a more linear format. Early on in Mexico, Challis had made the decision to focus more on the individual stars and their journey through the finals.

He approached Maradona during the group stage and asked for intimate access to him and his team during the World Cup matches. Challis explained to me that his project appealed to Maradona's ego, telling the Argentina captain, 'Let me get close to Argentina and the team – and we will get close – and we'll make you look great, because the world will see you in close-up. With television, they're covering every game in the World Cup and every player. We will be concentrating on you when we shoot Argentina games.'

Challis was behind the goal into which Maradona scored the two goals against England. The cameramen missed getting a clear shot of the handball but their continuous shots from two different angles of his dribble for the second goal have gone into football and cinematic history.

Challis explained to me the skill required to capture the footage of Maradona running at full speed with a telephoto lens. 'It is difficult. You're shooting on a long lens, if you're in fairly tight, you have to pull the focus to keep the subject matter sharp. We had a couple of specialist long lens cameramen, they worked for me for years. We started off, some of them, doing the World Cup in 1966.'

After the match, and given the thumbs-up by Maradona, Challis and a fellow cameraman followed the Argentina captain into the dressing room after his drug test and captured the never-to-be-forgotten footage of the returning hero morphing into team cheerleader as the squad broke into spontaneous song.

A year later, Challis and Gary Lineker were invited to Buenos Aires by Maradona for a special screening of the film, which became the second-largest grossing release in South America during 1987 after the multimillion dollar Hollywood blockbuster *Out of Africa*.

'We wanted to give our audience something that they hadn't seen on television,' Challis told me. 'We developed the technique with longer and longer lenses, which all grew out of a film I did in 1972 called *Vision of Eight* for the Munich Olympics.' A film so-called for the differing perspectives offered by eight filmmakers.

Part of the legend of *Hero* was created by its soundtrack, entirely composed by musician Rick Wakeman. The classically trained pianist was world-renowned for his progressive rock music and had already worked with Challis to provide the music on the official 1982 World Cup film. Enlisted to do the same in 1986, Wakeman told me he watched the 1986 World Cup quarter-final at home already thinking about the music he would put together for the film. Almost immediately after the tournament he saw the edited footage and began the task of writing the soundtrack. Reminiscent of the music used in the trailer for *Top Gun*, which was released a few months earlier, Wakeman created a portentous accompaniment for Maradona's movements against South Korea, which was also used for the match with England, as the footage illustrated both the significance of the match and some of the physical intimidation he suffered.

Wakeman also wrote the music and lyrics for the film's closing track, 'Special Kind of Hero', a song dedicated to Maradona's genius. It was performed by Stephanie Lawrence, a theatre actress who had ironically succeeded Elaine Paige in playing the role of another legendary Argentine in Andrew Lloyd Webber's *Evita* on London's West End.

Wakeman revealed to me: 'I knew they were focusing on Maradona so I had a route to go down. Everything that I was involved with was created especially for him.' To know, 40 years later that his music is still associated around the world with Maradona's greatest moments gives Wakeman a special feeling. 'That makes me feel very proud. I would have loved to have met Maradona.'

Minutes before kick-off, BBC Radio 1 announced that, after three weeks, 'Spirit in the Sky' by Doctor & the Medics had been replaced as the UK's number one single by Wham's 'The Edge of Heaven', a position the winners of the World Cup quarter-final at the Azteca would also seemingly occupy with Belgium or Spain to play in Wednesday's semi-final.

The original release of 'Spirit in the Sky' by Norman Greenbaum had been number one in May 1970, shortly before that year's World Cup. That had been replaced by the England World Cup Squad, whose world champion team had recorded the iconic single 'Back Home'.

By the time they were, and had been deposed, the song had been top of the charts for three weeks. In contrast, the 1986 vintage had released the forgettable 'We've Got the Whole World at Our Feet', which failed to make the top 40, peaking at number 66.

Never the biggest fan of the national game, Prime Minister Margaret Thatcher was spending the weekend at her country home of Chequers. A non-committal No.10 spokesperson said, 'I feel sure she will be taking an interest in the game.'

Never knowingly one to hedge his bets at a World Cup, the legendary Pelé was also tipping England to succeed. Writing in the Mexican *Excélsior* newspaper, the three-time World Cup winner said, 'England were among my four original favourites. In view of their improvement, I'm sticking with them.'

Argentina were on a win bonus of just over £20,000 a man to bring home the World Cup. The players from the already-eliminated Denmark reportedly received £25,000 each for merely qualifying for Mexico, their first-ever World Cup. England were on £30,000 a player to bring the trophy home but Bobby Robson insisted, 'They're here for pride not money.'

Neither pride nor money would be forthcoming from FIFA's Fair Play table. England went into the game as the most ill-disciplined team remaining in the competition. With five bookings in their four games so far, plus the red card shown to Ray Wilkins against Morocco, England had just six points in the rankings headed by West Germany and the Soviet Union going into the quarter-finals.

Of the 16 teams eligible, only the much-derided and already-eliminated Uruguayans sat below England, which had left them out of the running to collect the $200,000 gold Sport Billy Trophy. Joint-third going into the quarter-finals, it would eventually be won by Brazil after Thomas Berthold's quarter-final red card for violent conduct affected West Germany's score.

Going into the quarter-finals, Argentina and England were joint second-favourites to win the World Cup at 9/2 behind Brazil who had yet to concede a goal at the tournament. By the time the two teams played, Brazil had been eliminated and replaced as tournament favourites by their conquerors, the reigning European champions, France.

For the match itself, bookmakers William Hill made Argentina very slight favourites to win the game at 11/8 compared to 13/8 on England, with a draw at 9/4. A final scoreline after 90 minutes of 2-1 to Argentina was being offered at 7/1.

The King of the Lane

Thirty days before the World Cup started, Diego Maradona travelled to London to represent a Tottenham Hotspur side in Ossie Ardiles's testimonial at White Hart Lane. There he would play alongside two of his opponents in the World Cup quarter-final, Glenn Hoddle – who gave up his No.10 shirt for the Argentina captain – and Chris Waddle.

Ardiles had asked several current members of the Argentina squad if they were willing to take part in the game. Daniel Passarella was the only remaining international from the squad that, with Ardiles in the team, won the 1978 World Cup.

The Argentinian national team were gathered in Europe ahead of the World Cup. Like most of the others asked to play by Ardiles, Passarella said he required the permission of head coach Carlos Bilardo to travel. The one exception was Maradona, who promised he would be there.

Maradona was featured heavily in the matchday programme, produced well ahead of the game on 1 May. The Spurs players hoped Maradona may turn up as a guest of honour and appear on the pitch but few believed he would actually play. For much of the preceding week, they pestered Ardiles relentlessly about whether Maradona would come to London. Clive Allen recalls many asking, 'Come on Ossie, is he guesting?' To which Ardiles replied, 'I know nothing, I know nothing.'[3]

---

3   https://www.youtube.com/watch?si=NWo-NFCUgEyR02jo&v=rMc8RufviZU
&feature=youtu.be

Ardiles's son Pablo was 11 at the time. He remembers: 'Maradona had a bit of a reputation as being unreliable. My dad was nervous in the lead-up to the game as to whether he would turn up or not. Although my dad has always said that Maradona never let him down in all the time that he knew him and, true to his word, he was there for Dad's testimonial.'

The previous day, six of the Argentina side who would face England lost 1-0 in Oslo to Norway, a nation that had failed to qualify for the World Cup. The next morning, a dishevelled Maradona flew into Heathrow Airport to be met by Ardiles. The greatest footballer in the world was pictured walking across the terminal in a garish blue jumper, ferrying a luggage trolley with his four cases. Maradona had brought all his luggage with him as he would be flying directly on to Tel Aviv, rejoining the Argentina squad, who were playing another pre-tournament friendly away to Israel (Maradona would score twice in a 7-2 win, his third match in three different countries within five days).

Ardiles took him to a hotel in central London, where Maradona insisted on getting some sleep. The Spurs player had warned his former international team-mate that he would need to pick him up early to avoid the customary traffic on the Seven Sisters road. Maradona left the phone off the hook. When he eventually woke him up, Ardiles drove Maradona, now wearing a dark suit and red tie, to the stadium. Gridlocked outside the ground, Ardiles stopped a police car and asked to be escorted to White Hart Lane. Fans outside the stadium detained them even further, requesting autographs and photos.

Arriving in the dressing room just 45 minutes before the game, Maradona was filmed entering with Ardiles and his two sons. The rest of the squad were staggered that the world's most expensive football player had flown in to play alongside them.

Vinny Samways was a 17-year-old youth-team player at the time. He had occasionally trained with the first team during the week but was still a year away from his professional debut at Tottenham

Hotspur, but Ardiles had taken him under his wing and insisted that the teenager play some part in his testimonial game.

Ardiles introduced Maradona to every member of the Spurs squad one by one. Samways told me, 'He was a super, down-to-earth guy. He went round shaking everybody's hand. I don't think I washed my hand for a couple of weeks after that!' The teenage Samways was immediately struck by Maradona's torso. 'His physique was phenomenal. Obviously his thighs were ginormous but the top half of his body was just ripped like a boxer.'

Nevertheless, Allen recalls that Maradona disappeared into the treatment room before the game. 'He came back into the dressing room, he had ankles like footballs from the brutality that he'd taken in Serie A.'

It was at this point that Maradona realised he had not brought any boots to play in. Hurriedly, Ardiles asked around the changing rooms to enquire whether anybody played in size 6½ Puma boots and might have a spare pair. Allen, who like Maradona wore Puma Kings, raised his hand. He said he had two pairs, one he had worn all season and a newer pair he was breaking in. Maradona asked for the older boots but was eventually convinced to play in the newer pair, which he signed for Allen after the game. Allen still has the boots on display at his home, the only pair of boots he kept after his career finished.[4]

Pablo Ardiles told me that Maradona wowed the Tottenham players by doing kick-ups with a tennis ball. 'The players were in awe of Maradona. They appreciated they were in the presence of a footballing genius. Someone special. And there were some great players in the Spurs changing room.'

Sitting in the corner of the small locker room, Maradona was handed a succession of programmes and autograph books by the other star-struck players to sign. He did all of this without complaint as Ardiles translated.

—

4   https://www.tottenhamhotspur.com/news-archive-1/spurs-v-inter-the-day-maradona-played-for-spurs/

Ireland international Tony Galvin remembered, 'We were all queueing up for his autograph in the dressing room before the game. He'd never met the team before and we were all waiting for autographs. It was quite funny seeing all these footballers waiting with pens in the dressing room.'

Tottenham's Gary Stevens did not play in the match due to a thigh strain, but nevertheless made sure he was in the dressing room before the game to see the world's most expensive player in the flesh. He told me Ardiles introduced every member of the Spurs squad to Maradona, who was particularly keen to meet Glenn Hoddle. 'He seemed a nice guy but there was very little communication. His English was pretty much zero and, with the exception of Ossie, nobody could speak in his tongue either.'

Ahead of the game, Maradona got hold of a ball in the changing room and started doing some kick-ups to warm up. Hoddle responded by doing the same. Upon seeing this, Maradona made a comment to Ardiles in Spanish. The Spurs players asked him what Maradona had said, and Ardiles joked, 'Hoddle – flash cunt.'

However, Ardiles had already told Maradona about how highly he rated Hoddle. He had arranged an exclusive interview for Maradona with the *Daily Mirror* and, once the players were kitted up, the newspaper's photographer Monte Fresco took a picture of the two great No.10s, Hoddle and Maradona, standing together arm in arm.

Kick-off was delayed by 15 minutes due to the unexpected size of the crowd, which was the club's fourth-highest of the entire season and more than the combined attendance of Spurs' next two league games

That night, the two Argentines, accompanied by Ardiles's two sons, Pablo and Federico, came out after the two sides had assembled on the halfway line. Holding Maradona's hand, the elder Pablo told me what the Argentina captain said to him: 'We just walked out and he asked if everything was okay and if I was enjoying it. It was quite overwhelming for me personally, walking out in front of so many people. I wasn't used to it.'

The Argentines came out to the ovation of 30,536 fans at White Hart Lane who paid £110,000 in gate receipts. Once their opponents Inter Milan's appearance fee and other expenses were deducted, Ardiles walked away with around £90,000 from the night.

Pablo Ardiles admitted to me: 'I was quite shy and found being in front of 30,000 a little overwhelming. The stadium was filled to the rafters and there was a great energy about the place. My brother kicked a ball about with the players but I just wanted to get back and watch the game, to be honest! Then we had photos – me, Dad, my brother and Maradona – before we ran off to watch the game! I just remember there being such a buzz in the stadium. I think they gave Maradona a ticker-tape welcome. It was very loud. I was just pleased that I had met my football idol. Other than that, I almost certainly didn't appreciate what I was taking part in!'

As the players went through their paces to the soundtrack of Chas & Dave's 1981 FA Cup Final song 'Ossie's Dream', Maradona warmed up in the centre circle. He volleyed the ball into the night sky with the outside of his left foot and repeated the trick three times without it touching the ground.

In contrast to the figure of hate he would soon become in England, Maradona's first touch of the ball during the match at White Hart Lane brought a cry of 'come on my son' from the touchline, and when he sprayed an effortless ball across the pitch to the left touchline, the crowd began to chant 'sign him up, sign him up'.

Galvin recalls, 'I remember a pass got really hammered into him and he killed it dead – he was clearly thinking about the next pass before the ball had even arrived. And when he ran with the ball it was never further than three inches from his foot – this is something you just can't coach.'

Chris Waddle came on for Ardiles, unable to continue due to a persistent knee injury, after just eight minutes of the first half. Waddle said, 'For me, to play with Maradona was a dream. People always ask me who's the best player I've ever played with, and the best player I've ever played against. Diego Maradona was my answer to both questions.

'Nice guy, very humble, obviously didn't speak English, Ossie translated a lot. I think he enjoyed the occasion. He didn't know they'd man-to-man mark him on the night in a testimonial. They said, "We're not letting him run riot."'

Against opponents he knew well from Serie A, Internazionale, Maradona completed a second 90 minutes within 24 hours and played understandably within himself. He nevertheless elicited cheers from the Spurs fans with his ball juggling, one overhead-kick cross and a fierce shot that produced a point-blank save from the Inter keeper.

Maradona struck up a particularly natural understanding with Hoddle, wearing the unfamiliar No.11 shirt, who he enjoyed exchanging sharp passes with. As the first half wound down, the White Hart Lane faithful began singing 'there's only one Maradona'.

Watching from the stands were several Arsenal players, including Scottish international Charlie Nicholas. In an edition of *Football's Greatest with Jeff Stelling*, Nicholas said that after 20 minutes of the game, Maradona starting directing the other Tottenham players to give the ball to Hoddle at every opportunity. 'Maradona knew wherever he moved, Hoddle could find him.'[5]

Hoddle recalled that 'we couldn't converse before the game but the language started when we were on the pitch. I found him a down-to-earth bloke and after that match he told Ossie that he enjoyed playing with me. We know all about his skills but I was surprised by the lovely passes he laid off first-time. Playing in Spain and Italy has taught him how to cope with heavy marking. He was turning and showing his great runs, as well as knocking off great passes.'

Tottenham Hotspur manager Peter Shreeves admitted that 'Maradona did things I didn't think footballers could do. Anybody got £4 million to lend me?'

---

5 https://www.youtube.com/watch?si=XsZBmhvmChfbO7kR&v=_pieVL-POZFs&feature=youtu.be

After the match, Waddle was keen to find out what Maradona made of the occasion. 'We were saying to Ossie afterwards, "What did he think?" When we were saying that, Maradona came up to me in the dressing room and shook my hand. And through Ossie's translation, he said, "Very good player, he should play in Italy." I thought, *Wow, Maradona's just said I'm a good player.*'

Interviewed in the changing rooms after the game by Martin Tyler, Maradona was asked if he foresaw any issues if his Argentina side were paired against England in the knockout stages in Mexico. With Ardiles translating, Maradona replied, 'No, no problem at all.' He added, 'I felt like I was playing at home. I'm very happy that the crowd understood my only concern was to win the game and I tried very hard to win the game. I enjoyed it very much.'[6]

Speaking exclusively to the *Daily Mirror*, Maradona picked out the three England players he believed were world class – Bryan Robson, Kenny Sansom and Glenn Hoddle, who he described as 'the player with exceptional skill in the English game. He looks very much like our best players from South America. He has it all and, on top of it, has the English power. I've seen him a lot on television while I've been playing for Napoli in Italy and I've been very impressed.'

However, he feared the injury-prone England captain would not show his best form at the World Cup. '[Bryan] Robson will be a handicap to England if he is not fully fit. You must be at your peak physical fitness to cope with the stresses of a World Cup campaign.'

Maradona also said he had been impressed by the talents of two players about to play in their first World Cup. 'Waddle's goal against Russia [in March] was excellent. Lineker is fast and scores goals, but still has to prove himself at international level.'

Seven weeks later, ahead of the World Cup quarter-final, Maradona had now revised his opinion of England's striker. 'The players I'm worried about are Tottenham's man Hoddle, and Lineker,

---

6   https://www.youtube.com/watch?si=XsZBmhvmChfbO7kR&v=_
     pieVLPOZFs&feature=youtu.be

who has surprised us with his great goalscoring ability. But I'm confident Argentina will win. Our defence is strong and we will beat Hoddle in the hand-to-hand in midfield. England's central defenders are big and we will be able to turn them. It will be a difficult match. Tell the people in Argentina to pray for us.'

The Falklands Factor

'**S**port cannot compare in terms of significance and importance with actual war,' said Gary Lineker in 2020 to *France Football*, 'but, with those two countries, football is not that far behind.'

On the eve of the 1986 World Cup quarter-final, Mexican newspaper *ESTO* interviewed Argentina's forward Jorge Valdano. At the time, he believed that the upcoming duel between Argentina and England, four years after the end of the Falklands War, 'is ideal for confusing the idiots who do not realise that we do not need political conflicts to give a special flavour to the game'.

Speaking in 2016, Valdano admitted he was wrong. 'Thirty years later, it's very clear to me that the idiot was me because from then until now they've done nothing but confuse actions within the game, as if they were a political act, rather than part of a football match.'[7]

After England defeated Paraguay to qualify for a quarter-final showdown with Argentina, England manager Bobby Robson was immediately asked about the potential ramifications of the tie during the post-match press conference: 'I'm a football manager, not a politician. Don't ask me those sort of questions.'

Coming out of the stadium, captain Peter Shilton stopped to speak to a collection of reporters: 'Well, it's another game, we want

---

7   https://www.youtube.com/watch?si=lW1w6sX618Ri6j9Q&v=E_
     gH_9qKd90&feature=youtu.be

to win it because we want to go to the semi-final. We'll treat it just like any other match.'

The following morning *The Sun* featured a front page with the headline 'Bring on the Argies!' next to an image of Bobby Robson wearing a sombrero. The tabloid newspaper claimed they were reporting the chants of the 5,000 England fans at the Estadio Azteca who celebrated their first knockout victory at a major tournament since the 1966 World Cup Final by singing 'Bring on the Argies, we want another war'. In Mexico, a local newspaper advertising where fans could purchase tickets to the game billed the upcoming duel as 'the second version of the Falklands War'.

The Falklands War had taken the lives of 907 people, 649 Argentines, 255 from the UK and three from the islands themselves.[8] The conflict had officially ended on 14 June 1982, three days after world champions Argentina had kicked off their defence of the trophy in Spain.

At the start of the war in April 1982, Minister for Sport Neil Macfarlane issued a directive stating: 'I urge no sporting contact with Argentina at representative, club or individual level on British soil. This policy applies equally to all sporting fixtures in Argentina.'

After failing to participate at a World Cup since 1970, England – alongside Scotland and Northern Ireland – were one of three British sides preparing to play at the 1982 tournament at which Argentina would compete as the defending world champions.

Former Sports Ministers Hector Munro and Denis Howell called upon FIFA to kick Argentina out of the World Cup but this proposition was never going to gain support among the other qualified nations. Hosts Spain, in particular, had their own territorial dispute with the UK over Gibraltar and would have therefore backed Argentina's claims to the Falklands.

---

8   https://www.helpforheroes.org.uk/about-us/news/10-facts-everyone-should-know-about-the-falklands-war/

A member of the Conservative backbench sports committee, John Carlisle, reluctantly accepted the reality of the situation when addressing the House of Commons: 'If there is a disappointment, it is that our world partners in soccer and our European partners have not come out in full support of our own ideas, and against Argentina. Should a situation arise, FIFA would be under great pressure. My personal view is that the onus would be on FIFA to expel the aggressor and to allow the competition to go ahead.'

With Argentina certain to compete, the Falklands crisis now put the British sides' participation under question. When Macfarlane pulled out of a meeting in early May to launch a 'Spectators Guide' for fans travelling out to Spain, press speculation mounted that it was a clear sign that the three teams would not compete at the World Cup.

The three nations who had finished behind England, Scotland and Northern Ireland in World Cup qualifying – Romania, Sweden and Portugal respectively – were put on standby to take their place should the British teams pull out.

The 31-year-old England captain Kevin Keegan had waited his entire career to play at the World Cup but accepted that the players would have to follow their government's advice. 'We live in this country and earn our living here. If the Government says we can't go to Spain, that's it. The way things are at the moment, we couldn't possibly play against Argentina. There's no way we could do that – it would be hypocritical. We can't expect our lads to go to the Falklands and be killed, as they were on HMS *Sheffield*, and then face Argentina at football.'

Speaking to the House of Commons on 27 May, Macfarlane made clear that 'it is the Government's policy to discourage all sporting contact with Argentina, either here or in that country, at representative, club or individual level. Outside these two countries we see no objection to British teams or individuals competing in any international events where Argentina may be represented. This policy applies to all sporting events. I must emphasise that, however the Government view this situation, the final decision on whether to participate in the World Cup finals is one for the football authorities, and their players. Certainly the authorities have made clear their wish to participate in the World Cup finals.'

In actual fact, the UK Government did not have the power to ban teams from the tournament, confirmed by Macfarlane's superior, Secretary of State for the Environment Michael Heseltine, when addressing the Cabinet that month. They could, however, offer strong advice to that effect, and Cabinet briefings released in 2014 indicated the teams would 'follow a government call for a boycott'.

FIFA had threatened the home nations with the threat of expulsion from the next World Cup in 1986 and financial sanctions amounting to £1 million if they withdrew from the 1982 tournament. FIFA President João Havelange had already ruled out any notion on banning the reigning world champions from the tournament.

A motion led by Carlisle urged the Government not to put pressure on the three Football Associations to withdraw, believing it would hand a propaganda victory to Argentina. 'A military junta consisting of three men in a closed room is hardly likely to take notice of a democratic decision taken by the electorate of this country. Such a decision would, I suppose, in some people's eyes be a patriotic gesture, but it would be ignored by Argentina and in no way would it assist our efforts to remove the aggressor from the islands.'[9]

In his opinion, the three British teams should not withdraw from the 1982 World Cup unless they had to face Argentina in the latter stages, arguing that 'if hostilities are still in progress no honourable Member or any British person could envisage a Scottish, English or Northern Irish team running on to the same field as an Argentine team'. He cited discussions with English FA secretary Ted Croker 'who seems to be equal to the decision that he may have to take on the morning of that game'.

---

9   https://hansard.parliament.uk/commons/1982-05-27/debates/837b8bf1-e401-411b-b432-ecd12bb46f78/Argentina(SportingContacts)

On the very eve of the World Cup, Macfarlane wrote a private letter to Prime Minister Margaret Thatcher claiming that the escalation of the conflict meant his position was beginning to shift. 'Up until a week or 10 days ago I have taken the line that it was up to the Football Authorities to decide whether they should participate. However, the loss of British life on HMS *Sheffield* and Sea Harriers has had a marked effect on some international footballers and some administrators. They feel revulsion at the prospect of playing in the same tournament as Argentina at this time.'

In contrast – after narrowly failing to qualify for the World Cup – the Football Association of Ireland (FAI) had hastily arranged for themselves a money-spinning tour of South America to provide opposition for nations preparing to play in the tournament. Organised by an Argentine agent, matches were scheduled against Argentina, Chile and Brazil.

When Ireland manager Eoin Hand travelled to ask Manchester United manager Ron Atkinson if he would be willing to release his players to travel to South America, his response was that Hand could tell the FAI to 'fuck off'. Speaking to the *Irish Times*, Hand remembers telling Atkinson he would need an official response. 'Fuck off, that's my official response.'

Other English clubs followed suit. Arsenal manager Terry Neill prevented his Republic of Ireland internationals David O'Leary and John Devine from travelling to Buenos Aires. Neill said, 'I don't feel it is right that our players should be involved in anything to do with Argentina. It's a delicate situation and there's obviously the question of their safety.'

With the prospect of only being able to field a team consisting of League of Ireland players, the match in Argentina was eventually called off four days before the players were scheduled to depart, but the tour to South America went ahead. The FAI remarkably failed to alter their initial travel arrangements and flew to Santiago via Buenos Aires.

Many of the Irish players held UK passports and were understandably nervous about flying into a country where British journalists were being arrested. In his autobiography, *Born to be a*

Footballer, Liam Brady said, 'There were a few sweating on that flight when we landed in Buenos Aires. The late Michael Robinson, one of our English-born players was convinced he'd be arrested.'

The Irish squad had to wait ten hours at Ezeiza International Airport not knowing whether they would be allowed to fly on to Santiago, detained or deported. Hand recalls that 'we were held up in Buenos Aires for a long, long time. We weren't allowed out of the airport while they were checking that we were what we said we were; an international football team. It was awful.'

The day after the war broke out, Tottenham Hotspur's Argentinian international Osvaldo Ardiles was booed mercilessly by opposition fans during the FA Cup semi-final against a Leicester City side featuring Gary Lineker. A banner in the Spurs end suggested that 'Argentina can keep the Falklands, we'll keep Ossie'.

Speaking to the *Daily Mirror*, Ardiles confessed, 'That match was the most difficult game of my life. I could hear the Leicester supporters shouting insults but my heart was lifted by the Tottenham fans chanting "Ossie, Ossie".'

The next morning, Ardiles flew out of Gatwick airport, returning to Buenos Aires to play in a friendly international against the Soviet Union ahead of the 1982 World Cup. In the circumstances, he felt he could not return to England, missing the end of the season and the FA Cup Final.

Back in Argentina, Ardiles was quoted as saying to his country's media that 'if there is a war, I'll never go back. I'll do everything I can to help my country. I would be very sad to leave Spurs. But my country comes first. For England, the Falklands are just a political problem. But for us Argentinians, it is a question of identity and unity.'

Ardiles had a year left on his contract and would eventually return to play for the club until 1988. His manager Keith Burkinshaw knew that his player's hand had been forced upon returning to Buenos Aires: 'I knew what Ossie was going to say when he got home. He told me he would have to say it.'

The hero of the previous season's FA Cup Final, Ardiles's compatriot Ricardo Villa, had not travelled to Birmingham for the semi-final due to injury. However, having not been picked for the national team since 1978, he was not summoned to return home to Argentina ahead of the World Cup. Added to Villa's concerns was the fact that his wife Christina was pregnant with their second child. Vowing to stay in the country unless he has kicked out, he told the *Daily Mirror*, 'It worries me the British Government might say all Argentinians must pack up and leave. I want so much to play in a Cup final at Wembley again.'

In Ardiles's absence, Villa played in the next nine Tottenham Hotspur matches as the conflict between the UK and Argentina over the Falklands escalated. Speaking to the *Independent* in 2006, Villa recalled that 'sometimes I was booed, but that was all. An English player in Buenos Aires at the same time could never have stayed. It was easy for me to stay here.'

The club did not feel that Villa needed extra protection. Burkinshaw urged the club's supporters to 'judge him as a footballer, not concern themselves whether he is English or Argentinian'. At the time, Villa never spoke out about the political situation between the two countries.

One of those games was a European Cup Winners' Cup semi-final away to FC Barcelona, which required Villa to leave and then re-enter the country. The Home Office confirmed to the club that 'there is now a rule that any Argentinian leaving the country at the moment requires a special re-entry visa. He would have been ill-advised to leave without one.'

In the end, the club made the necessary arrangements but Burkinshaw, who had personally gone to Argentina to sign both players in 1978, was prepared to leave Villa in London unless they could guarantee his admission back into the country.

Villa had been the match-winning hero of the 1981 FA Cup Final, scoring twice in the 3-2 replay win over Manchester City. His second was a Maradona-style slalom through the opposition defence, a goal that cemented his place in English football folklore to this day.

After playing in the final league game of the season at Ipswich, Burkinshaw declared, 'He will definitely play at Wembley unless something drastic happens on the political front.' Yet four days later, Villa was left out of the Tottenham Hotspur matchday squad for the 1982 FA Cup Final against Queens Park Rangers. The showpiece match would be broadcast live on BBC and ITV, as well as around the world. As part of the pre-match presentation, each player would be introduced to Princess Anne, the daughter of Queen Elizabeth II. Anne's brother Andrew was part of the naval task force sent to the Falklands on behalf of Her Majesty's Armed Forces.

The Tottenham Hotspur manager refuted suggestions that pressure had been exerted on him to withdraw Villa from selection. However, on the day before the FA Cup Final, a Royal Marines Commando unit launched Operation Sutton, an amphibious landing on to the disputed islands.

The same day, Burkinshaw informed the squad that Villa would not play, following a training session at Cheshunt. He insisted to the media that it had been a mutual decision. 'There was no outside pressure on me not to play him and I certainly didn't consult the government. It is a real blow for the club but in the circumstances there can be no other decision. He is under intolerable pressure. I am sad for him because he deserved to play. I wanted him to play but world events have overtaken us. I am sure the English public would have given him a tremendous reception but this cup final of ours is a big occasion and is seen all over the world. There are a lot of countries where it might have been interpreted differently if he had played.'

With Villa unavailable, midfielder Micky Hazard was selected, but he nevertheless felt for his friend who was 'not able to come back to the place of his biggest glory and maybe relive that moment. He was sort of deprived of that opportunity because of nothing that he did wrong.'

Villa elected not to be at the stadium to watch the FA Cup Final, choosing to stay at home to watch the match on television. In the dressing room before the game, Hoddle said to the team, 'Let's win this for Ricky.' Hoddle scored the winning goal in the replay.

Three weeks before Tottenham Hotspur retained the trophy without him, Ardiles's cousin José was shot down and killed by a British Sea Harrier. The body of José Ardiles was never found. Osvaldo Ardiles went to the 1982 World Cup not knowing for certain whether his relative was dead or being held prisoner by the British. Years later, his uncle came to England to learn the truth from the Ministry of Defence.

Despite that personal loss, Ardiles's son Pablo, who travelled back to South America with his father, told me, 'There was a lot of propaganda at the time, about how Argentina were close to winning the war. Which was nonsense of course.'

FIFA President João Havelange was unconcerned about the prospect of the two nations, so recently at war, meeting at some point during the 1982 World Cup. Speaking during the tournament, he said, 'England and Argentina have not said that they will not play each other. FIFA are not worried and will be happy if it so happens that they do play.'

The unique structure of the World Cup draw in 1982 meant that England could not face Argentina until the final but there was every chance that Scotland would have to meet them in the second group phase should they make out of the first round.

Initially, during the World Cup draw in December 1981, which was televised live to millions around the globe, Scotland had been pulled out to face Argentina in the opening match of the 1982 World Cup. Embarrassed FIFA officials were forced to start again and reallocate Scotland after they realised that they had forgotten to apply their own predetermined procedures to keep the four South American qualifiers apart.

It was Belgium who were eventually paired with Argentina in the opening match at Camp Nou in Barcelona. However, such was the feeling within the UK that ITV elected not to broadcast the match live, restricting coverage of the showpiece occasion to a few clips on the evening news.

In the event, Scotland went out on goal difference and it was the winners of their group, Brazil, who would have to face Argentina, ending their neighbours' reign as world champions with a crushing 3-1 win in Barcelona. England went out three days later at the same stage.

However, playing in Spain opened the eyes of the Argentina squad to the truth they had been hidden from by the media censorship within their country's military dictatorship. In *Touched By God*, Maradona recalled, 'I remember well when we got to Spain in 1982 and saw the first uncensored coverage of the war. It was a massacre, a pile of legs and arms and all those Argentine boys snuffed out in the Malvinas, while those military sons of bitches kept on telling us we were winning the war.'

Jorge Burruchaga was 19 at the time. Recently signed by Argentinian top-tier club Independiente, he recalls that, but for his talent in the game, he may have died fighting for the country: 'I was in the military at the time but was saved by football. After the war I visited the base I had been assigned to and heard about the people who didn't come back. It was tough. Those kids never came back.'

No peace treaty had been signed since the start of hostilities so the nations were still technically at war in 1986. Informal talks had taken place between the two governments but Thatcher was refusing to meet Argentina's new democratically elected President Raúl Alfonsín until his country dropped their claim of sovereignty over the Falkland Islands.

The war had been a financial disaster for Argentina, which was facing an international debt of $50 billion. Inflation in the country had never been under 100 per cent in each year since 1982. The banning of trade between the two nations had begun to thaw as the British had restarted the import of Argentinian fresh fruit and corned beef.

On the sporting front, a team of schoolboys had travelled from Buenos Aires to play in England in 1983. Following a season in which he left the First Division to play for Paris Saint-Germain on loan,

Ardiles had returned to London to play for Tottenham Hotspur. In the summer of 1984, Spurs had even given a trial to the hero of Argentina's 1978 World Cup triumph, Mario Kempes, as a potential replacement for the departing Steve Archibald.

In the immediate aftermath of the Falklands War, all Argentines entering the UK were required to apply for a visa. Ardiles, who had lived in England for four years but had returned to Argentina with the rest of the 1982 World Cup squad, was refused a work permit. Applying again from the British Consulate in Paris, with the help of Tottenham Hotspur secretary Peter Day, Ardiles was denied an entry visa to the UK. Yet, a couple of months later at the start of 1983, there was a turnaround and Ardiles returned to play for Spurs in January.

Pablo Ardiles was seven years old when the war broke out. He told me, 'We moved to France and travelled a lot between Argentina and France. It was a very unsettling time for me. I have very few memories of the time – I think I have probably blocked them out. I didn't understand why I couldn't be in England with my friends. I really didn't enjoy Paris, even though it is a great city – one of my favourites now I am older – but at the time I didn't want to be there. I wanted to be in England. We also went back to Argentina. I didn't really fit in in Argentina. It was time I didn't really feel at home anywhere. I had family in Argentina that I loved. It was a strange time. It affected all of us very much. We loved England and we loved Argentina.'

At international level, all major polo and rugby matches between the two nations had been cancelled. However, after the 1986 World Cup draw had paired them with Uruguay, the Scottish Football Association (SFA) pursued a pre-tournament friendly against Argentina to prepare their national team to face a South American opponent.

Scotland originally pinpointed the March international window for a game between the two sides at Hampden Park, with the two countries' representatives meeting in Mexico City after the draw for the group stage on 15 December 1985. The SFA was keen to line up a glamorous opponent for what would be the 100th international appearance for Liverpool player-manager Kenny Dalglish. SFA Secretary Ernie Wise believed he had a verbal agreement with his Argentinian counterparts when he left Mexico. Upon his arrival back in Glasgow he instead discovered that they had arranged to play in Paris on the same date, against Michel Platini's France.

A spokesman for the Argentinian Football Association told the *Daily Record* that 'there are diplomatic reasons why there would be problems about a game in Britain at this time ... perhaps some other time'. In the end, Dalglish's landmark cap – he remains the only Scottish man to represent his country 100 times – was won against Romania.

Walker hoped 'some other time' could be the following month, in between Scotland's match against England at Wembley and Argentina's trip to play Norway in Oslo. The SFA sought out government permission from the UK Foreign Office for what would have been the first meeting between Argentina and a British side since the Falklands War.

With diplomacy in mind, Walker said, 'Perhaps we have had too many physical battles recently. Now it's time to have a match where skill will be the only factor. If we were to meet the Argentines, it could help resolve other problems.'

Ultimately, the match could not be arranged. Walker claimed that the diplomatic situation had nothing to do with it: 'Argentina want to play us as part of their European tour, but the fee they are asking is exorbitant. They will have to lower their demands if they really want to play at Hampden.'

The arrival of the Argentina squad in the UK may have quelled some of the hysteria generated by the tabloid press from both nations ahead of the tournament. Instead, that first encounter took place during the pressure cooker of a World Cup quarter-final. Scotland would have to wait until the eve of the following World Cup in 1990 to entice Argentina – without Maradona – to play at Hampden Park.

The day after England beat Paraguay to ensure a knockout tie against Argentina at the 1986 World Cup, the UK Foreign Office took the unusual step of issuing a statement: 'We see sporting occasions of this kind as wholly consistent with the British government's efforts in seeking to normalise relations between Britain and Argentina. It is, of course, up to the governing body of the different British sports associations to decide whether to engage in competition with Argentine teams. Naturally we hope that the England-Argentine match will be played and watched in the sporting spirit that such an occasion demands.'

FIFA President João Havelange concurred with the sentiment: 'Obviously fair play will be very important on Sunday but you can be assured this game will, above all, be one of discipline and technique. It will go down in the history of the World Cup for the behaviour of the players who have come here to play football, not to engage in politics. We have all confidence that there will not be any major incidents on or off the pitch.'

However, at ground level, *The People* newspaper reported that England fans in Mexico City had regularly been signing, 'What's it like to lose a war?' 'Bring on the Argies', and 'Who do you think you are kidding, Galtieri?' to the theme tune of 1970s Second World War sitcom *Dad's Army*.

Tickets for every game at the tournament were split into five categories (A–E). Notionally, the cheapest category D ($10) and E ($3) tickets were only sold to Mexican residents to prevent locals being priced out of attending matches in their own country. Tickets in the other categories were priced at $20, $30 and $50 (£12, £18 and £30). These might seem a bargain now when general sale tickets for the 2026 World Cup Final range from a staggering $4,185 to $8,680. Yet in 1986, the most expensive seats in an English First Division stadium were priced under £5.

Most of the tickets for the 1986 World Cup quarter-final had been sold as part of 'season tickets' covering each game at a particular stadium. British travel agents were offering a set of tickets to all 13 matches in Mexico City for £650, way beyond the budget of the average English football fan. In the preceding season, the most expensive season ticket at Old Trafford covering all 21 league matches plus priority on cup games was £96.

Mexican fans who had purchased category D and E season tickets for the Estadio Azteca in order to see their team play its first four games there were now free to sell on their quarter-final tickets at the stadium in a lucrative black market.

Mark Woodroffe was a 25-year-old Norwich City fan who at the start of June 1986 was, in his own words, 'bumming around the United States'. After watching England's victory over Poland in a hostel in Santa Monica, he decided, together with his best friend Nick, to drive to Mexico City in the Ford Ranch Wagon they had purchased a few weeks earlier for $500. Having recruited three others from the hostel, they set off on their 3,000km road trip. Following a hairy three-day journey across a desert and through a tornado they made it to outside the Azteca, where they slept the night before the Round of 16 match in the car they had christened 'The Belgrano', with a Union Jack stuck on the back window.

The next morning they easily found touts selling tickets for the equivalent of £10. In this light, Pamela Ibarrola, a spokesperson for the British Embassy in Mexico admitted, 'There is no chance of segregating fans. Tickets have been sold for a long time now and it would be impossible to keep them apart. Even on the streets of the city and outside the stadium itself, tickets can be readily bought. We are just hoping that a strong security presence will keep everything in order and the fans are sensible.'

Two days before the game, British Consul Bob Webb and the FA's police liaison officer Les Walker met with Mexican authorities, requesting extra security inside the Azteca due to the lack of segregation. Ibarrola confirmed that 'the Mexican authorities have been made aware that there could be complications, and they have assured us they will lay on extra security inside the Aztec stadium'.

Among the celebrity fans heading to the game was the lead singer of AC/DC, Brian Johnson. The good behaviour of the England supporters had convinced the Newcastle United fanatic to make the last-minute decision to take his wife Carol to the Azteca Stadium. Speaking to Newcastle's *Sunday Sun*, Johnson said, 'I was worried about going in case the fans caused a riot. I didn't want to be an Englishman in Mexico if our name was dirt. But the fans have been brilliant, and I was so excited about watching Peter Beardsley since he came into the team that I couldn't resist going over.'

Also attending would be 31-year-old Joe O'Connell from Sligo. The Irishman was visiting his brother-in-law in Florida and was given the choice between watching Barry McGuigan fight Steve Cruz in Las Vegas or travelling to the World Cup. He chose to fly with his wife to Mexico City. Supplied with free tickets for the quarter-final through a contact in the British Embassy, his concern as an English-speaking couple in a foreign country was not the threat of hostile Argentina fans identifying them as British, but the depths of poverty they encountered in a city still recovering from the devastating effects of the previous year's earthquake.

Looking out on the morning of the match from the ninth floor window of their high-rise hotel in the city's affluent Zona Rosa, they saw people living in tents on top of adjoining buildings, and row upon row of temporary shelters pieced together from sheets of corrugated metal. Later, given two tickets for the final, O'Connell had to forego the once-in-a-lifetime opportunity as the only available flights out of the city were several days later, and his wife Anne could not bear to witness the suffering of everyday people any further.

'She had seen enough of the poverty,' O'Connell told me. 'That upset her more, watching families on the street begging for food. While I was only thinking of the football, my wife was looking at all this because she's a very sentimental person. What really changed her mind is when we went on a trip one day to some of the pyramids outside Mexico City. We had to travel through areas where there were shanty towns; we'd never seen shanty towns before, never seen anything like it in my life. You had tens of thousands of people living on the side of hills. It would really affect you. For my wife, it had an awful effect on her. She found it quite hard to come back into a plush hotel.'

For the Argentines living in England, the emphasis was on keeping the occasion low-key. One told *The Telegraph*, 'On Sunday we will gather round the telly, just among friends, with plenty of good Argentine wine and an asado [barbeque] cooking over a slow fire, and we'll pray like mad that Argentina wins.'

Another, who wished to remain anonymous, claimed a tin of corned beef had been hurled through his front window at the beginning of the Falklands War. He hoped an Argentina victory would not lead to more of the same. 'The English are good winners but poor losers.'

The most famous Argentine in England during the World Cup was the new star of women's tennis; 16-year-old Gabriela Sabatini had just finished playing at the Eastbourne championships and had recently been voted the second most popular person in Argentina – ahead of Maradona – behind only President Alfonsín. Speaking to the *Sunday Express*, Sabatini admitted that, despite playing in the first round of Wimbledon the next day, she would be watching the World Cup quarter-final. 'I watch it all the time. I see Argentina win, and I hope, yes, they will win when they play England. I like Maradona very much – oh yes. What will I do if they win? A party? No, I don't know what I'll do.'

In Argentina itself, one of its MPs, Miguel Alterich, requested that a one-minute's silence be observed before the game in memory of the soldiers who died in the Falklands War. Eight Argentinian senators – all Peronists – made a last-minute plea to President Alfonsín to pull the national team out of the World Cup so they would not have to play the country that 'had taken possession of land belonging to Argentina'. Both suggestions were rejected by the government.

The Argentinian Minister of Sport, former rugby player and national team coach, Rodolfo O'Reilly, was more conciliatory: 'We are convinced that our players will put all their enthusiasm into this game and concentrate exclusively on playing football.'

However, on the Falkland Islands themselves, the residents of Port Stanley saw the match as an opportunity to make Argentina pay for their invasion and occupation. Peter McKay, a 23-year-old mechanic, told *The Telegraph*, 'It's impossible not to think of it that way. Every Argentine footballer was quick enough to support the invasion, but now they conveniently want to forget it. But I'm afraid we can't. I want England to give them a damn good thrashing.'

With English teams having been banned from competing in European club competitions the previous season as a consequence of the Heysel Stadium disaster, The FA was understandably concerned that further outbreaks of hooliganism on the world stage would undermine their attempts to reintegrate their teams into UEFA tournaments.

While the English fans had arrived in Mexico branded as 'animals' by the local press in Monterrey, the majority did not live up to their fearsome reputation. Indeed, two days after their victory over Poland, in which the England supporters had led celebratory conga lines around the Estadio Universitario, the nation's English-language paper ran a story headed 'Hooligans, bah! Monterrey loves the English.'

'The labelling of the English as animals has stopped in the local press ... And the people of Monterrey have fully embraced the young Englishmen who have played friendly matches with local youths to prove they are better than the label suggested.'

FA Secretary Ted Croker concurred, playing down the risk of potential confrontations with Argentina fans: 'I think the behaviour of England supporters on this trip so far has been exemplary. As far as we are concerned, sport is sport, and politics is politics. I know they overlap in certain areas but I believe sport bridges gaps between countries far more easily than politicians can. The game is a wonderful opportunity to build a bridge between our two countries.'

To prove that sport and politics do not mix, Croker chose to attend the England v Paraguay match with Admiral Carlos Lacoste, the one-time head of the ruling military junta in Argentina. Croker revealed that Lacoste was keen for England to defeat his fellow South Americans and set up an encounter with Argentina. 'Without wishing any ill-will on his neighbouring country he was also hoping that our two nations should meet.'

Lacoste had been the head of the World Cup Organising Committee, assuming that role after the original choice General Omar Actis had been murdered by a car bomb. Investigative journalists in Argentina later found evidence that Actis had been killed on Lacoste's orders.

When Roberto Viola was ousted in a coup d'état in 1981, Lacoste served as interim president of the state for 12 days in December before being succeeded by Leopoldo Galtieri, the man who would order the invasion of the Falkland Islands the next year.

After democracy was restored to Argentina, Lacoste was handed a role as a South American representative at FIFA. Many Argentines thought his presence in Mexico was an outrage. Speaking many years later, 1978 World Cup-winning goalkeeper, Ubaldo Fillol, confessed that Lacoste had once threatened his life. 'One day Lacoste called me and put a revolver on top of the table. He told me, "If I want to, I can make you disappear and nobody will find out."'

Nonetheless, Croker went on to say, 'We will treat this as a normal match at the World Cup. I think what the admiral was saying was that there have been political differences between us in the past but not sporting differences. I share that opinion.'

Nevertheless, it was not a view shared by the British tabloids. Two days before the match, *The Sun* inevitably led the jingoism with the infamous headline: 'It's War, Senor' (sic), stating that 'troops on alert for Argy battle, gunships and tanks standby'.

At the height of the battle between the country's red tops, the *Daily Star* used those headlines as a stick to beat their rivals with. 'There's one way we will not go ... this newspaper that is. And that's to follow the idiotically exaggerated reporting about security for the game. This is not a war, senor. This is a football match that could be spoiled by a lunatic fringe spurred on by lunatic jingoism.' On the back pages of the same edition, they at least attempted some subtlety in their racism by informing the country: 'don't let this Diego go by'.

In light of all this, Labour MP George Foulkes, the shadow minister of foreign affairs, made a complaint to the Press Council alleging that 'a lot of the media are turning this match into a re-run of the Falklands War. They appear to be trying to whip up hostility again. We should be urging the supporters of the two teams to ignore these hysterical and inflammatory outbursts on the part of some sections of the British press.'

However, under the headline, 'Field of human conflict', *The Times*'s feature writer Alan Franks believed the tabloids were tapping into the feelings of the general public. 'This is one of those few occasions when the popular press, echoing the 1982 headlines of "Gotcha!" and the rest, is not wholly guilty of hyperbole. The fixture in fact is rather more than a mere game of football, in the same way that a Test Match between England and the West Indies is rather more than a mere game of cricket. Both have become metaphors for the greater puissance of the competing nations.'

The next day, *The Sun* toned down it's rhetoric in its 'The Sun Says' editorial column. Under the headline 'Sport not war', they attempted now to be the voice of reason, urging fans to show restraint and that 'if anti-Brit feeling erupts on the terraces, flags are burned and slogans chanted our fans don't have to be provoked. Let them for once turn the other cheek.'

Writing on the back pages the day before the game, John Sadler spoke of his concerns that the beautiful game could once more be tarnished by hooliganism: 'After more than 20 years writing on sport around the world ... for the first time I feel a sense of fear. And fear should have no part in the build-up to an event, be it a World Cup or an Olympics. But after the horrors of the Heysel Stadium, the attention of the world will be trained on the Aztec's potentially explosive mix.'

'We are very unhappy to hear headlines like that,' said Robert Webb of the British Consulate in Mexico City. 'Everyone here is trying to play it low-key. It is just a football match as far as everyone in Mexico is concerned. Headlines like that can only stir things up. Security inside the ground is not as much in evidence as we would like, although we understand the Mexican authorities have many plain-clothes security men mingled among the supporters. But, to be fair, it is hard to cause trouble in the stadium. It is simply not built for charging around it.'

Outside the stadium was a different matter. The *Daily Star* spoke to some of the Argentina fans in Mexico. Victor Rossi, a 42-year-old clerk from Santa Fé, warned the English about confronting the notorious *barra bravas* (fierce group). 'They are dangerous animals. They still want to fight the Malvinas war. For once, England can be proud of its fans.'

During Argentina's match against Bulgaria, some of their fans had burned a Union Jack on the stands of the Estadio Olimpico. The match had been played on 10 June, the anniversary of the day in 1829 when Luis Vernet had been appointed governor of the 'Islas Malvinas' by the Buenos Aires government. The 25-year-old Jorge Marquez had lost his cousin in the Battle of Goose Green, a pivotal defeat for Argentina during the Falklands War. He was realistic about what was likely to occur: 'Most people want no trouble. But if I am honest there is a hooligan element from our own country – and yours too – that will clash. I think it is inevitable.'

To prove the point, Brian Dear, 24, of Yeovil said to the *Daily Mirror* that 'they are our country's enemies. I don't want trouble but if those bastards burn Union Jacks, I know I'll lose my rag.' Daniel Withers of Hull told *The Sun* that 'if Argentinian fans start saying the islands are theirs, then there could be trouble'. Mick from Rugby went further. 'We will kick the Argies to pieces,' he told *The People*. 'I don't go for trouble,' he insisted, 'I am not armed, I just use my fists, but any hint of bother and we'll give them a good hiding. I'm waiting to meet up with some of the National Front fans.'

Argentina's goalkeeper Nery Pumpido seemed to be tapping into the feelings of many on the terraces when he insisted that 'it's special because of tradition but it is also special because of the Malvinas. Not that I think that is a bad thing because it will make us play all the harder. To beat the English would constitute a double satisfaction, for everything that happened in the Malvinas.'

However, publicly at least, this was not a view voiced by many of the other players who were at pains to downplay the political significance of the match. The erudite forward Jorge Valdano said 'It will be an interesting game because the two teams play different styles. The fact this is a World Cup quarter-final game is sufficient motivation for political issues not to enrich or dirty the contest.'

Head coach Bilardo responded to repeated questioning about the war with the English words 'only football'. However speaking to Mexican newspaper *ESTO*, he was more honest. 'I have my feelings, my way of thinking, but at this moment I am in a sports competition and I cannot express it. I will externalise it another time. Now, you know that not all people think the same – that it is very difficult to escape – because I have many friends who have had a lot of pain, but at this moment keep in mind that Argentina only thinks about the sporting part.'

Maradona spoke to the world's media for 75 minutes penned into a corner attempting to deflect the conversation away from the recent war between the two nations. Asked by *The Times*'s Spanish-speaking journalist John Carlin what impact he thought politics would have on the game, he responded, 'Look mate, I play football. About politics, I know nothing. Nothing, mate, nothing.'

At one point he was almost tripped over as photographers followed his every move. He asked, 'Why is it the English want to talk about that?' Another player quipped, 'Because it's easy for them to talk about it. They won.' Maradona later reacted angrily to the persistent line of interrogation. 'Why do you keep asking the same questions? We are not taking guns on to the field, we are not going to shoot anyone. We are going to play football. It will only be a football game, we are not going to resolve anything by putting the ball in the goal. How can I talk of war when last month I was cheered on to the field at Tottenham Hotspur by 30,000 English fans?'

Speaking many years later in his 2005 memoir *El Diego*, Maradona admitted he had lied back in 1986. 'Bollocks was it another match! In a way we blamed the English players for everything that happened, for all the suffering of the Argentine people. I know it seems like madness and a nonsense now but truthfully at the time that was what we felt.'

In his autobiography *Playmaker*, Glenn Hoddle conceded that 'it was bigger than football for them. They had extra emotional edge, a deep yearning to beat us, and it was like their players were the medium for a nation yearning for revenge. The footballers were the only ones who could get one over on the English, and it gave them extra motivation on the day. They were able to tap into something deeper, something more visceral.

'We couldn't fool ourselves into feeling those emotions. They simply didn't exist. Our motivation was more straightforward. We were simply desperate to reach the last four of the World Cup and we felt that we were good enough to beat Argentina – as long as we found a way to stop Maradona.'

Despite the political sensitivities surrounding the match, BBC commentator Barry Davies told me he did not recall receiving any special instructions from the corporation over language to avoid during the game: 'The BBC didn't do that so often. I think they trusted their commentators a bit better.'

Determined not to give Argentina any extra motivation to defeat them, England manager Bobby Robson had become an expert in treading on political eggshells before international games. With English clubs a year into an indefinite ban from European club competitions following the Heysel Stadium disaster involving Liverpool and Juventus fans, the threat of hooliganism was a constant factor around the national team during the 1980s. Robson's media officer Glen Kirton told me the manager and players had got used to fending off inflammatory questions from the press a year earlier: 'There'd been a practice run the year before because we went to Mexico in 1985 for a mini-tournament. The match against Italy followed on immediately [one week] from Heysel. So there was tension in the air about the relationship between England and Italy. 'There'd been plenty of practice in what you should say and what you shouldn't say.'

Nevertheless, the day before the game, a group of England fans were supposedly ambushed on the central square around El Ángel de la Independencia monument, attacked from both sides of the Paseo de la Reforma by Argentina fans representing the Boca Juniors' *barra bravas* known as 'La Doce' (the 12th man). Following a 20-minute battle, the English fans had some of their flags and banners stolen as prizes in the fight. Union Jacks and the 'West Ham NF' flag prominent at earlier England games in Monterrey were subsequently taken back to Buenos Aires and displayed by 'La Doce' at the Estadio Bombonera, the home of Boca Juniors.

Inside the stadium, 'La Doce' draped their stolen Union Jacks from the Perspex barriers on the upper tiers of the Azteca beneath a gigantic Argentina flag and their trademark blue-and-yellow banner representing the colours of Boca Juniors. On *News at Ten*, ITV's Terry Lloyd reported that the display was a sign that the rival fans were mixing on the stands, stating that 'from early on, it was clear that Union Jacks were mingling with Argentine flags'.

However, what might have seemed like a show of solidarity in the modern age, was anything but. The *barra bravas* were provocatively displaying their acquisitions from the pre-match confrontation between the two nations. When one of those flags was burned, it provoked English fans on their left to attack them. The baton-wielding Mexican police were quick to intervene, separating the two lines of fans. A bearded Argentine was captured on film wielding a black cosh.

At the ground, fans had to go through metal detectors, a first at the tournament, as the Mexican police imposed a 'ring of steel' outside the stadium. A Mexican newspaper offered this warning to any would-be troublemakers: 'Riot police will fill your orifices with tear gas and drive your head into your shoulders like a nail.'

David Robinson, aged 21, told the *Rochdale Observer* that he had never experienced such security measures at a football match: 'It didn't stop the Argentinians sneaking in iron bars and canisters of tear gas through.'

In his excellent book, *Mexico on Fifty Dollars a Ticket*, Mick Worrall said that his newspaper was confiscated at the gate 'in case you tear it up and throw it'. Simultaneously, Worrall witnessed that Argentina fans carrying flagpoles, drums and drumsticks were waved through. Television pictures from the game showed a fan in the first row of the upper tier brandishing a live snake!

The *Irish Independent* described how the Mexican police, army and security forces smothered the venue, both inside and outside the stadium: 'Automatic rifles were cradled by some, others toted machine guns while some gently smacked three foot wooden batons into the palms of their hands as a subtle warning to supporters not to get out of line. The authorities identified two main sets of English fans, and one group of Argentines. As a precaution, they were surrounded by hand-picked security men, dressed in beige-coloured tracksuits and wearing trainers for mobility. The Mexicans clearly intended to contain and quash any violence instantly.'

Of the 20,000 security personnel deployed, the majority were outside the ground. The few inside the stadium were in the moat between the pitch and the stands among hordes of photographers more interested in capturing any fighting off the pitch than incident on it. Standing in the front row, Mark Woodroffe recalls watching the action confronted by 'dozens of Mexican soldiers pointing rifles at us throughout the game. They looked more scared of us than we were of them.'

Ahead of kick-off, Mick Worrall claimed that Mexican fans began to taunt and abuse the English fans in the stadium and several small fights broke out during the game, many captured on film. Another Union Jack stolen by Argentina fans in the city centre was set alight by a man on the lower tier as the game kicked off.

Many Argentinian banners at the game referred to the country's claim to the South American islands, including a Santa Fé flag with the words 'Malvinas Siempre Argentinas' (the Falklands are Always Argentinian) written along the bottom. Many supporters wore T-shirts to the same effect.

At the opposite end, English fans unfurled a banner over a balustrade on the top balcony reading 'Exocet Lineker – EFC' (Everton Football Club). The French-built Exocet missile was deployed by the Argentinian navy to sink the HMS *Sheffield*. It was now used to describe the sharpshooter who the England fans hoped would sink Argentina's World Cup hopes. The banner was confiscated by the police during the first half.

Another more innocuous banner hanging from the top tier in between England flags from West Acton and Bingley, West Yorkshire was one addressed to a woman – 'Carol, please marry me'.

The Sun reported that 'the match turned into a terrifying ordeal for innocent England fans as Argy thugs brutally attacked them. Waving Las Malvinas flags, they launched at least four major assaults in the Aztec stadium. The worst scenes came just one minute into the match after they set fire to a Union Jack being waved by one group of England supporters. Riot police wielding 3ft batons hauled apart rival fans as they punched and kicked each other behind the Argentine goal.'

Ultimately, the stadium medical facilities treated 51 casualties from the crowd of 114,580. Only two, both Mexicans, were taken to hospital, one with breathing difficulties, the other with gastroenteritis. Police later said there were no arrests made during the game.

In comparison, the day before, around 100 arrests – including 15 Germans – were made in Monterrey after hosts Mexico had been eliminated in a penalty shoot-out by West Germany. Mexican fans, allegedly shouting 'death to the Nazis' had tried to enter a hotel containing German fans, who retaliated by hurling objects including chairs and beer bottles at them. Twenty people were reported injured.

At the end of the game, some Argentina fans unfurled a 6ft by 4ft banner with the slogan 'Death to Tatcher [sic] the player number 12' written on it in Spanish, with a skull and crossbones symbol. After the match, it was widely reported in the British press that around 20 English fans hid under a bridge on the Avenue Calzada de Tlalpan leading away from the stadium and attempted to ambush a larger group of celebrating Argentines. Having had bottles and stones hurled at them, the Argentines retaliated by chasing the English fans down the wide avenue, using their flagpoles as weapons. It took the arrival of 300 policemen to break up the violence.

Woodroffe told me that he and Nick got separated from their three other friends and ended up in a side street confronted by two Argentines, and two policemen pointing guns at them. They made their excuses and managed to escape without harm. This was later corroborated by the Associated Press, who reported that the fans were held at gunpoint for several minutes after being chased by two policemen. The incident began when English supporters began throwing beer bottles at the entrance of a hotel. A British diplomat was told the fans were reacting after Argentina fans ganged up on two Englishmen in a car.

Police Lieutenant Jesus González later confirmed that no one was arrested and the action was taken to discourage further incidents. The English press reported that fans from both sides were treated for cuts and bruises and around a dozen were briefly detained.

When they returned to their hotel, Woodroffe found people in the reception watching a television documentary on *Los Hooligans*, featuring footage of the England fans' worst rampages through history before cutting to a news programme detailing the confrontations in Mexico City that day. Woodroffe saw himself on the screen shouting abuse at Maradona from the stands.

The Holiday Inn

Bobby Robson had promised the players before the tournament that if they reached the semi-finals, their wives and girlfriends would be flown out at the FA's expense for the final week of the World Cup. Having travelled out previously to spend time with the squad during their pre-tournament camp in Colorado, a 250-seat chartered plane was ready to fly the families out to Mexico City to arrive on the Tuesday at an estimated cost of £20,000. Robson's own 82-year-old father, a former miner, was also due to jet out, having just been issued with a new passport.

An FA spokesman allegedly told the *News of the World*: 'I know some teams, like France, have had their ladies out in Mexico all along. But we agree with manager Bobby Robson that too much ooh-la-la can put players off their stride. Everyone seems delighted with our arrangements.'

In hindsight, this may not have been the case. Alvin Martin was one who was impatient to see his family. He told me, 'Every individual is different but I struggled with it. Sarah, my daughter, was two and David was born in the January. You miss your kids at that age.' Martin was more fortunate than the majority of the squad. His brother had flown out to watch the whole tournament and was one of the few family members out in Mexico, alongside Kenny Sansom's 61-year-old mother Rose.

Rose Sansom had travelled at her own expense and was staying by herself at the same hotel as members of the British media. In between matches she spent her time sightseeing the streets of Mexico City. Speaking to the *London Evening Standard*, her son revealed: 'She goes all over the place, my mum. When I played for Crystal Palace, she never missed a game.'

In March, Bobby Robson, together with his liaison officer Alan O'Dell and team doctor Vernon Edwards had visited Mexico City to choose potential accommodation for the team should they reach the later stages of the World Cup. They settled on the Holiday Inn close to the airport. They were satisfied that the double glazing shut out the noise of the aircraft and that both the rooms and restaurants were of sufficient quality.

Yet, when England flew to Mexico City from Monterrey for the Round of 16, they checked into the four-star Hotel Vallé de Mexico close to their new training base. Sick of travelling an hour and a quarter each way from their previous hotel in Saltillo to their first-round training facility, and now playing at a higher altitude, the players yearned for less of a daily commute in the summer heat of a Mexican morning.

In Mexico City, England trained at the Reforma, a sports club that reminded everyone in the squad of home. With a lush football and cricket pitch, a swimming pool and 22 tennis courts, it was a haven for ex-pats and British descendants.

The president of the club was a German national called Sigurd Burmester, a former Luftwaffe pilot shot down over Budapest in February 1945 and captured by the Russian army before emigrating to Mexico City upon his release. The *Manchester Evening News* reported that a British background was a requirement for membership of the club.

In contrast to the soaring temperatures of Monterrey, the capital city proved to be a bit of a culture shock to the squad. The sky was overcast and the air was full of smog. In the midst of the rainy season, the locals warned of afternoon downpours and, almost like clockwork, torrential rain fell every day around 5pm, preventing the players from doing anything outside in the evening.

Everton's Gary Stevens told me about the problems of adapting to living and playing at the high altitude of Mexico City: 'Monterrey had a bit more of a holiday feel about it. It was less busy, less frantic. It's actually the flight of the ball that gets you more than anything else, you're sort of under-running crosses and passes in the first couple of training sessions but you quickly get used to it.'

Everton team-mate Trevor Steven recounted to me his wonder at the surroundings. 'I think it was an adventure. I was 22. The whole thing about being in a World Cup and the size of the tournament was not lost on any of us. We were all ticking a box, as far as our dreams were concerned. To go into Mexico City, we knew we were going into extreme altitude and a city that was just a complete hubbub of noise, continually day and night. It's difficult to rationalise that four years earlier I was at school and then all of a sudden you're in a World Cup tournament and going towards a quarter-final and likely to play.'

While the new hotel was close to the Reforma club, it was also sat next to an industrial estate between two major motorways, constantly clogged with traffic. The only television channels available were Mexican ones and the players were finding it difficult to get through to their families in England on the hotel's telephone system.

Their new accommodation also lacked air conditioning, and the plumbing made noises akin to 'a spectacular concert' during the middle of the night. The England players quickly dubbed the hotel 'Fawlty Towers' and the press labelled it a '£14-a-night doss house'.

In his World Cup diary, *So Near and Yet So Far*, Robson said the reporters 'saw a story and started to tell the players what a dump it was, looking for a reaction'. During a meeting with the squad, a couple of the senior players, including captain Shilton, complained about not being able to sleep. Everton's Gary Stevens told me, 'One of the two of the players found odd things in their bread and food, so we ended up moving up hotels.'

'It made logic, and common sense, to try the hotel that we were in because we were seven minutes from our training ground,' said Bobby Robson, admitting defeat. 'Having had to endure long journeys down the motorway daily, the players were naturally trying to get out of that situation. We've moved out because of noise, just pure noise. The hotel was alright, they loved us and they tried very hard to supply us with the right accommodation. What they can't do is change the noise, they can't stop the traffic in the early mornings.

'On that basis, and that basis only, we have decided to move hotels for the benefit of the players. Not all of the players – many of them have slept quite well, some haven't.'

Peter Reid joked, 'Imagine a room on the hard shoulder of the M62; that's what it was like!'

The England players moved soon after watching Argentina defeat Uruguay, two days before their own Round of 16 match against Paraguay. They relocated to the Holiday Inn, Robson's initial choice. He now hoped the move would work in England's favour, the upgrade providing the players with a psychological boost at the perfect time, which they may not have appreciated had they moved straight there from Saltillo.

Trevor Steven told me the new hotel was 'probably 25 per cent better and not ideal. It had a great view over the motorways. Not much to see, not much to look at. It was pretty much the industrial Mexico City that we were in. But we weren't there for that. We weren't there to look around and to sightsee, we were there to do a job.'

Holders Italy, who opened the tournament at the Estadio Azteca three weeks earlier, were also staying at the Holiday Inn. Upon England's arrival, Mark Hateley chatted to his club colleague Paolo Rossi. In fact, alongside Ray Wilkins, there were more AC Milan players in the England squad than the Italian. Many of the Italian players complained about having been away from home for so long.

In the morning, Italy left to play their midday Round of 16 match against the European champions France. The England players went into the dining room where the world champions had enjoyed their pre-match meal. On their self-imposed drinks ban, the English players were amazed to see bottles of wine next to the Italians' plates.

The next day, the Italians were checking out after losing 2-0 to a Michel Platini-inspired France in the city's Olimpico '68 stadium. The deposed champions offered the England players their good wishes as they waited in the lobby. Bobby Robson had come down especially to see them off. His Italian counterpart Enzo Bearzot gestured to Robson that his players did not have anything left to give – 'dead minds, nothing'.

Terry Butcher told me the departure of the reigning World Cup winners illustrated how far England had come in two matches. 'To be in a position where we could have been knocked out in the group stage, to then be staying on and still playing in the competition when Italy left felt really nice.'

The players trained early in the morning as most games would kick off at midday. The FA brought their own chef, and the squad's sugar and iron levels were monitored through regular blood and urine tests.

In 1970, wary of foreign cuisine, the FA transported their own food to Mexico. Much of it ended up being set on fire at the airport as it was not cleared by Mexican customs, who cited the risk of importing foot and mouth disease into the country.

This time, mindful of upsetting their hosts again, they brought over only a few essentials from back home. Skips arrived filled with HP Sauce, mustard, tins of baked beans and cases of Mars bars. The players were encouraged to adopt a high-carbohydrate diet ahead of games, with plenty of pasta. Honey and chocolate were consumed on the day of the game.

The squad were usually back in the hotel by 2pm and left to entertain themselves for the rest of the day. CNN was the only English-language television station available to them and, due to the intense heat, the players were banned from sunbathing after 11.15am.

Mindful of the high number of tabloid photographers sent out to Mexico, Bobby Robson stressed to the players the importance of behaving at all times: 'I want no trouble. We all know they're out there, so if you go out into town, go in twos and with an FA fella with you. These people are here for one reason only, so be ultra-careful.'

Many of the players had brought portable Walkmans with them and passed the time listening to music. Glenn Hoddle chose The Eagles, Gary Bailey listened to Dire Straits, while Kerry Dixon preferred Lionel Richie.

Manager Robson was staying in room 222. He found time to escape the pressures of managing his country at a World Cup by reading espionage novels by John le Carré or listening to his own episode of *Desert Island Discs*, selected on the BBC Radio 4 show that was recorded alongside Michael Parkinson just before the World Cup. As well as saying he would take a copy of *Roget's Thesaurus* and a set of golf clubs as his luxury item, his musical choices would have seemed as distant to his players as theirs now seem to us: 'Pomp and Circumstance' by Elgar, 'Try a Little Tenderness' by Frank Sinatra, 'A Nightingale Sang in Berkeley Square' by Mel Tormé, 'Dance of the Swans' by Tchaikovsky, 'September Morn' by Neil Diamond, 'Slaughter on Tenth Avenue' by Rodgers and Hart, 'The Girl from Ipanema' by Astrud Gilberto, and 'I Dreamed a Dream' by Patti LuPone.

Captain Peter Shilton was in room 509 with another player born in Leicester who, 11 years his junior, had idolised him as a youngster, Gary Lineker. The goalkeeper was mockingly referred to as 'Shilly' after Bobby Robson had accidently called him that during a training game. Now aged 36, Shilton was playing in his second World Cup, having won two European Cups with Nottingham Forest, and he had also just been featured on the popular *This is Your Life* television series on ITV, underlining his status as a national celebrity.

According to his former Forest team-mate Viv Anderson, now in Mexico with the England squad, Shilton was in no doubt about how good he was. 'Do I think he believed that he was the best goalkeeper in the world? Absolutely he did! He was never short on confidence, Peter, in fairness.'

Reid elaborated, 'He was single-minded. He was very driven in himself, very driven. He used to look after himself. He trained to the maximum all the time, always finished with shots against him. He was a fitness fanatic.'

No one would get to know the goalkeeper better than Lineker. 'For most of my England career, I was room-mates with Peter Shilton. I used to do as I was told. He used to snore quite badly, I had to just roll him over. He's a noisy sleeper was the goalie.'

The men who arrived in Mexico as England's captain and vice-captain – Bryan Robson and Ray Wilkins – also shared a room. Injury and suspension had cost them their guaranteed starting positions in midfield. It was not the World Cup either had expected it to be. Robson told me, 'Obviously it was a bad time for us. In 1982, the two of us played in all the games and we had a great time.'

Peter Reid was the beneficiary of their misfortune. He told me, 'It was difficult for them two lads. Even though they weren't involved after the first couple of games, they were desperate for us to get results. I think that showed the spirit among the lads.'

After his shoulder had been dislocated against Morocco, Bryan Robson could have gone home to have it pinned but elected to stay in Mexico. He explained to me that Bobby Robson wanted him, as captain, to remain out there: 'He wanted me to stay for the morale of the squad. I actually wanted to stay as well. Even though it was frustrating for me with the injury, I wanted to still be a part of it, and Bobby Robson did. Obviously Ron Atkinson, he didn't, because he wanted me to get back and get the operation on my shoulder.'

Bobby Robson had made a personal plea to his captain to have the shoulder pinned after it had come out five months earlier. However, with Manchester United in pole position to end their 18-year wait for a First Division title, Atkinson did not want his talisman to miss any games, so Bryan Robson delayed the surgery.

Looking back on it now, he realises it would have saved him several more painful dislocations: 'The frustrating thing for me was that I had the operation when I got back and, ever since, the shoulder has never, ever given me a problem. So when I actually first did it against Coventry at Old Trafford [in January 1985] before the World

Cup, I know I would have had no problem, if I'd had the operation there and then.'

Terry Butcher was rooming with Viv Anderson and sometimes passed the time listening to psychotherapy self-help recordings on his Walkman, which featured a soothing voice encouraging visualisation and a metronome to regulate the player's tension.

Speaking to ITV Sport, Butcher explained: 'Last season at Ipswich, we had a doctor come to the club, approached us and he gave us some tapes, which he made himself, which gave us some ideas about positive thinking, helped us relax before games. About half an hour before kick-off, I just sit down in a corner and relax and just control my mind. Really, he's saying everybody can be masters of their own mind. It's your mind really, you worry too much or you worry too early before the game. He's saying you can just control that and get worked up at the right times.'

In 1986, there were few allowances made for a player's mental wellbeing. Back in London, ITV panellist Mick Channon was incredulous: 'I can't believe it. He's a big lad, he wants to get out there and get stuck in, that's all I would say.' 'Very scientific approach Michael,' joked presenter Brian Moore.

Butcher's room-mate Anderson had his own problems. The right-back had gone to the 1982 World Cup and not seen any action after his rival for the position, Mick Mills, was handed the captain's armband in the absence of the injured Kevin Keegan. Now in Mexico, he was sitting idle once again as Bobby Robson selected the younger Gary Stevens of Everton instead of him.

In the privacy of their rooms, Anderson complained that Bobby Robson 'didn't know what he was doing' and was 'fucking useless'. Butcher, armed with his newfound self-help techniques, told Anderson he needed to 'get over it and go to sleep'. which Anderson later admitted was 'probably the best advice I could have got'.

Alvin Martin was rooming with Peter Beardsley, who earned himself a reputation as the organiser of the group. Martin recalled: 'It helps when you've got a decent room partner and we got on well.

We liked the same things.' They would certainly have had plenty to joke about.

Just over a month earlier during a First Division match at Upton Park, Martin had scored a penalty past Beardsley to complete a unique hat-trick in an 8-1 win for title-chasing West Ham over Newcastle United. Beardsley had been forced to play in goal after Newcastle's two other keepers had both been unable to continue after being injured during the game. Therefore, Martin ended up scoring three goals in the same match against three different goalkeepers. Martin later said his England team-mate had pulled faces to distract him before he took the kick.

Aware that he would be making his World Cup debut against Paraguay in the absence of the suspended Terry Fenwick, Martin told me, 'I'd flown my dad out for the Paraguay game. He was staying in the Holiday Inn. The FA were really good in terms of what they did for my dad. I must admit, a couple of the players did come up to me and said that when it had been mentioned on television that my dad was there, it got a few of the lads into a bit of bother. I think a few of their parents didn't know why they weren't out there as well!'

Everton's Peter Reid shared with Aston Villa's Steve Hodge, the least experienced international in the squad. Neither had expected to play at the start of the tournament but both were now the lungs of England's reshaped midfield. Reid joked that 'he didn't need to do any training in Mexico because he spent every hour of the day running around doing errands for me. Open the door, get the drinks in, turn the telly on, fetch me a sandwich, Hodge did the lot and never uttered a single word of complaint.' The Everton midfielder explained to me that 'back in the day, the senior pro ranked, so he was almost my gofer when we were in the room making cups of tea or coffee'.

Reid celebrated his 30th birthday two days before the Argentina match. When the squad returned to the Holiday Inn after training, the hotel staff presented him with a special cake in the shape of a football pitch, replete with two sets of players, two goals and a scoreboard.

Later, Hodge also brought Reid a chocolate cake laid on by ITV for the benefit of the television cameras. Reid said, 'I remember getting abuse because of a few grey hairs coming out. I looked older than 30 years of age. I've still got a card that all the lads signed. Some of the – let's say, friendly messages of abuse – were brilliant.'

Hodge described Reid as a 'real social animal'. Reid explained to me how the players passed the time in between training sessions: 'There was a putting green, we had a lot of quizzes and the time difference made it very difficult because TV wasn't great then, so we sort of had to make our own entertainment.'

Kerry Dixon shared with John Barnes. The two liked to escape by playing late-night tennis with whoever else they could find. At their hotel in Saltillo, the squad had enjoyed access to a floodlit tennis court and, on their first day at Vallé de Mexico, they were therefore understandably delighted to find an indoor court next to the hotel.

On the evening of Friday 13th, Dixon, Barnes, Chris Woods and Chris Waddle played for two hours until Dixon, chasing a ball across the court, smashed himself on the bridge of his nose following through with his racquet. He recalled that there was 'blood everywhere'. As Dixon received four stitches in the medical room, the rest of the squad gathered outside, laughing at his expense. Dixon said in his World Cup diary, 'Feel a right idiot. Have to put up with jibes for a couple of days.'

The next morning, fearing the wrath of Bobby Robson at breakfast, Dixon found he too saw the funny side, calling the injury 'just one of those things'. For a couple of days, Dixon – nicknamed 'Ernie' after legendary comedian Ernie Wise on account of his hairstyle – required assistance from the other players to shampoo his blonde locks as he held a waterproof gauze over his face.

The players had a cinema room with a video recorder, where they often gathered after dinner to watch films. During the tournament, they had watched action movies such as *Back to the Future*, *Commando*, *Delta Fox* and *Stick*. Trevor Steven recalled that, in the group stage, some had sat through film noir parody *Dead Men Don't Wear Plaid* for ten consecutive days.

Finding ways to pass the time was essential as venturing out into the world's most populous city was not really an option. John Barnes told me, 'Mexico City isn't really the place you want to venture out, especially during the World Cup when everywhere was going to be busy. We trained, we stayed at the hotel, we watched TV. Just being at the World Cup was an exciting time, so everybody was looking forward to the matches.'

In 1984, after scoring his first England goal, against Brazil at the Maracanã, a Maradona-style slalom from the halfway line past three defenders and the goalkeeper, Barnes had been cruelly exposed to the prejudices prevalent among some of the England travelling fans at the time. Awaiting to board their flight to Montevideo, a group of supporters aligning themselves with the far-right National Front began singing racist songs and claiming that Barnes's goal was not valid due to the colour of his skin. The spectators then boarded the same plane as the England players and treated them to the same offensive chants during the flight.

In Mexico, England supporters had been photographed holding a white flag with 'West Ham NF' scrawled across it. Barnes told me he was aware of the presence of National Front supporters in Mexico but did not feel threatened by it. 'They were just there, standing there with the National Front flags, they didn't approach me and do anything to me. They never said anything. They were just standing there having pictures. They weren't being aggressive towards me or shouting out. They were just making a point that they supported the National Front. Even in 1984, when they stood there outside the plane where Brazilian photographers were taking pictures of them, they never approached me or Mark Chamberlain at all. They were just trying to make a point.'

Everton team-mates Gary Stevens and Trevor Steven shared another room. When Steven and Reid came into the England side for the decisive group stage match against Poland, Stevens was liberated;

playing in the right-sided trident he had flourished in under Howard Kendall, feeling more confident in his ability to push forward and join the attack. He told me, 'We knew each other's game inside-out. I was well aware of Trevor's strengths and hopefully he was well aware of my strengths. When we were playing for Everton back in the halcyon days, we liked to push up and squeeze teams. I started off my career more as a forward, then I became a midfield player and eventually ended up at right-back, so I was always keen, probably because of that, to get over the halfway line. When I got the opportunity to get past Trevor, I knew that he could do a job. If I was a bit over-zealous, I knew he'd fill in for me.'

Steven told me, 'We needed a change in the system and that was agreed in a team gathering. It was the consensus that we had our backs to the wall, so let's play a system that everyone's really comfortable with. A strict 4-4-2, in a typical sense, is what we played. I wasn't a winger, I was tucked in. Steve Hodge did the same thing on the other side.'

According to Kenny Sansom, Stevens and Steven were known affectionately as 'The Hustlers' because they were always playing pool together. Steven told me, 'I wasn't a betting person, I wasn't a gambler so I certainly couldn't be a hustler! Gary and I were probably the quiet ones. I was probably even more quiet than Gary was, really in awe of the people I was with. We just got on with things nice and quietly. Me and Gary kept our noses pretty well clean and got on with the jobs in hand.'

'We were very much aware that the security was quite high,' Stevens told me, 'so we weren't really encouraged to go out. If we did, to see some of the tourist areas, then it would be very much as a group.'

The other Gary Stevens shared with Terry Fenwick, a player who would join him at Tottenham Hotspur the following summer. Stevens remembered that 'there wasn't a great deal to do. It was a very basic hotel.'

He filled the time with his own endeavours. Together with long-term friend and music consultant Tony Norman, he helped set up and organise the official England fan club. Over 5,000 children joined to receive a supporters' pack in return for a membership fee of £3.99. For that sum, each fan received a full colour team poster, action pictures of Bryan Robson, Gary Lineker, Peter Shilton and Glenn Hoddle, a World Cup pennant, badge, sticker and newsletter, as well as a 'limited edition' postcard from Mexico signed by one of the squad.

To that end, Stevens regularly sought out his fellow players in the hotel to obtain signed cards, which were sent home to those in the fan club. Speaking to the *Wolverhampton Express and Star*, Stevens explained: 'I give the players a hundred or so a day to sign. I think they dread me appearing with my bundles, but really they know it's in a good cause and encouraging the right sort of supporter for England.'

It seemed that some members of the squad found the openness of the Holiday Inn uncomfortable. Local children thronged the communal areas as the players spoke to the press. When fans discovered where the England team were staying, they were free to mill about in the foyer of the hotel chatting to the players and asking for autographs.

Terry Fenwick told me, 'Going into Mexico City, the hotel there was huge. I think there was a fashion show going on at the same time. So we had all of the things going on with a World Cup, because of the Falklands War, we're all over the United States' television, journalists chasing us everywhere. In amongst all of this, Bobby Robson was brilliant. I think he's possibly the best man-manager I've ever come across. He'd come knock on your door, make sure everybody was as comfortable as they could possibly be.

'He was doing as much as he could but it was just far too much for us. When he got to the hotel, it was too big, too open. There was so much going on within the hotel that we were pretty much out there for anybody that wanted to have a chat. Sometimes it wasn't as nice as we would have liked.'

Chris Waddle, who roomed with Mark Hateley, told me this affected the players: 'We were basically under lock and key. When there's a group of lads together, you train and get back to the hotel and you have your meal and whatever – lads get bored. You can only watch so many videos, you end up getting a little bit "can we sneak out, can we get out of the hotel, can we go somewhere?"'

Having been dropped from the team ahead of the Poland match, Hateley was dealing with his own issues. In his autobiography *Top Mark!*, he admitted that 'it was a depressing time personally and Chrissie Waddle who was sharing with me worked hard to keep my spirits up. He was good but I was as down as I had ever been. It's a strange situation you can find yourself in: you are genuinely happy the team is doing well and that the lads are getting results – but you still want so much to be in there as a part of the whole thing.'

Tottenham's Gary Stevens was close to Hateley, the two of them both graduating to the senior team after playing together under Dave Sexton in the U21 European Championships two years earlier. Stevens said, 'On one occasion, we booked a car through the hotel reception to take us downtown in Mexico City to have a look at some of the earthquake damage.' The harsh realities of the poverty in some parts of the city was striking. 'It shocked us the fact that there could be a building stood there, looked perfectly fine, and next door to it was a pile of rubble where the adjoining building obviously couldn't withstand the earthquake. That was something we did, because I think we were a little bit bored. I think the times were very different then. Rather than the FA going out on an advanced reconnaissance mission to see what hotel we should stay in, set up the rooms for us and have a games facility for us, we just stayed at whatever hotel was allocated by FIFA.'

The two reserve goalkeepers, Chris Woods and Gary Bailey, also shared a room. At that time, no goalkeeper had ever been sent off in a World Cup. There as back-up to Shilton, the undisputed number one, they knew their role was, barring an unlikely injury, in all probability limited to being good tourists. Having the time to notice which model of car was seemingly omnipresent in Mexico City, Bailey told me he recalls sitting on the steps of their hotel with

Woods and betting on how many Volkswagen Beetles passed by in five minutes.

Woods, who would have to wait another four years to replace Shilton as England's first-choice goalkeeper, explained: 'It is part and parcel of a footballer's career really. You're just really pleased to be there and be part of the squad. Obviously, we knew Shilton was playing.'

An apprentice at Nottingham Forest, Woods had been Shilton's understudy as a teenager when Brian Clough signed the England goalkeeper in 1977. Eight years later Woods broke into the senior international squad, only to find the same man ahead of him. 'I'm pretty sure Shilts would have thought he was the best goalkeeper in the world. When he came to Forest, I was so grateful to think that I could actually work with him and learn from him. Obviously, I left Forest. When we met up again, I was playing regular first-team football and I was sort of playing number two to him again. It wasn't quite so frustrating because I knew I was going back to my club and playing.'

That club would soon be Glasgow Rangers, as their new player-manager Graeme Souness had already lined up the Norwich City goalkeeper as his first signing in a revolution that would eventually lead to six of the England 1986 World Cup squad playing north of the border at Ibrox.

Adding to the players' boredom was a self-imposed alcohol ban, which the England players were committed to. A year earlier at the Copa Ciudad de Mexico, some of the players had enjoyed a few nights out drinking in the capital, only to later struggle on the pitch in the heat and altitude.

The players had been warned by team physician Dr Vernon Edwards that alcohol hindered the acclimatisation process, and Hoddle admitted that 'we learnt a lot as players. It wasn't the staff. We came away from that thinking, *Crikey, if we qualify for the World Cup and get there, there's no way we could do that.*'

After England won their three group stage matches at the 1982 World Cup, manager Ron Greenwood had told his players to 'go and get drunk'. They went out in the next phase, failing to score a goal in two matches. That would not be happening in Mexico.

During the squad's pre-tournament training camp in Colorado, the players' wives and girlfriends had been flown out by the FA for a few days of relaxation for the squad. Several dinners were laid on, during which the players had enjoyed their last beers before the tournament.

Stevens of Tottenham Hotspur told me, 'There was a concerted effort that all the boys pretty much decided that if we have a day off or a night off, that we are not touching any drink. And to the best of my knowledge, everybody stuck to that. I just think deep down, we believed we had a really good squad of players and that actually we had a chance of going the distance in the World Cup. So I remember that clearly, and Ray Wilkins, he was certainly leading that. Kenny Sansom – who's had his issues with alcohol – I remember looking at him and thinking, *My God, you mean this, you're serious!* Being one of the younger members of the squad and being very inexperienced as far as England internationals were concerned, I was kind of all for it. To be honest with you. I think it was kind of something as a younger player, as I was at the time, I never found that an easy aspect, the "you've got to drink with the boys, if you want to play with the boys". I always felt I was being railroaded into having a drink just because that's what the drinkers wanted to do.'

The day of the Argentina match marked one month since the England players' last taste of alcohol. Hoddle said 'it hit us that it was going to be tough'. Tottenham Hotspur's star midfielder was rooming with Arsenal's future captain Sansom, a player who would later admit to being an alcoholic. Humour was one way of distracting the players from their lack of booze. 'We had a good bunch of lads,' said Hoddle. 'Kenny Sansom was a funny, funny guy.'

In his autobiography, *The Man with Maradona's Shirt*, Steve Hodge recalled that after watching the 1984 blockbuster movie *Beverly Hills Cop*, Sansom used to wander through the hotel singing

'The Heat is On'. One day Bobby Robson misheard him, 'The heater's on? Well turn them bloody off!'

Hoddle and Sansom had labelled themselves as 'The Blues Brothers', entertaining the rest of the squad with their impersonations and giving the other players nicknames. Sansom said, 'We were a good double act. He sang and I told jokes.'

Hoddle revealed that Sansom could have been a showman, quickly picking up accents and honing his many voices in their room. 'Kenny is the England football team's great comic. He is simply a brilliant mimic. His impersonations of Prince Charles and Norman Wisdom are his star turns. It is quite an experience sharing a room with him – he gets me at it, and before long we are both rolling about in stitches.'

According to Sansom, Waddle was known to the group as Barry Norman, after the film critic, due to his interest in movies. The 'funny bastard' Reid was called Freddie Starr after the stand-up comedian, who, like the midfielder, hailed from the Liverpool suburb of Huyton.

Sansom had also christened Hodge 'Mr Forgetful', as the Nottingham Forest midfielder had developed a reputation within the squad of getting things mixed up, such as which tracksuit to wear on different occasions, often being the only one to appear in the wrong attire. After losing a training top on the squad's first day in Colorado, Hodge admitted to Bobby Robson, 'I'm like that boss, I forget things, you know.'

On the flight to Mexico from Vancouver, Hodge had forgotten the gate number from which to board the connecting plane at Los Angeles. Standing at gate 28, he was tracked down by an FA official who informed him that 'We're at 33, everybody is waiting for you!' Hodge had to run through the terminal before having to endure the ribbing of his team-mates on the flight. Bobby Robson said they needed to 'put a tag on him at the airport in case we lose him!'

Behind the laughter, Hoddle was coming to terms with his own faith after having experienced a spiritual awakening on England's recent game in Israel three months earlier. Since visiting the birthplace of Jesus on a squad trip to Bethlehem, Hoddle had started to go to church with his wife Anne. Still in the process of trying to work out what his new religious feelings meant, he admitted to feeling cut off from the people closest to him in Mexico. Isolated in the England hotel, he prayed every day for guidance. Hoddle's faith in justice on the sporting field would soon be put to the test.

Chris Waddle, who admitted to feeling homesick when he first joined any new club during his career, also felt the effects of being in a foreign country away from his family and friends for so long. 'It's very hard. Obviously the results went against us at the beginning. You start thinking, this isn't going to be a great journey, it's not going to be a great trip, what's going to happen? People don't realise – listen, everyone wants to play in a World Cup, it's the greatest thing you can do as a player, to play for your country. If you can get to the World Cup, then wow! But, sometimes it's very mental. It's on your mind – four walls, hotel, you get to another hotel. You want to be active, you want things to take you away, taking your mind off games and thinking about things.

'You can't really have that freedom, which you'd like, to get out of the way. It's very difficult. People think, *Oh I'd love to go to the World Cup*, yeah of course you would, and I wouldn't turn it down. I wouldn't say I didn't want to go, but it can get to you a little bit. You're sitting around a hotel every day. You're looking for things to release and get away from it, and it's very difficult to do that.'

As well as providing the squad with videos of all the matches at the tournament to watch, ITV supplied them with recordings of race meetings from back home. Not knowing the results, the players then watched, betting on the outcomes.

The night before the Argentina match, the players had dinner at 7pm before having a racing evening. Resident bookmakers Shilton and Lineker were joined by Dixon in taking the bets off their team-mates.

Viv Anderson remembers that 'they came out with crap odds, that's all I used to know. I could have got better odds somewhere else.' Not surprisingly, Dixon reported that they 'cleaned up'. The players went to bed at 10.30pm ahead of the next day's kick-off at noon.

Argentina had been the first team to arrive in Mexico, touching down on 9 May, the day before four of the England squad were preparing to play in the first all-Merseyside FA Cup Final between Liverpool and Everton. The South American team stayed at the training facilities of the capital's biggest club side, Club América, 3km from the Estadio Azteca where the team hoped to end up playing in the World Cup Final. At the time, Club América were coached by former Argentinian footballer Miguel Ángel López, known to everyone as 'El Zurdo' (the left-hander). López was an old friend of Argentina coach Carlos Bilardo from their days together playing for Estudiantes de la Plata.

López had recommended the Club América facilities to Bilardo should they be drawn to play in Mexico City. The ever meticulous Bilardo had López on standby on the day of the draw in December 1985 as well as other trusted friends in the other Mexican cities where they could play. When Argentina were drawn in Group A, playing two of their three games in the capital's Estadio Olimpico '68, Zurdo was called and the Club América facilities secured.

One of the few bases to have training pitches and accommodation on the same site, the Argentina players had been living for seven weeks in secluded grounds covering ten acres and surrounded by forests. However, they were not in the lap of luxury. Their base only had one television in the communal dining room, where the players would congregate to watch the other World Cup matches, and one landline telephone from which they could call family and friends back in Argentina. Like a scene from 1970s hit sitcom *Porridge*, which was set in a prison, the players had to queue up for their turn to use the beige rotary-dial handset mounted to the brick wall.

The players regularly ate outside, all sat together around a long table next to the training pitch. Maradona's father Don Diego shovelled coal underneath an open-air grill upon which huge slabs of beef and sausages were barbecued. The squad were treated to this slice of traditional slow cooking, known as *asado*, twice a week.

Unlike the English – in a foreign land among people who spoke a foreign language – the Argentines were able to read the Mexican newspapers that were delivered each morning as well as their own *El Gráfico*, which arrived once a week from Buenos Aires, a few days after it was published back home.

The small rooms with their exposed brickwork, a dangling lightbulb and two basic beds, were described by Maradona as 'a whorehouse with no whores'. There were only enough rooms for 16 of the players. The remaining six – Valdano, Trobianni, Brown, Passarella, Ruggeri and Almirón – stayed in makeshift rooms created in a shed area, called 'the island' by the other players, separated with cardboard partitions.[10]

Maradona was in room six, sharing accommodation with fellow striker Pedro Pasculli. They decorated the bare walls with World Cup posters, taped-up photographs and letters from home, adding something new every day. Next to Maradona's pillow was a picture of his girlfriend Claudia leaning over a balcony, with the words 'I love you' written on it in pen. Above that was the 1985 cover of *Para Cantarle A La Vida* (To Sing To Life), an album by Argentine singer, Valeria Lynch.

Directly above Maradona's pillow was a small relief of Our Lady of Luján, a 16th-century Argentinian statue of the Virgin Mary. Higher up was a World Cup poster provided by his sponsor Puma, and other assorted football memorabilia. To the right was a *Playboy* centrefold, a woman in suspenders who Maradona joked was his motivation.

Filmed by Néstor Clausen on a handheld camcorder, Julio Olarticoechea kept the often-bored players entertained by recording a video diary at the camp. The joker in the pack, Olarticoechea pretended to be a reporter interrogating the players, wearing a white

---

10   https://www.youtube.com/watch?feature=shared&v=86AMgQ_q_EY

plastic hat with the name of his daughter Gisela written around the top. Burruchaga and Pumpido assisted by shining makeshift spotlights to illuminate the speakers in the otherwise dark rooms.

In one such interview, Olarticoechea asked Maradona how it had been for him not having sex for nearly two months. The captain replied that it was 'very, very tough. We had all been warned by Bilardo that it would be like this and I think we are professional enough to do as we are told. Anyway, at times likes this we all have a hand that comes in useful.'

Before every match, the players visited the Perisur mall, 8km away, for ice cream after lunch at Helen's bar, which they believed brought the team good luck. The squad leisurely walked through the mall, visiting the stores and signing autographs for afternoon shoppers.

The excursions also helped win over the Mexican public, a country that had historically viewed Argentines as arrogant. Speaking to *ESTO*, Bilardo said, 'I believe that this national team is not like that, this squad has showed that it has another image. They demonstrated that they are humble people and, if you want to prove it, without me saying it, come with us to Perisur, and you are going to see how the players interact with people, how they enter shops, how they walk with the girls and with the boys.'

As they progressed through the tournament, more and more locals became aware of the squad's pre-game visits and saw it as an opportunity to meet the best footballer in the world. In his autobiography, *El Diego*, Maradona claimed that, at least at this stage of his career, he was not inhibited by the constant attention: 'To me it was like another training session. I'd run around the corridors of the shopping centre with three hundred people running after me, until I slipped into a shop – it could be an electronics shop or a hairdresser's – and I would stay there, feeling hundreds of eyes staring at me, focused on me, from the other side of the window. I was happy. Very happy. It was adulation but it didn't bother me, not at all.'

After each game, players would dine at Mi Viejo, a restaurant in the Polanco district owned by former Argentinian footballer Eduardo

Cremasco, another former team-mate of Bilardo at Estudiantes de la Plata.

The erudite Jorge Valdano, one of only four players in the squad to play in Europe, arrived at the camp with two suitcases, one full of suits and shirts, the other full of books to read. The rooms the Argentina players stayed in didn't even have closets.

Nevertheless, speaking to *El Gráfico* before the start of the knockout phase, and perhaps anticipating a future encounter with England, Valdano revealed that he was reading *The Soccer Tribe* by Desmond Morris, often staying up until 2am in the morning.

The quarter-final was the third of Argentina's games to kick-off at midday.

The day after England secured their place in the last eight and a tie against Argentina, the South Americans invited Bobby Charlton to their training camp. England's most decorated footballer had played in both previous World Cup encounters between the two nations, scoring in the 3-1 victory in 1962 before collecting the only caution of his international career during the tempestuous 1966 quarter-final.

The 48-year-old was working as an analyst for BBC Sport at the tournament and wore the corporation's branded red polo shirt. With the cameras whirring, he took part in a stage-managed shooting session, testing Argentina's goalkeepers with a few trademark drives. England's greatest-ever footballer was then photographed speaking to Diego Maradona, the man who sought to emulate him as the talisman of a World Cup-winning team.

The night before the game, José Luis Brown claims that Maradona was unusually quiet. 'He didn't say a word, not one. After dinner, he shut himself in his room. That night he didn't listen to any music, he didn't make jokes either. He didn't do anything. We thought he was feeling unwell. At two in the morning, he went out on to the balcony looking into the distance, he was pensive. I approached him and asked, "Diego, is something wrong?" With a smile, he said, "What are you doing awake? Go to sleep."'

Changing a Winning Formula

On the morning of the decisive group stage match against Poland, Bobby Robson had been awoken by several phone calls from back home in England. One came from North Heaton, a suburb of Robson's home town of Newcastle, from a Mrs Porter. The cockney pensioner was at pains to tell the England manager that the transatlantic call was costing her a fortune but she could not let the day go by without wishing Robson good luck. She singled out her favourite player, Peter Beardsley, then of Newcastle United, for special praise. England won 3-0 with Beardsley excelling.

A week later, on the morning of the Round of 16 match against Paraguay, Mrs Porter rang again. 'I've been dithering all day whether to ring you. I can't really afford it, but if it didn't go well I would think it was my fault for not wishing you good luck.' England again won 3-0, with Beardsley scoring.

After two successive matches on Wednesdays, the quarter-final was scheduled for Sunday. This time, Mrs Porter rang a day early on the Saturday morning. She explained to Robson, 'I thought you would have too much to do on Sunday, so I decided I would ring you now when you have a bit more time.' She once again said she could not afford the call.

Ahead of the quarter-final, Robson insisted that 'I expected us to qualify (from the group) and win the next game. Now we are going for the big stakes and the kind of success that could be so important for the future of our game and please so many people back home. We are now in the position I expected us to reach when we set out. Anything more will be a bonus.' The bonus would be to repair the faltering reputation of the English game abroad, so battered the previous year after the fatal tragedies at Bradford and Heysel.

The match was seen by many as a direct confrontation between the world's best player and world's best goalkeeper, Peter Shilton. His understudy Chris Woods told me the England captain was not fazed by the prospect of an apparent duel. 'Shilts was a very focused goalkeeper. He worked his socks off. You go into a game and you don't think about other players, what they're going to do or how they can do it. You just go out and perform to what you think you can do.'

England had not conceded a goal at the World Cup in three matches. Carlos Manuel's mishit winner over Peter Shilton was the only World Cup finals goal to be scored against him in his last eight matches at the tournament going back to 1982. Argentina had just conceded two but, unlike England, had the experience of coming back from going a goal behind in a match. They recovered to earn a well-deserved 1-1 draw against world champions Italy in the group stage.

Nevertheless, Terry Butcher believed the team that scored first would win the game: 'The players feel that if we can score the first goal against Argentina, then we are going to take some beating.'

Not since Bobby Robson's first game in charge in Denmark four years earlier had England failed to win an away match in which they had taken the lead. The national team had not lost a game where they took the lead since their humiliating reverse to Norway in Oslo the year before that under Ron Greenwood.

'That's why I feel we must try to hit Argentina early on,' added Butcher. 'Then we will be in a position to dictate to them.'

Despite their best efforts, England did not manage a shot on target until midway through the second half. It would be another 38 years until England again failed to register a shot on target in the opening half of a knockout match at a major tournament.

With Peter Reid ultimately declared fit, Bobby Robson could have named an unchanged side to start against Argentina. However, deep into the tournament, the manager suddenly had a fully fit squad to choose from. With the exception of third-choice goalkeeper Gary Bailey, whose top-level career would never fully recover from the knee cartilage injury he suffered before the tournament, every other player was fit and available for selection. Kerry Dixon had re-joined training after his 'freak injury' requiring four stitches, as had captain Bryan Robson. With Peter Reid's ongoing ankle problem rendering him doubtful to play, Bryan Robson was a serious contender to replace him in a holding role.

Bryan Robson told me he believes he could have adapted his natural box-to-box game to play alongside Hoddle. 'I could do both roles that Bobby wanted. If he wanted me to do more of an attacking role, I could do, which I more or less did because of Ray Wilkins being in the team. But if he wanted me to do more of a sitting role, in front of the back four, and allow Glenn to go forward and get on the ball, I could do that. I think myself and Glenn had some really good games for England. The two of us could balance off, because I knew I had to do more of a defensive role when I played with Glenn.'

Bobby Robson concurred, stating in his *World Cup Diary* that 'it would not put his shoulder so much at risk as charging into the box and it is a job he could do to great effect. I was also aware of the psychological effect his appearance would have on the Argentinians.' However, the day before the game he took his captain aside and explained to him that Reid would play if he was fit. Bryan Robson agreed: 'Quite right. You can't change that team.'

However, Bobby Robson did change the team. Added to the fit-again players, two were now free from suspension. Ray Wilkins had been forced to miss two games after becoming the first Englishman to receive a red card at the World Cup finals during the goalless draw with Morocco, but was now available.

Former England captain Emlyn Hughes was adamant that Wilkins should not be brought back. In his newspaper column he said that Wilkins 'should take no further part in the campaign, for it has been proved that his role is as old-fashioned as Robson's 4-3-3 tactics'.

Another former international agreed. Speaking to *Today* newspaper, Alan Mullery argued that 'Wilkins is definitely not the man to come in if Reid is not fit. He would just get in the way of Hoddle and destroy the successful pattern we have established in the last two games. In our first two matches he was insignificant because Wilkins's presence pushed him put to the right and restricted his special talents. By holding the centre of midfield Reid has got the best out of Hoddle. Wilkins would just want to play in his space.'

Hoddle knew the absence of Bryan Robson and Wilkins had liberated him. He accepted that the England team would never be shaped around him to promote his unique gifts in the same way Bilardo had built his Argentina team around Maradona.

'I'm not moaning about that,' said Hoddle. 'I'm just happy that, suddenly through things I didn't expect to happen I've found myself playing where I'm happiest. Going down to ten men (against Morocco) made us get behind the ball. We kept solid as a team in the last two games and I think we have learned a lesson.'

Also available again was Terry Fenwick, who had been suspended for the game against Paraguay after picking up two yellow cards in the group stage. He was replaced for the Round of 16 match by West Ham United's Alvin Martin, who had gone to the World Cup off the club's best-ever league season, ultimately finishing third in the First Division behind double winners Liverpool and runners-up Everton.

With Martin and Butcher playing together in central defence, England had never lost a game and had only conceded two goals. Writing in the *Daily Mail* two days before the match, Jeff Powell was in no doubt who should play against Argentina: 'Alvin Martin's most convincing performance yet alongside Terry Butcher appears to have closed the door on Terry Fenwick's return from suspension.' David Miller in *The Times* agreed, suggesting that 'Fenwick's malign habits could inflame Argentina. He is not really the answer.'

Speaking to the West Ham United website in 2022, Martin revealed, 'I thoroughly enjoyed playing against Paraguay. The atmosphere was contagious and against tricky opponents we took the game by the scruff of the neck. Personally, I was pleased with my own performance. I knew what I wanted to do and I did it. Terry Butcher and myself knew that we had completed a good job. There was camaraderie between us and we felt the partnership was right. We had beaten Paraguay 3-0 and looked good doing it too.'[11]

Martin not only helped England keep a clean sheet against Paraguay but he almost scored early in the second half when his diving header from a left-wing Hoddle free kick flew past the far post. However, England might have conceded twice before they took the lead and, with the score at 2-0, Martin appeared to pull back Paraguayan centre-forward Roberto Cabañas in the area. Referee Jamal Al Sharif waved play on but it was a clear penalty.

Fenwick had played in every group game but his performances had inspired little confidence going into the quarter-final against the world's best footballer. In the first match with Portugal, Fenwick had been bamboozled by a similar left-footed dribbler, substitute Paulo Futre, clearly fouling him in the penalty area, but once more England somehow avoided conceding a spot-kick. Then, in the must-win final group match against Poland, Fenwick had presented the ball to Smolarek in the opening minutes, eliciting a counter-attack that only a save from Shilton and a vital toe-poke from Butcher prevented from resulting in the opening goal. Moments later, Gary Lineker scored the first of his life-changing hat-trick to spare England from first-round humiliation. In addition to his second booking of the World Cup, Fenwick had later torn his groin muscle and had to be nursed through the second half of the game.

The day after the Paraguay game, manager Robson unusually decided to give the entire squad a full day off. Most elected to recuperate and take the opportunity to sunbathe, while others, like Martin, chose to go shopping. Fenwick, however, volunteered to do an extra training session.

---

11 https://www.whufc.com/en/news/world-cup-hammers-1986-pride-and-confusion-martin-and-mcavennie

Speaking before the tournament, Robson said of Fenwick, 'He is a lad who always thinks he should be in the team, which is an attitude I like, but he will have to learn to control himself in Mexico and to temper his natural aggressiveness with cool judgement.'

Robson's first choice to partner Butcher in the World Cup was the man who would ultimately play alongside him so successfully four years later in Italy. England coach Don Howe had identified the 22-year-old Mark Wright, then playing for Southampton, as a man ideally suited to play in Mexico. 'He could be ideal for those conditions. Mark can play the ball from the back. If Mark can concentrate for a full 90 minutes, he could form a tremendous partnership with Terry Butcher.' Wright had started five out of England's six matches during the previous season, including the standout 1-0 win away to the Soviet Union in Tbilisi.

Just ten days later, playing at White Hart Lane in the FA Cup semi-final against Liverpool, Wright collided with his own goalkeeper, Shilton, and broke his leg in two places. Robson felt that 'if he had been able to play, he would have come back a hero because the football would have suited him ... His time would come.'

Now having come in for Fenwick against Paraguay, Martin believed the place in the starting line-up was his. He told me, 'I thought I was going to be playing.' His father had joined his brother out in Mexico City and, given a rare day off by Bobby Robson after the Paraguay game, the three went shopping.

The night before the game, Robson revealed his line-up after dinner: 'The team is going to be the same ...' causing Martin to relax in his seat, 'except for one change. I'm going to bring Terry Fenwick back for Alvin Martin.'

At the time, a stunned Martin looked around the room for reassurance. 'I looked along the line to a couple of the lads. You know, they give you that nod of compassion, but it makes you feel worse sometimes.' Looking back all these years later, Martin recalls, 'It was all done in a matter of fact manner really. There was no malice in it from Bobby Robson. He was a gentleman and we all respected him.'

Martin was not even named among the five substitutes and watched the game from the stands sitting next to Viv Anderson. 'I think my dad was more disappointed than me, that I wasn't actually going to play against Maradona. It was a total shock to me. Things had gone particularly well in the Paraguay game, I expected to play. So when we went down for the team meeting, I expected to come back to my dad in the hotel and tell him that I was in the team, but obviously I didn't.

'I had to have a walk around the hotel instead. It was a bombshell really. You're looking around the room because you're a bit stunned. You're expecting to play and it's a massive game and then all of a sudden, you're not in it within a flash of a second.'

The starting line-up would not be officially released until the next morning so Martin had to be careful who he could confide in. 'You've got to go and tell your family. It wasn't the case that you could go and tell anyone, at that time, you knew you had to keep your cards close to your chest in terms of who you let know because obviously you didn't want anyone finding out what the starting line-up was.'

Ultimately, Bobby Robson had changed a winning team. Speaking to ITV's Jim Rosenthal about his team selection just ahead of the quarter-final, Robson said, 'I don't have to explain that to anybody, I don't even have to explain it to my chairman and, if I did, I wouldn't be in a job, I don't think. Terry Fenwick did well in the earlier stages. I'd made up my mind about him anyway. What we do need is, in the event of people losing form or suspensions or injuries, people who can step in and do the job and, if necessary, have to step out.

'It's tough for Alvin Martin because he did play very well, his best-ever international match under me. So it was a tough decision – cruel – I understand how the lad feels. Terry Fenwick would have been disappointed also, so you can't please everybody in this game you know, it's a matter of selection.'

Fenwick told Rosenthal that he did have sympathy for Martin: 'I must say, I feel for Alvin, he's a smashing lad and he's done great when he's been in. But I'm ever so pleased, I'm there myself.'

In the ITV studio, Jimmy Greaves was asked for his reaction to Robson's choice. 'Shocked and stunned. I really felt that Alvin Martin came in and did a great job and, with due respect to Terry Fenwick, I thought he was struggling in the early games. He doesn't normally play in that position and I think he was getting caught out quite a lot.'

The straight-talking Mick Channon agreed: 'I'm surprised they played Fenwick. I think he had a nightmare in the first three games. He nearly got us knocked out the competition [against Poland] with a bad square pass.'

Martin was never told why he was dropped. 'I honestly don't know,' he told me. 'You don't ask him, there was so much going on at the time. I wasn't the sort of player to go up to his room and knock on his door and start yelling and shouting. That wasn't me. I got on particularly well with Terry Fenwick. Maybe he wanted somebody who was a little bit more mobile alongside Terry Butcher, I don't know. With all due respect to Terry Fenwick, he wasn't a lot quicker than me anyway!

'It's one of them things, you think, *Should I have asked him why?* I never really got an explanation. Really, once he's made the decision, I'm not going to change that, that's the way I always looked at it. It's not as if knocking on his door is going to make it any better. It was done as far as I was concerned.'

Working for the *Daily Telegraph* at the time, Michael Calvin told me that Fenwick was 'a cute operator' with the media, always making himself available. 'He liked the press attention, he courted the press quite well. He always had a good line. It was so surprise that he went into coaching. I think Bobby knew his own mind. Maybe he thought Terry Fenwick was a more effective enforcer.'

Speaking to *Shoot!* magazine earlier in the year, captain Bryan Robson revealed what the manager expected of his centre-backs. During the January friendly in Egypt, Bobby Robson urged Mark Wright to 'mark, rattle and dig' the opposition forwards. Considering the way Fenwick handled Maradona during the game, his renown as a player able to do all of those things may have been decisive in Robson's thinking.

According to Fenwick, he had earned the right to be recalled due to his performances for England since 1984. He told me, 'I just think over that period of time, the two years, I'd built a bit of confidence with Bobby. He recognised what I was about. I was a very vocal player, captain of my club, Queens Park Rangers. I kept the team together, kept on lifting everybody. I was always giving good information. That was me as a captain wherever I went. Everybody could hear my voice, organising the team and keeping everything nice and tight and sticking to the manager's game plan.

'We might have been a little naive in our tactics. I fully expected to go man-for-man with Maradona, but Bobby didn't want that. Keep it as is, Big Butch and myself at the back. We'd been fairly solid I think, quite strong with two good characters, very determined players working together.'

Yet, in his World Cup diary, *So Near and Yet So Far*, Robson admitted he would have kept faith with Martin had he not got himself needlessly booked against Paraguay for 'ungentlemanly conduct' following an off-the-ball incident with Roberto Cabañas, which prevented a quick restart. Robson called it a moment of 'silly petulance'.

Butcher was also carrying a yellow card from the first game against Portugal, so a second booking would rule either out of a potential semi-final. Robson felt he could not go into the match with two central defenders potentially inhibited by the threat of suspension, so Fenwick came back in. That logic was rendered immaterial within ten minutes of the game starting as Fenwick got himself booked for a lunging foul on Maradona and was forced to play out the remainder of the match on a knife-edge.

After the first two quarter-finals had been decided by penalty shoot-outs, Robson also resolved that Fenwick would be one of his five penalty takers, having selected Lineker, Reid, Steven, Beardsley and Hoddle for the Paraguay match.

In an interview for ITV Sport the day before the game, and fully aware he was one of those down to take a penalty, Reid lamented, 'We know who's gonna take them … I just hope it doesn't go to penalties.' Jimmy Greaves joked, 'So you know the team then, can you tell us what the team is?' By the end of the quarter-final, Reid and Steven had been substituted off.

Robson also shuffled his five substitutes. Before the tournament, FIFA had recommended that all 11 non-playing members of any World Cup squad would be allowed to sit on the bench and potentially be available to come on. Yet four days before the World Cup began, FIFA backtracked and only permitted five substitutes to be named, from which two could come on.

From the game against Paraguay, Viv Anderson and Mark Hateley were cut from the 16 named for the quarter-final, with Ray Wilkins back in as a substitute and Chris Waddle also returning to a bench with no recognised defender or striker.

After starting the first two games, Waddle was dropped to the bench for the decisive group match against Poland, appearing as a late substitute. Four days later against Paraguay, he was left out of the 16 altogether as Barnes was brought in. He told me, 'The gaffer comes to us and just said, "Look, I'm going to look at something else but you'll get back involved, don't worry." It was sort of, one of them. I don't know what he had in his mind.'

After starting in the final group match of the 1982 World Cup, Glenn Hoddle had also been dropped for the second phase and knew exactly what his Tottenham Hotspur team-mate was going through. Hoddle claimed that it had not been easy to cheer Waddle up. 'I just told him that he had been unlucky and that he must keep going and not sulk. With that attitude he made more appearances as substitute than might have been the case if he had allowed his head to drop.'

Waddle watched the Paraguay game from an executive box in the Azteca alongside Kerry Dixon, another who had been cut from the 16 against Poland. Waddle admitted, 'I was a little bit disappointed but, to be perfectly honest, I sort of got a breather. I watched the game from the stand and sat in a box. The lads did well, I never got involved obviously, but was back in for the next game.'

How to Solve a Problem Like Maradona

On the day of the match, the *News of the World*'s front page featured the headline 'Randy Argy's Love Antics'. On pages 12 and 13 they detailed 'World Cup Romeo's naughty nights on the town in Mexico', alleging that 'Dirty Diego' was cheating on his long-term girlfriend Claudia Villafañe with three women who were described respectively as 'dusky', 'blonde' and 'raven-haired'.

Villafañe was quoted as saying, 'I'm very jealous. He's a megastar and so handsome. All the girls want to make love to him.' Writing in the *Daily Express*, Louise Court could not understand what the fuss was all about. 'From a woman's eye view, Diego's a dead loss. Short, dark and snappy, he has all the appeal of a bull terrier.'

In her opinion, the most desirable players at the World Cup were earning their living closer to home. 'The winners, after scores of action replays among every World Cup widow of my acquaintance, are undoubtedly England. Nothing jingoistic, of course. Simply that Glenn Hoddle has the best legs in the business. Glorious Glenn has thighs that put the rest in the shade.'

Nevertheless, it was Maradona who was courting the world's media attention both on and off the pitch. While two of his alleged affairs involved women back in his adopted home of

Italy, the third involved a Mexican television presenter Edith González.

Maradona is said to have frequently sneaked out of the team's hotel to meet celebrities at house parties thrown in his honour. González claimed that during a dinner at the Antigua Hacienda de Tlalpan restaurant, Maradona had offered her money to sleep with her. 'He was infatuated. He told me he had finished with his fiancée and wanted me.'

What the *News of the World* did not report on was the story of another Italian woman named Cristiana Sinagra. Maradona went to Mexico knowing that Sinagra, a 21-year-old Neapolitan, was six months pregnant with his child, the result of a long affair.

Speaking on Asif Kapadia's 2019 film on Maradona, his personal trainer Fernando Signorini said, 'Diego travelled to Mexico certain about Cristiana Sinagra's pregnancy and this was something that really affected him. But, luckily, he had his dad, who always made sure Diego kept his feet on the ground.'

Diego Armando Sinagra was born less than three months after the World Cup. Seven years later, the Court of Naples legally recognised him as Maradona's son and he changed his name to Diego Armando Maradona Junior. Despite the striking resemblance, it would take Diego Senior over 20 years to recognise Diego Sinagra as his son.

Bobby Robson had his own problems. In the days leading up to the match, in the words of one player, the England manager seemed to be 'transfixed' on how to contain Maradona. 'I've got 24 hours to devise a way to stop him,' he fretted ahead of the game. 'It won't be easy. Other teams have already tried everything. They've assigned one man to mark him, they've closed down space, they've let him go while attempting to cut off his service. All to no avail. Everyone will come to the Azteca Stadium on Sunday to see how we try to handle him. Let's just say that without Maradona, Argentina would have no chance of winning the World Cup. That's how great he is.'

Speaking about Maradona ahead of the game, his strike partner Jorge Valdano admitted, 'He is the soul of our team. He is our great offensive key. Without him we would have to change our whole tactical scheme.' Asked how he would stop Maradona, Valdano smiled and said, 'I would mark the man.'

Howard Wilkinson, then manager of Sheffield Wednesday, was acting as one of Robson's spies in Mexico, scouting out potential opponents and reporting back to him. The morning after the Paraguay match, after giving his players the day off, Robson sat at a table outside the hotel listening to Wilkinson's tactical assessment of their next opponents.

Four years later in Italy, Wilkinson famously equated playing a World Cup quarter-final against a Cameroon side shorn of four players through suspension to 'a practical bye to the semi-finals'. Now, speaking to the *Daily Star*, Wilkinson said of Maradona, 'He is an outstandingly gifted player and so far has looked impossible to contain. But he actually only imposes his brilliance for little more than five minutes in any match. If England can contain him in those minutes, I don't believe Argentina have got anyone else in the side to fear. Without Maradona, Argentina would be quite an ordinary side.' In the event, Maradona would not even need five minutes of brilliance to eliminate England, just 230 seconds.

In an age before mainstream access to foreign leagues, the last time many English viewers had seen Maradona in action was during the 1982 World Cup. Then, during the second phase, the 21-year-old had been stifled by the brutal man-marking of Italy's Claudio Gentile before being provoked into retaliation in the next match, which meant his first World Cup ended with the ignominy of a red card against bitter rivals Brazil.

In Mexico, Maradona had been man-marked in every game but four years of playing in European football with first FC Barcelona and then SS Napoli had taught him how to utilise his prodigious talent at the highest level. In four World Cup games so far in 1986, he had scored once against Italy and provided the direct assist for four of Argentina's six other goals.

Against Uruguay in particular, Maradona rose to the challenge of playing against one of Argentina's historic rivals. Despite the close attentions of Miguel Bossio, he laid on chance after chance for his team-mates, hitting the crossbar himself with a wicked, curling free kick and having a thrilling breakaway goal dubiously ruled out by the referee for a raised foot.

Dave Sexton, who had led Chelsea to their first European trophy in 1971, was working alongside Robson in Mexico as another scout for the England team. Since 1982 he had been employed by the FA as the national U21 coach, twice winning the European Championships in that age group. They were the only occasions on which England's men won that tournament until 2023. In 1984, Sexton's team was spearheaded by player of the tournament, Mark Hateley, who had started the first two games at the 1986 World Cup alongside Lineker. Also in Mexico from that squad were midfielders Gary Stevens and Steve Hodge.

In his role as scout, Sexton was in Puebla to watch England's possible quarter-final opponents – Argentina and Uruguay – slug it out in the first World Cup encounter between the South American neighbours since the 1930 final. After Uruguay had players sent off during the two matches preceding the Round of 16, a fractious duel was predicted. Instead, Sexton witnessed a Maradona masterclass, arguably his most complete performance of the tournament.

Speaking on *ITV News* before the game, Sexton labelled Maradona as 'the little pocket Hercules, with exceptional speed. I watched him on Monday and he laid on four gilt-edged chances, he took the ball right to the line and squared it across and they just couldn't get a final touch to it. He's a brilliant all-round player and, in actual fact, he does spend a lot of his time in midfield. Well I hope he does spend most of his time in midfield when he's playing against us!'

Former Arsenal manager Don Howe was Bobby Robson's right-hand man throughout his tenure as England manager. Renowned for his defensive strategies, he was recommending that England did not man-mark Maradona. Speaking to the *London Evening Standard*, he said, 'My inclination would be for us to play our normal game and share the responsibility for Maradona around the team. The most important thing of all is that we stop him making those devastating runs. The best way to do that is for our nearest player to jockey him on to his right foot and slow him down until reinforcements arrive.'

In Argentina's four previous games, they had utilised Maradona as a playmaker behind two centre-forwards, usually Pasculli, who scored against Uruguay, and Real Madrid's Jorge Valdano, the scorer of three goals in the group stage. Sexton was therefore expecting a similar line-up against England. 'Now he's got two other strikers up there with him. One of the features of their game is if they get into a right crossing position or a left crossing position – in fact, they've scored a couple of goals from this – they're very good at hitting crosses right across to the back post, curlers away from the goalkeeper, and big Valdano's coming in at the back.

'And number 19 is Ruggeri, an exceptionally good jumper, very athletic, he leaps very high, and he's always the one at the back of the free kicks. He nearly always gets his head to it and gets a header in, or knocks it back across the goal. So we'll have to be on our toes against him.'

Presciently, Sexton also predicted that Argentina could be vulnerable to the out-and-out wingers England had discarded after the first two games. 'They don't appear to be great shakes down the flanks,' he said. 'So I think we could get quite a lot of joy from the wide men. They're not happy against a direct side, which we've proved that we can be.'

Robson may have taken Sexton's advice into account when he named both Chris Waddle, who was not in the 16 against Paraguay, and Watford's John Barnes, previously unused during the tournament, among his designated five substitutes for the game.

Speaking to BBC Radio, Robson said, 'There's no doubt Maradona is a very unique player and he has grown up and learnt to ride all the things that happen to him. There are few players who can win a game in five minutes. He is one of them, Platini is another. I don't want to disturb my team too much to cater for Maradona but we will have to be very conscious of him, and when he gets the ball, it's red alert. We will have to get to him and crowd him. I think if you man-mark him he will tear the man who is marking him apart.'

Speaking to *The Sun*, Manchester United manager Ron Atkinson, working in Mexico as a television pundit for ITV, concurred. 'We can forget putting one man on him. We just don't breed that sort of football animal.'

Atkinson's team had subdued Maradona during a famous match at Old Trafford two years previously in which his Manchester United side knocked Barcelona out of the European Cup Winners' Cup. On that occasion, Atkinson had entrusted a 19-year-old Graeme Hogg to mark Maradona. He now believed the key to stopping him was to cut off his supply line, singling out Sergio Batista as the man to target. 'He's the grafter who gets busy and wins the ball. And when he does, his first instinct is to look for Diego. England must stop him dead in his tracks. They must put pressure on Batista every second, hustle and hound him through the game, and we might just kill Maradona as well.'

England's playmaker Glenn Hoddle, who a decade later as his nation's manager sent out his side in a 1-2-5-2 formation similar to the one employed by Argentina in the quarter-final, said, 'I don't think we should change the way we play because of him. If you have someone to mark him – Kenny Sansom would be ideal – you'd have to reshape your whole side.'

Centre-back Butcher agreed: 'You have to play it the way you see it on the day. He is such a quality player, he can improvise so quickly and get you into trouble, he can make nonsense of a pre-match plan. He gets himself out of trouble no matter how many people are around. He always seems to come out of a crowd with the ball at his feet.'

Ray Wilkins, then playing for AC Milan, spoke from his experience of facing Maradona. He explained how Italian defenders played against him: 'They compel him to make his own mind up by standing off him. They allow him to pass, because he tends to look for winning balls – and very few of those come off. They're patient with him and we'll have to be patient as well. We must stay close to him but not fly in because he'll always go past you into space. Then he's dangerous. He's a robust, determined little man. Very tough because of the way he's been marked over the years. A winner.'

On ITV, the former England captain Kevin Keegan, who had played against and swapped shirts with a teenage Maradona during a 1980 friendly match at Wembley, argued that 'you've got to take special measures for special players, and I think Platini and Maradona are the two special players in the world. You ignore them at your peril.'

In a 1983 FA Cup third round replay at St James' Park, the then Newcastle United captain had been man-marked out of the game by a young Brighton defender called Gary Stevens, and Keegan now felt that he was the man to do a similar job on Maradona. 'He's the sort of guy who could go, and he's got the discipline to do that. I mean he's not a great user of the ball, but he has done that type of thing before, he's played at the back.' Former Liverpool great Ian St John offered a withering response: 'I think Maradona would destroy him.'

However, one man who agreed with Keegan was former England midfielder Alan Mullery, who 16 years earlier during the previous World Cup in Mexico had been asked to man-mark Pelé in the group stage match against Brazil in Guadalajara. He felt that Stevens, now at Tottenham Hotspur, was the man to do the same job on the Argentina captain. Speaking to the *Sunday People*, Mullery said, 'We've got to put a man on Maradona and play ten against ten or we'll be ruined. He's destroyed every team that has given him room – we can't make the same mistake. Unfortunately, [Alvin] Martin is too slow for individual marking, and I would go for Stevens as the only one with sufficient pace.'

The man who selected Mullery to shadow Pelé and also enlisted Nobby Stiles to shackle Eusébio in the 1966 World Cup semi-final agreed that Maradona had to be man-marked. Speaking in his newspaper column in the *Daily Mirror*, Sir Alf Ramsey picked him out as his player of the tournament so far, saying, 'What I love about him is that he's always involved, whether he has the ball or not. We'll have to mark him man to man, we'll always have to be goal side and never let him run at us. If we can tie down Maradona, then we can beat Argentina. While we are basking in what was a magnificent result against Paraguay, it is worth remembering we are still vulnerable at the back.'

Stevens himself was not fazed by the prospect. 'Marking Maradona would not be frightening,' he said ahead of the game. 'It would be a great challenge and I would relish the prospect of marking one of the world's best players with a place in the World Cup semi-final at stake. He has two arms and two legs, the same as me, and although there is no disputing his talent, it would come down to who has the biggest heart. I do not believe it would be a negative tactic because all football is about one against one situations all over the pitch. And if you win most of those, the chances are that you will win the game as well.'

Stevens told me that in the days before the game Bobby Robson and Don Howe asked him if he had ever done a man-marking job on anyone. He joked, 'If I was less honest, I probably should have said, "Of course I have," because it would have got me into the game. In the end, the decision was made that they wouldn't go man-for-man with Maradona. Possibly if I had got the job, I might still be in hospital now with a twisted body, I don't know!

'At the time, I don't think there were many better athletes than me in the game. On the running stats, endurance, I think I would have been right at the top end with anybody in that England squad at the time. So the physical aspect wouldn't have been a problem to me.'

With the benefit of hindsight, Stevens told me how he would have approached the task of shackling Maradona: 'It's how I used to play really. Could I be in a position which stops the ball going to my direct opponent? Can I be in a position that denies them passing the ball to him. If it is passed to him, can I nick in front and pinch it before it gets there? If it gets to him, can I hold him up and force him into an area, for instance away from our goal, into our numbers, or to actually force him to pass the ball. To this day, the last thing I ever wanted to do was make a tackle, because arguably that was the last resort.'

If Stevens had played, commentators around the world would have had to deal with an England team starting with two players going by the name of 'Gary Stevens'. Everton's Gary Michael Stevens had now established himself as England's first-choice right-back ahead of Viv Anderson since making his debut at the Estadio Azteca against Italy the previous year.

The two Stevens had never started an England game together, but three times Gary A. Stevens had come on to play alongside Gary M. Stevens – for 13 minutes against Scotland in April, for 15 minutes against Morocco in the group stage and a whole 33 minutes against Paraguay in the Round of 16. In that time, the pair had combined in the move that led to England's third goal scored by Gary Lineker. On BBC commentary, John Motson had distinguished them by referring to their club sides – Gary Stevens of Everton, Gary Stevens of Tottenham. Mexican commentator Hugo Enrique Kiese differentiated them by putting emphasis on their middle names. Eventually the 'Stevens' was dropped altogether and they became known simply as 'Gary Michael' and 'Gary Andrew'.

Gary Andrew Stevens had come on against Paraguay to replace the hobbling holding midfielder Peter Reid. Having carried an ankle injury into the end of the domestic season, Reid had suffered a heavy knock to it against Poland and then again against Paraguay. The Everton midfielder had first sustained the injury at the City Ground during a 0-0 draw away to Nottingham Forest on 26 April. Going over on his ankle during the first half, he had typically played on but left the ground on crutches, reportedly in tears, fearing he would miss out on the World Cup.

Nonetheless, two days later, Bobby Robson selected Reid in his 22-man squad and he returned to play before the end of the domestic season, starting in the FA Cup Final. However, it was an injury that could be aggravated at any time. The day after the Paraguay game, Reid explained how the England medical team dealt with any post-match flare-ups: 'In the first 24 hours, we just hammer it with ice and keep the old fingers crossed.'

Yet, two days before the Argentina match, Reid's ankle remained tightly strapped up. Robson admitted that 'Reid has injured his ankle, and although an X-ray showed no serious damage, there is only a slight improvement today. His ankle is still very sore and painful and he is limping heavily.'

Reid appeared determined to play through the pain barrier: 'When the old adrenalin starts flowing you can fight your way through a bit of pain. I am not a betting man, but if I was, I would put money on myself playing. There's no swelling and like everyone else in the squad I want to play in this one.'

Robson appeared to leave the final decision to the player himself: 'He's a gutsy little fellow. He wants to play and we want him to play. But he is a very responsible person, an old head, and he won't say he's all right if he isn't. We will leave it to him and respect his decision.'

Reid told me, 'I had an initial problem and it was still giving me jip when I got back from Mexico. I kept getting a whack on it, but then it was alright. I got a knock on it against Poland, missed a day's training, which was good because you needed a rest over there. Looking back, I had a problem, definitely yeah. I know you can tell! I could run, but then, if I got any sort of contact – and I mean minimalistic – I was going down, and I'm thinking, *Christ, almighty, this is not right.* Whatever else I was, I never went down easily. I thought at the time it was a small fracture. It was severe pain.'

It was an injury that caused him to miss the majority of the following season in which Everton regained the league title from neighbours Liverpool, limiting him to just 16 appearances in the First Division.

Speaking to me years later, Reid admitted that he was in fact carrying a much more serious injury. 'It turned out to be a trapped nerve in my shin. It was stuck to the bone and that's why I kept getting pain in it. I had to go down to a hospital in Beaconsfield, Bon Secours it was called, and a surgeon, Mr Williams, did the operation. I thought I was going mad because no one could diagnose this injury but he went in and released the nerve. Any time I got a knock on that, it was like someone sticking a knife in me. I'm always grateful for that surgeon finding that.'

The Everton midfielder was a major doubt for the quarter-final with Stevens or Ray Wilkins on standby to replace him. The PFA Footballer of the Year in 1985, Reid had finished fourth in the World Soccer Player of the Year Awards, behind only Michel Platini, Preben Eljkaer and Maradona himself. Nevertheless, he knew he would probably not play in another World Cup. Speaking to the media at the time, he said, 'There is no way I would play if I was not fully fit. It would be too much of a risk, too much of a gamble. There is not even a temptation to cheat, for if I played and broke down, I would be letting the country down in a match I believe we can win putting us through to the semi-finals.'

In a post-match debrief the day after the Paraguay match, Bobby Robson had opened the floor to the players for their thoughts on the performance. Stand-in captain Shilton emphasised that he felt that England had been less solid in defence after Reid had been substituted, making it clear who he believed should start against Argentina.

Certainly after Reid's departure, the game against Paraguay had become more stretched, with chances at both ends. However, with the South Americans two goals down and committing more men forward, this may have happened anyway.

Nonetheless, Reid's presence and personality had been credited with being pivotal in the tactical change that had brought success in the previous two games. In particular, his ceaseless harrying and cajoling of others kept England's two banks of four together, making them difficult to break down.

Writing in the *Daily Star*, former England international turned ITV Sport pundit Mick Channon suggested that the absence of Reid in England's reformed midfield would now be a fatal blow to the nation's hopes. 'If he's out then we can book out tickets home. He's that important.'

With England three goals up against Poland, television viewers were given a glimpse into Reid's own particular brand of motivation when Butcher overhit a long pass to him, conceding a throw-in. A Scouse yell of 'fucking hell, oi!' was audible to a worldwide audience. Luckily, for those not used to hearing that sort of language on BBC1, the later kick-off meant it had already gone past midnight in the UK.

Bobby Robson had been contemplating replacing Reid in the deep-lying holding midfielder position with an apparently fit-again Bryan Robson. The England captain had reportedly trained for a week since his latest shoulder dislocation against Morocco and was in contention to play against Maradona, an opponent he had overcome two years earlier when Manchester United had eliminated FC Barcelona in the European Cup Winners' Cup at Old Trafford, a night when 'Captain Marvel' scored twice in a 3-0 win, sending his side through 3-2 on aggregate.

Bryan Robson told me, 'I was joining in a little bit of training because now it didn't matter. My shoulder had come out five times. I could just put it back in myself. So it was painful but at least I could still join in with a bit of training.'

'Bryan Robson is fit and available for selection,' declared Bobby Robson at a pre-match press conference. 'If he was not in that category, I would have sent him home ten days ago.'

When he went off against Morocco two weeks earlier, the England captain had dislocated his shoulder despite going into the World Cup wearing a harness developed in Australia for rugby league players. Speaking to the *Manchester Evening News* two days before the game, Bryan Robson admitted he had now given up on using it. 'The harness did not help the last time I played and if I am selected I will not wear it.'

He told me that left him caught in a Catch-22 situation. 'It was a little bit different to rugby where you could play with a harness on, it gives you a real good support around your shoulders. In football when you go to kick the ball, it sort of makes you go off balance, so I just didn't feel comfortable in the harness, one little bit, even though I knew if I'd played with the harness, my shoulder would not have come out. It was just so weak that there's no way I could have played without it, but there's no way I would have played to the best of my ability if I'd worn the harness.'

Bobby Robson added, 'He has done extra training and the situation is really no different than when we left England six weeks ago. He is here to play. If Bryan Robson is called upon to play, Bryan Robson will be physically fit. But he still has a clinical problem and, yes, it would be as much a risk as ever to play him.'

Manchester United's chairman Martin Edwards said the club would not be asking England to send Bryan Robson home early to have an operation on the shoulder. 'We have been assured that there will be no lasting damage to Bryan if the shoulder went again.'

Edwards had been assured that Robson would be ready for the start of the new season even if his shoulder was not pinned until after the end of the World Cup. He was not. Robson missed Manchester United's first four league games of the season, none of which they won. Their manager Ron Atkinson was sacked shortly afterwards and a new man who had never coached in the English league was hired, Alex Ferguson.

Speaking to *The Sun* after the tournament, Bryan Robson admitted, 'Every time it goes on me, I'm in agony. The pain is unbelievable, it kills you. But even though it has tortured me at times I was always prepared to take the risk and play on out here.'

Yet looking back now, he revealed to me that England had indulged in a pre-match subterfuge: 'I think it was more of a smokescreen so they didn't really know what team it was going to be. My shoulder was that weak, any sort of off-balance movement or somebody to pull my arm, anything like that and the shoulder just came out. There wasn't really any realistic chance of me being able to play in the game unfortunately. It was one of them, if I just lost balance or did a slide tackle and I went on to my right side with my right arm, there's no danger, it definitely would have come out. It was just too sore to play.'

The day before the game, the two injury doubts, Reid and Lineker, did not participate as the rest of the squad went for an early morning training session across the city. Reid came through a fitness test and convinced Robson he was fit to play as long as he suffered no reaction overnight.

Lineker, never the best trainer, sat out the session as a precaution to rest a recurring groin strain, but the sharpshooter demonstrated his readiness to play by firing an imaginary gun with his fingers at cameramen filming him at the Holiday Inn. Bobby Robson told reporters, 'I'm very confident he will play.'

That evening, Reid and Lineker spoke to the ITV panel of Brian Moore, Kevin Keegan, Ian St John and Jimmy Greaves live from the Holiday Inn in Mexico City. The interview went out just before 2am UK time after the players had watched two hours of sterility between Mexico and West Germany in the second quarter-final. After missing training, Lineker was quizzed on his readiness for the quarter-final.

'Yeah, I'm fine,' insisted Lineker, wearing an ITV Sport T-shirt. 'I tend to get a little bit stiff around the groin area after games and I just need an extra day off.' 'Really?!' quizzed Moore. Off camera, Reid next to him could barely conceal his giggles. 'You wait until you get to our age, son' remarked Greaves, eliciting roars of laughter, 'but never mind Gal, keep going mate.'

Reid also declared himself fit: 'I've done a wee bit today and it's gone quite well so I'm fit for selection. I've told [Bobby Robson] that today.' He also argued against going man-for-man on Maradona. 'Well, I think you've got to look at your own game. Obviously Maradona is a danger but you can't change your style. You've just got to try and accommodate him when the back four get to him. You can't do anything special because if you try and go one-for-one, he'll batter you. So we've just got to play our normal game and hopefully it's good enough.'

In the end, Reid did play as Robson named an unchanged midfield and forward line for the third successive game. Speaking to the BBC's pitch-side reporter Kevin Cosgrove before the game, Reid revealed, 'I did a little bit yesterday, no reaction at all, so looking forward to it now,' reassuring Cosgrove by joking, 'Wait till you see me!'

Speaking to the *Liverpool Echo* at the end of the World Cup, Reid had nothing but sympathy for the displaced Captain Marvel – who would again have his following World Cup in 1990 curtailed by an injury in England's second match. 'It should have been the highlight of his career. Having said that, he still had a tremendous attitude and encouraged us all the way.'

In the event, it would be Argentina who changed their tactics to counter the developing strengths of England, who were now playing without an orthodox winger and with a four-man midfield. Argentina brought an extra man into their midfield, the diminutive but gifted Héctor Enrique in place of their match-winner in the Round of 16, goalscorer Pedro Pasculli.

Speaking two days before the game, it appeared that Maradona did not know that his room-mate would not be playing. 'Valdano and Pasculli will give them plenty of problems and we think we can exploit their slow centre-backs. They do not like the ball played quickly across the ground.' Pasculli was also certain he would start, telling the media the same day, 'I am going to score at least one goal against England.'

However, coach Bilardo pulled Maradona aside before the game to tell him that he would be dropping his former Argentinos Juniors strike partner to accommodate an extra midfielder. He explained that 'you can't play against the English with a pure centre-forward. They'd devour him, and the extra man in midfield will give Maradona more room.' Maradona said Pasculli cried in their room when the news was broken to him.

Speaking to the *Daily Mail* in 2020, Pasculli claimed, 'I did not cry. I was unhappy because I had played well and scored the winning goal. But the coach always thought of the opponent when he picked the team and I respected that. Myself and Diego talked. He is a champion, he knew how to give peace and the right advice.' Pasculli would not play at the tournament again.

Another who would take no part was Argentina's captain in 1978, Daniel Passarella. Having been named ahead of Brown in Bilardo's first line-up at the tournament against South Korea, Passarella had been sidelined with enterocolitis, or so-called 'Montezuma's revenge'. Much conjecture still surrounds his condition. Some put it down to the stress caused by a team meeting prior to the tournament in which Maradona asserted his authority over Passarella by calling him out over his supposed failure to accept him as the new captain. Others in the squad blame it on the ice cubes used by Passarella drinking whisky late at night. The man himself – insisting he ate and drank the same as everyone else – has hinted he may have been poisoned by someone within the camp.

Suffering from diarrhoea, the man nicknamed El Kaiser had lost six kilos while in Mexico. He returned to training after missing the opening two games underprepared and promptly pulled a calf muscle. After a short break in Acapulco, he had returned to camp in a bid to prove himself fit, only to be diagnosed with an ulcer in his colon the day before the England match.

On the morning of the game, Argentina's *Crónica* reported, 'In addition to his gastric disorder, it emerged that Passarella has suffered some sort of psychosomatic disorder due to his frustrated participation at the World Cup.' The former captain, who would go down in history as the only non-Brazilian man since the Second World War to win two World Cup titles, would watch the game from a Mexico City hospital.

Maradona was clear about who would pose England's biggest threat: 'We will worry about Lineker because he always scores goals and about Hoddle because he is a phenomenal player. Hoddle is a player of brilliant touch and accurate passing. But England will have more worries than us. I saw them against Paraguay, they are strong, but we are not afraid of them.'

Left-back Oscar Garré had started all four of Argentina's games up to that point but was suspended for the quarter-final. In the 30th minute of the game against Uruguay he had collected his second yellow card of the tournament for a crude body check, one of a succession of fouls on Enzo Francescoli. In his place, Bilardo handed a first start to Julio Olarticoechea, used as a substitute in each of the previous games. The man nicknamed 'El Vasco' (The Basque) on account of his ancestry had impressed Maradona with his fitness and the way he had adapted to the altitude of Mexico.

Both Olarticoechea and the tough-tackling Ricardo Giusti were deployed as wide midfielders with the job of restricting the space for England's flank players, Trevor Steven and Steve Hodge. Maradona and Valdano, the designated forwards, would often drop deep to flood the midfield. Bilardo admitted, 'Even my own father tells me I should play with two wingers, but we no longer have as many great forwards.' He added, 'The match will be decided and mostly played in midfield. We will have to be careful to avoid the danger of those constant high and low centres of the English.' His tactics worked perfectly as Steven and Hodge were never allowed to get sufficiently forward into positions to provide the crosses from which Lineker might score.

Bilardo's predecessor, the 1978 World Cup-winning coach César Luis Menotti, believed England's improvement against Poland and Paraguay was due to the introduction of Beardsley alongside Lineker. 'They made the mistake of playing only to Hateley. Now they have two points of attack.' Menotti predicted that Argentina 'will keep the ball on the ground, they will put a lot of pressure on the English defence and they have Maradona in inspired form'.

Robson told his players that Argentina's new tactics were 'a negative change in their formation to protect themselves'.

The Two One-Off Strips

The 1966 World Cup Final enshrined the idea of England wearing red shirts as an alternative to their regular strip of white shirts and navy-blue shorts. However, the fact that the men's team won their only major international trophy wearing red was because of Argentina.

Fifteen years earlier, the South Americans were invited by the FA to play at Wembley as part of the 1951 Festival of Britain. Instead of embarking on their usual post-season overseas tour, England played a series of matches at home as part of a range of events aimed at boosting the post-war mood by celebrating the country and its achievements.

In May 1951, Argentina remarkably became the first overseas nation to play England at Wembley Stadium. They arrived in London with their usual white (*albi*) and sky-blue (*celeste*) striped shirts. On the morning of the match, the Welsh referee for the game, Benjamin Mervyn 'Sandy' Griffiths, made a ruling that altered English football history. With the match to be filmed in black and white on a cloudy afternoon, Griffiths decided that, due to the poor visibility, England's white shirts offered insufficient contrast to Argentina's stripes. Up until that point, England's alternative shirts had always been navy-blue, but, beingtoo similar to Argentina's *albiceleste* colours, this was unsuitable too.

Therefore, for the first time ever, England wore a hastily assembled 'third' strip of red shirts with white shorts. England won

2-1. They wore red shirts a year later during a famous 3-2 victory away to Austria in Vienna, then again at Wembley in 1954 when defeating world champions West Germany, victories that implanted the idea of the colour as being 'lucky' for England.

In contrast, England's navy-blue shirts became associated with humiliation. The team had worn the colour during the 1950 World Cup defeat to the United States and then donned the same shirts in Lima against the white-and-red shirted Peruvians in 1959. England lost 4-1. They never wore navy-blue again for the remainder of the century.

Argentina were the designated home side, or 'Team A' in the 1986 World Cup quarter-final. By right, it was England's duty as 'Team B' to change strip if there was any clash of kits. So why did Argentina wear their away strip, a decision that precipitated an extraordinary chain of events?

During England's last World Cup finals match against Argentina at Wembley in 1966, both sides had worn their home shirts. On a sunny afternoon, the plain England shirts this time sufficiently contrasted with the Argentinian stripes. To avoid a clash of shorts and socks, both sides had deviated from their usual combination, with England wearing white shorts and Argentina changing to play in dark socks.

Four years earlier, Argentina had lost 3-1 to England in Rancagua, Chile. During that group stage match, England were also the designated home side, forcing Argentina to wear their dark-blue away shirt and black shorts, as they would in Mexico City. England once again wore an all-white strip.

It was an all-white strip for England in 1998 when they met Argentina during the Round of 16 in Saint-Étienne. Manager Glenn Hoddle said, 'It takes your mind straight away to 1966 and the quarter-final we won.' This time it was not a lucky omen as England went out in a penalty shoot-out.

Four years later, England were again the away team against Argentina in their meeting at the 2002 World Cup. They changed this time into their traditional away strip of red shirts and white shorts, which did not clash in any way with Argentina's home kit. England won.

In 1978, Argentina won the World Cup wearing Adidas shirts but two years later they signed a kit deal with French manufacturers Le Coq Sportif, displaying their rooster logo on the shirts worn during their unsuccessful defence of the trophy in Spain.

The 1986 World Cup draw forced Argentina to kick off all of their group stage games at midday, in the hours of maximum heat and humidity, in addition to the high altitude of Mexico City. To mitigate this, the meticulous Argentina coach Carlos Bilardo had made a request to Le Coq Sportif that they provide the squad with a special lightweight home shirt made of Aertex fabric. Designed like a honeycomb mesh, it allowed air circulation and did not get weighed down by absorbing excessive perspiration. The fabric had also been worn by England during the 1970 World Cup in Mexico. Jorge Valdano remarked that the shirts were so light they were 'practically made of paper'.[12]

With no kit clashes during the group stage, Argentina wore their breathable *albiceleste* home shirt in all three games. However, a duel with their *celeste*-shirted neighbours Uruguay necessitated a change in the Round of 16. Uruguay's away shirts, also made by Le Coq Sportif, were white, so Argentina wore their dark-blue away shirts.

Remarkably, Le Coq Sportif had not supplied the Argentina squad with an Aertex fabric away shirt, only a cotton one. Not so much of a problem, it was thought, as for the first time Argentina kicked off at 4pm local time on an overcast afternoon. However, the weather changed all that. During the second half, the heavens opened for the second successive Mexican afternoon during the Round of 16. While the thunderstorm that afflicted the previous afternoon's thriller between Belgium and the Soviet Union in León only began at the

---

12   https://www.youtube.com/watch?feature=shared&v=VyNMzo2sdEU

end of extra time, the Argentina and Uruguay players were deluged throughout most of the second half of their tight affair.

The cotton fibre Argentinian shirts were thus soaked through and slowed the players down as they held on to their 1-0 lead. Maradona recalled, 'Our blue jerseys started weighing us down like sweaters.' After the match, Bilardo asked kit-man Tito Benrós to compare the weight of the sodden shirt worn by central defender José Luis Brown against a clean Aertex shirt. The staff were amazed to discover it amounted to carrying a few extra kilograms. Facing another white-shirted team six days later, this time with a noon kick-off, FIFA informed Argentina that, following a draw, they would have to change shirts once more. The players were adamant they would not wear the same material again.

Bilardo took a pair of scissors to the original away shirt and pierced holes in it to provide improvised ventilation, a solution Maradona labelled as 'totally ludicrous'. The finished product resembled a moth-eaten shirt. The prototype created for Jorge Burruchaga was gifted by him to kit-man Benrós and subsequently displayed in the museum of Racing Club. In March 2024, the randomly holed shirt was sold by Graham Budd Auctions (now BUDDS) for £7,000.[13]

Despite a request from Bilardo to produce an Aertex away shirt, Le Coq Sportif were unable to supply a suitable replacement in time, so Rubén Moschella, the administrative officer from the Argentinian FA, was sent shopping in Mexico City to find a similar set of blue jerseys also manufactured by Le Coq Sportif. Moschella visited six stores but only found two candidates, which he recalls being 'very cheap'. Neither were Aertex but had an open V-neck design as opposed to the more claustrophobic round neck of their designated away shirt.

Bilardo was not enamoured with either but nonetheless asked Maradona, who was passing by the room. Striped and shinier than

———

13 https://bidlive.budds.com/past-auctions/srgrah10065/lot-details/cf5cbd48-2aa3-48f6-b58a-b11601869b9b

their usual jerseys, the captain commented, 'What a nice shirt. We'll beat England in that one.' The decision was made.

The staff then worked out how they would apply the badge and numbers to the new shirt. A prototype was created with a rubber shield and thin white, angular numbers ironed on the back, but they were deemed unsuitable.

One of those test shirts was gifted by Maradona to the Costa Rican linesman Berny Ulloa, another to the Brazilian referee Raimundo Arppi Filho, both of whom officiated during the World Cup Final a week later. Shortly before he passed away, the shirt dedicated personally by Maradona 'with affection' to Arppi Filho, was put on sale by the referee through BUDDS Auctions. The prototype, never used in any match, sold for £6,500 in March 2023.[14]

Once again Moschella improvised, experimenting with a silver cloth that was covered in glitter and manufactured to be used on American football shirts against the new blue shirts. The numbers were cut out with scissors and ironed on to the shirts by Benrós. The unofficial silver numbers covered the players who wore them during the match in sparkles.

Moschella returned to the store and purchased 38 shirts, two for each of the 19 outfield players in the squad, one to wear in each half. Four women who worked as housemaids at the Club América facility serving the players their food were then given the task of sewing the Argentina badges on to the new shirts. Unable to find badges identical to the ones on the modern-day shirt, they instead used an older version from the early 1980s. The crest on the shirts against England is therefore missing the laurel leaves beneath the Argentina badge that were added in 1982. The downward angle serif on the 'F' of the 'AFA' is straight, unlike the more embellished font used on the home shirt.

---

14 https://bidlive.budds.com/past-auctions/srgrah10050/lot-details/b78d3f18-fbbf-49d1-9f75-afaa00fc3ed

Glenn Hoddle poses for a photograph with Diego Maradona during Osvaldo Ardiles' testimonial 52 days before they faced each other in the 1986 FIFA World Cup quarter-final

Gary Lineker shows off his 'lucky' Adidas boots. Their mysterious disappearance before a match away to Oxford United may have cost Everton a second successive league championship title

Jorge Burruchaga's cotton jersey worn in the round of 16 match against Uruguay. Head coach Carlos Bilardo pierced holes in it to illustrate the ventilation he desired for the shirts he wanted his team to wear in the quarter-final. In 2024, this prototype sold for £7,000 at auction. (©: BUDDS. COM)

Two of the greatest footballers in World Cup history exchange words ahead of the World Cup quarter-final between their two nations

England's talismanic captain is reduced to shooting a camera from the sidelines. Could he have made a difference to the outcome? 'They had a Maradona, we didn't have a Robson' lamented the England manager afterwards

The four men directly involved in the Hand of God goal – Diego Maradona, Ali Bin Nasser, Bogdan Dochev and Peter Shilton – exchange pleasantries before the incident which would shape all of their lives

'This is football, not rugby'– not for the last time in the match, Terry Fenwick brings down Maradona. The yellow card he earned for this challenge was a decisive factor in the rest of his performance

'Quit breaking my balls' – Maradona and Costa Rican linesman Berny Ulloa lighten the mood during a first half of few notable incidents

'We practised the move the day before!' Kenny Sansom (centre) vents his fury at Peter Reid as the teams come off at half-time after England's perfectly executed free kick routine was undermined by one player's forgetfulness

'A Renaissance painting depicting a tragicomedy.' A Chelsea fan and a man, incongruously wearing a shirt and tie, engage with one another in a photograph which has taken on a life of its own on social media

The future chairman of Velez Sarsfield Raúl Héctor Gámez (holding his shirt) unloads his pistols in a fist-fight with the English fans – 'I don't want my grandchildren to find out'

La Mano de Dios – one of the most recognisable photographs in history shot by a Mexican, Alejandro Ojeda Carbajal, but since credited to Englishman Bob Thomas

Maradona (not Terry Butcher) applies the final touch to the Goal of the Century

Norwich City fan Mark Woodroffe lets Diego Maradona know exactly what he thinks of him after the Argentina players had celebrated their two-goal advantage in front of the England fans

Most of the badges were not even sewn on all the way around; four stitches were used at the top and bottom and thus came away from the shirt in the middle. The label on the shirts worn in the quarter-final also uniquely read 'Hecho in Mexico' (Made in Mexico) as opposed to 'Hecho in Argentina'.

Resident cameraman Néstor Clausen filmed the kit being put together in the communal area of the training camp, and team-mate Jorge Burruchaga remarked that 'this is incredible. There is one day left to play against England and these women are fixing our shirts.'

In 2025, England's unused substitute in the quarter-final, Gary Andrew Stevens, allowed me to compare his shirt from the 1986 World Cup with that of the player he swapped with at the end of the Argentina match, Óscar Ruggeri. In spite of being taller than Stevens, Ruggeri's shirt is visibly smaller than his counterpart's. The Argentina crest is only loosely sewn on to the shirt at the top and bottom and pinches the fabric of the shirt around it, having been hurriedly sewn on in mid-air rather than professionally while being laid flat.

Stevens showed me that his fingers could fit under the badge, which came away in the middle. The silver numbers on the back, designed to be worn on shirts in another type of football, are unusually tacky. With its textured glitter, they have the feel of Christmas wrapping paper.

No two Argentina shirts used that day looked the same, with the crest and numbers in visibly different positions on each one. Burruchaga laughed about it years later, recalling, 'In the afternoon before the quarter-final against England, the women were sticking those numbers on. The silver ones were ugly and the crest is ugly.'

The England shirts worn during the 1986 World Cup also featured so-called shadow stripes. After ten years of wearing a strip manufactured by the Leicester-based suppliers Admiral, England reverted to the Manchester-based kit-makers Umbro in 1984. Umbro had last supplied the England shirts at a major tournament for the previous World Cup in Mexico but, unlike then, they were now permitted to display their diamond logo on the front of the kit. For the first time ever, the Three Lions badge was displayed on the players' shorts.

A survivor of the polyester Admiral kit worn at the previous World Cup, Hoddle remembers how the players suffered in the afternoon heat of Bilbao. 'In Spain at that World Cup, that was blisteringly hot, and we played with a shirt that was really dreadful to play in heat. We learned from that and we explained that as players.'

A year before the World Cup, England were invited to Mexico to play in a warm-up tournament against Italy and the hosts in Mexico City, the 'Copa Ciudad de Mexico'. There they experimented once more with an Aertex shirt, but this was ultimately not used during the World Cup the following summer.

For the first time ever, England wore a special tournament inscription underneath the Three Lions badge during the World Cup. The words 'FIFA World Cup Mexico'86' (no space) were embroidered in navy-blue into the fabric on the left breast. Unlike the shirts worn in Europe earlier in the year, the elasticated navy-blue cuffs on the shirt sleeves were removed to offer the players more ventilation in the oppressive heat of Monterrey, where England played their three group stage matches.

Known for his style on and off the pitch and also renowned for wearing his shirt outside his shorts, Hoddle was an admirer of England's 1986 World Cup shirt. 'They were beautiful. Not only were they beautiful to wear, they looked great and it felt good. So at least we were ahead of them in one way. Our shirts were ready!'

Umbro estimated that England reaching the last eight of the World Cup would lead to a 50 per cent increase in sales of replica shirts and more jobs at their four factories. For the tournament, England had been issued with two away strips, their traditional red shirts and white shorts and a new all sky-blue kit.

During the previous World Cup in Mexico, believing that darker colours absorbed more heat, the FA had also opted for a sky-blue away kit rather than their traditional red shirts. They wore the all-blue kit against the white-shirted Czechoslovakia in the final group game but viewers complained that the colour offered insufficient contrast to their opponents on the black-and-white televisions owned by the majority of the population in 1970.

Sitting in the dugout, England manager Alf Ramsey also admitted to having trouble picking out his own team from their opponents: 'I think the choice, and it was my choice, of pale blue, as a second colour was a bad one. Where I sat looking from the shade into the sun, it was very difficult to distinguish the players.'

England thus reverted to their third-choice red kit for the quarter-final against West Germany. However, four years on from winning the 1966 World Cup Final in red, this time the shirts did not prove lucky, as the reigning world champions were eliminated in extra time after leading 2-0.

Now back in Mexico 16 years later, the FA once again opted for an all-sky-blue strip as the first away kit, with the red shirt as a third choice. Alone, the white and sky-blue shirts would have been considered too similar in tone. FIFA's Equipment Regulation 6.2.4. stipulates that 'where a First-Choice Playing Kit item is predominantly light in colour, at least one equivalent Alternative Playing Kit item should be predominantly dark in colour, and vice versa'.

During a briefing a month before the tournament, FA officials told the media that they considered red to be 'too dark' a colour to wear in the heat of the Mexican summer. Ironically, the team's best performance during the preparatory tournament in Mexico City the previous year had been in red shirts. Wearing Aertex shirts for the last time, they soundly defeated the white-shirted West Germans 3-0 at the Estadio Azteca. It would be the last victory over the Germans for 15 years.

England had the option of wearing red in the 1986 quarter-final, as they would when they eventually defeated Argentina at the World Cup in 2002, but decided to stick with their white shirts, forcing Argentina to change. However, both of Argentina's kit choices involved dark shorts and white socks, the same as England's home strip.

Article 6.5 of the Equipment Regulations state that 'where FIFA or the Match Officials consider that there is an insufficient contrast between the colours used on the Playing Kits of two Teams … they may require one Team to switch to, or to combine, different items from its different Playing Kits as necessary in order to achieve a clear distinction'. Therefore, England were forced into a mix-and-match of a strip. They could have worn the white shorts and red socks of their third kit, as they had on many previous occasions when facing South American opposition, such as Brazil and Chile. They instead changed their shorts and socks to their designated second choice of sky-blue.

Ironically, facing a country they had gone to war with just four years earlier, England played wearing the exact colours of the Argentinian flag, *albiceleste*, white and sky-blue. Like the one-of-a-kind Argentina shirt, this kit combination has never again been worn by England.

The Men Who Captured History

If the 1986 World Cup quarter-final was played today, there would have been almost 115,000 photographers inside the Estadio Azteca, each with the potential to shoot high-resolution pictures and videos on their camera phones.

That was not the case then. Amateur photographers were rare and most of the cameras in the price range of the average football supporter were of the point-and-shoot variety, without the technical capabilities necessary to capture anything more than a stadium overview.

In 1986, Joe O'Connell went on holiday having borrowed a 35mm camera from his friend in Sligo. With no idea of how to operate it, or even how to open it to insert the film, he had to visit a camera shop in Florida to ask for help from the shop assistant.

Having learned how to use it, he took it to Mexico City and had it with him in the Estadio Azteca, so decided to take some pictures. Speaking to me from the north-west of Ireland, O'Connell said he spent a lot of the game squinting through the viewfinder: 'You really wouldn't know what has happening down on the pitch. You just sort of said, "This is going to be a nice move, maybe I'll just take a photograph."'

Developed a few days later, O'Connell's photos were stored away in his attic and forgotten about for 36 years until discovered one day by his son Ruaidhri in an old box. 'They could have easily been thrown out,' admitted O'Connell.

Amazed to find a picture of Maradona jumping for the ball with Shilton, Ruaidhri, with the help of a friend, released the photographs his father had taken through a new website called Betting America in the lead-up to the 2022 World Cup. In Argentina, the images, taken from the opposite side of the stadium to most of the official photographs, went viral on social media.

Joe O'Connell's photograph of the 'Hand of God' is taken from the top of the stadium in almost perfect focus. It captures the anguished expressions of Maradona and Shilton in mid-air as they both grasp at the ball. After three decades of endless debate over the incident, it was football's equivalent of discovering Abraham Zapruder's film of the Kennedy assassination, offering a fresh perspective on an infamous moment in history.

O'Connell told me, 'For that photograph, I wasn't aware what happened. I didn't even know that a goal was scored until I took the camera down from my face. All the people around us – they probably thought that we were English – they kept pointing to their hands. I didn't know what the reason was, I didn't realise it was even a goal. When I think about it now, it was so funny, I hadn't realised what had happened. They've seen it and they were at the very top of the Aztec stadium. You wonder how the officials haven't seen it right.'[15]

In 1986, almost every newspaper in the UK printed in black and white. Colour photography was something reserved for books or magazines released after the event. On 6 March, however, the Manchester-based businessman Eddie Shah launched *Today* newspaper, the first-ever in the country to use computer typesetting and full colour printing. They immediately hired a 23-year-old as their staff sports photographer.

Eddie Keogh is now the official photographer for the England men's national team but in 1986 he was a relative novice who was told he would be sent to the World Cup, working alongside the more

---

15   https://bettingamerica.com/maradona-hand-of-god-photo

renowned photo-journalist, Tom Stoddart, in the Estadio Azteca. Keogh was behind the goal into which Argentina scored both their goals and told me he had no idea Maradona had handled the ball for the first. Speaking to Shutterstock in 2018, he explained why he missed out on the money shot: 'I pulled the trigger a split second too late, the ball had just left his hand.'

Keogh and Stoddart's colour photographs were published in *Today* two days after the match. Only three pictures were used in a full-page spread. Keogh explained: 'While working for *Today* newspaper, they would only use a couple of pictures per day, and if there was no game or training, we would set up funny pictures with the players and that was our day's work.'

Now photographers can process and send endless images around the world within minutes, but in 1986 the process was far more laborious. The images reached London via the World Trade Center in New York, having been flown across Mexico to the offices of the *El Informador* newspaper.

Keogh explained the journey to me: 'I personally flew to Guadalajara with the film, where we had it processed, and *Today* newspaper somehow had a relationship with a company called Scitex who could transmit the colour transparency. I'm not joking, the machine that did this was the size of a small lorry. The cost must have been crazy.'

The match, like all of the showpiece matches in Mexico for the 1986 World Cup, kicked off at noon local time. This not only suited the major television companies in Europe as it allowed them to broadcast live coverage in the prime-time evening slot, but it minimised the contrasting effect of shadows dissecting the playing surface, which was more prevalent later in the afternoon.

The noon kick-offs put player welfare to one side to ensure the clarity of the television coverage was not affected, but it created problems for photographers working in brilliant sunshine. Keogh told me, 'The light was really tricky as the sun was almost directly above, creating horrible shadows over players' eyes. I was also working on transparency film, which is unforgiving if you get the exposure wrong.'

Many of the photographs with which the match has become associated were made famous long after the match was played. Perhaps the most perplexing story is of one taken at half-time that had nothing to do with events on the pitch but has since taken on a life of its own on social media. Shot in the stand behind one of the goals, it shows two men completely incongruous to each other and everyone around them. One is muscular, heavily tattooed and bare-chested, wearing only a pair of Chelsea FC replica shorts and a white T-shirt tied around his head. The other is skinny and is perhaps the only man on the terracing wearing a shirt and tie.

The bare-chested man appears to have thrown a punch at the shirted man that has left him reeling. A subsequent photo shows him floored, as a third man, another bare-chested Chelsea supporter, stands over him with his fists raised ready to back up the man who had apparently thrown the punch.

In the background, the electronic scoreboard timestamps the image at 12.51, a few minutes into the half-time interval, which means this altercation is unlinked to the brawl that occurred shortly after and is described later in the book. Nonetheless, the uniqueness of the photograph, arms flailing, faces contorted, all watched by a wide range of startled onlookers, has given the image the feel of a Renaissance painting depicting a tragicomedy.

Explanations of what is actually happening in the photograph have varied, with each man labelled at different times as being either an Argentinian or English hooligan. The most plausible theory is that the bare-chested Chelsea fan is attacking an English journalist, but that is disputed.

Even the identity of the photographer is a matter of intrigue. Sergio Dorantes was a 40-year-old Mexican of Native American origin. Born into a poor family, his academic abilities earned him a place in one of Mexico City's best schools where he learned English. In 1970, he moved to the UK, working initially as a catering assistant in a hotel, then a mechanic on Formula One cars. In England, he discovered a talent for photography and eventually became a press photographer, working for Associated Press at the 1986 World Cup.

After the tournament he returned to live in Mexico and became internationally renowned. Yet in 2003 his career was suddenly ended when he was wrongly accused of the murder of his former wife, Alejandra Dehesa, who was stabbed to death at the Newsweek offices where she worked. Dorantes fled to the United States before eventually being extradited in 2007 and imprisoned in 2008. He was released four years later with the judge conceding there was no evidence against him after the only witness placing Dorantes at the scene of the crime recanted his testimony and admitted he had been bribed by the prosecutor.

As the historical significance of the game spiralled with every passing year, so more and more photographs were released to demonstrate the confrontation between the two nations. Several later emerged of the two teams coming out on to the pitch up the steep ramp leading out from the changing rooms situated behind the north goal.

As part of the renovations for the 2026 FIFA World Cup, new changing rooms are being constructed next to the dugouts, with the players emerging from a standard tunnel on the halfway line. Before the stadium was closed, the two teams always had to enter the pitch from the underground catacombs of the concrete bowl into the light.

Shot from pitch level, overlooking and behind the players, one of those photographs was taken for *El Gráfico* in Argentina. This was used by Diego Maradona in his book on the tournament, *Touched By God: How We Won the Mexico '86 World Cup*. A more widely used photo of that scene is now owned by Getty Images and was taken by Englishman Mike King, then working for *Allsport*. Maradona, at the head of the Argentinian line, is obscured by the taller Pumpido behind him. For once he is not the centre of the focus as the camera perfectly captures the other 21 protagonists ahead of a game dominated by the one player you can't see.

In the days before international players habitually shared club sides and sponsorship agreements, there were no pre-match greetings between the two teams, just two clear lines of 11 men, separated by their nationality. The vertiginous stands of the Azteca dwarf the footballers, highlighting the magnitude of the occasion, the sky only visible at the very top of the photo. The sweep of the stands from the left and right seems to curve in opposite directions to create a dizzying effect encapsulating the blur or emotions the players must have experienced.

It is every inch an image of combatants entering the gladiatorial arena. In fact, during Ridley Scott's *Gladiator* film from 2000, a very similar scene was created with two lines of men walking up a sloping ramp into the open light of the Colosseum.

Maradona said it was 'a picture I always remember, a really great, special shot'. In his recollection of that moment 'all I could hear was the clicking of our cleats on that metallic floor. There was no more talking at that point, not between us players or to any of them.'

King, who previously worked as a freelancer for Bob Thomas Photography, had been recruited by Steve Powell and Tony Duffy for *Allsport* in 1982. Four years earlier, Powell had captured what many believe to be the greatest sports photograph of all time, a shot of Maradona seemingly confronted by six Belgians during the opening match of the 1982 World Cup. That photograph became symbolic of Maradona's genius only after the events of the 1986 World Cup quarter-final when he became the player he had promised to be in 1982 – one actually capable of singlehandedly taking on and beating six players on the world stage.

In 1982, *Allsport* had no fixed presence at the World Cup but four years later, with the recruitment of King alongside established football photographer David Cannon, they sent a crack team to cover the finals in Mexico. To keep costs down, the team stayed at a rundown bungalow in Mexico City and rented a car for the duration of the tournament. King, a wannabe rally driver, had sourced a second-hand grey Ford for $1,500, which survived several near misses on the Mexican roads.

In the second half of the match, King sat close to a Mexican freelancer Alejandro Ojeda Carbajal to the left of the goal that Peter Shilton was defending. Unlike King, who joined the Bob Thomas Photography Agency straight from school, Ojeda was a part-time healthcare worker who first photographed the dogs whose hair he cut. After covering the 1968 Olympics in Mexico, Ojeda also worked at the 1970 World Cup on home soil before being sent to the 1974 and 1978 finals in West Germany and Argentina.

Both photographers were ideally placed as Maradona ran to that corner of the pitch after scoring both his goals. After the match, Ojeda raced back to the offices of *El Heraldo de México* newspaper to process his Kodak Ektachrome colour film in the hope he had captured a good one of Maradona celebrating his two goals. In the darkroom, one of the other photographers noticed that one of the negatives had captured something else. He told him, 'Ojeda, you have the photo of the World Cup.' It was an image that would become one of the most famous photographs ever taken.

Even the day after the match, there were still some who wanted to believe that Maradona had headed the ball past Peter Shilton. A Mexico City tabloid newspaper, *Unomásuno*, published a black-and-white image from behind the incident, with Shilton's outstretched arm obscuring Maradona's fist. The caption underneath claimed it proved the veracity of the first goal: 'According to the photo by Aarón Sánchez, there was no hand in this shot by Maradona.'

In an age before multiple close-ups from every conceivable position, television viewers were limited to the four long-range angles provided by the host broadcaster, and exclusive footage from the two pitch-side cameramen working close to one another for the BBC and ITV. None provided conclusive proof of deliberate handball.

Many photographers had captured images from different angles of Maradona jumping with Shilton before the disputed first goal. Of the hundreds of pictures of the incident that were being circulated, most revealed Maradona above the England goalkeeper, leading with his left fist, but none definitively caught him making contact with his hand.

None except Ojeda's. The picture he had taken was perfectly exposed, caught from the right angle with Maradona and Shilton like two frozen figures contorted and momentarily fixed in mid-air, and Maradona's left hand in full contact with the Adidas ball. For any doubters, it was the incontrovertible proof that the first goal had been punched into the England net.

Ojeda's photograph was used on the front page of the next morning's *El Heraldo de México* and he reportedly turned down an offer of $10,000 from the BBC for the photograph. A year later he won the 1987 Mexican National Journalism Award for his image.

However, search for the image now and there is little mention of Alejandro Ojeda Carbajal, his name airbrushed from history. The iconic photograph, like King's and so many others, is now owned by the Getty Images Picture Library, founded in 1985 by Mark Getty, the grandson of billionaire J. Paul Getty, and Jonathan Klein. The picture is now credited to Bob Thomas, the 28-year-old English photographer who at the time owned his own eponymous sports agency. How he came to own the rights to Ojeda's photograph is shrouded in mystery.

Speaking to me about it, Thomas admitted the details surrounding the photo are subject to a confidentiality agreement and he is only therefore willing to answer certain questions. He did say that, like Ojeda, he was positioned 'behind the goal where Maradona scored his goals. I knew immediately that he had punched the ball into the net for the first goal.'

'I saw the image in the local morning newspaper the following day,' Thomas admitted. It is said that, realising the potential value of the photograph, Thomas went to the offices of *El Heraldo* and purchased a copy of the original slide for somewhere between $5,000 and $10,000.

According to another photographer who spoke to Ojeda in the days after the match, the Mexican had no knowledge of what happened between his newspaper and Bob Thomas, whether the Englishman made copies of the photo or obtained the original image. Thomas told me, 'In the circumstances, the content matters more than any quality considerations.'

Juha Tamminen was working as a freelance photo-journalist at the 1986 World Cup. He told me, 'Bob Thomas had a nose for important photos and probably did hundreds of duplicates of it. I don't think he bought the original. During the 1990 World Cup in Italy, Bob did that with some of my photos, and he gave me back my originals … He paid me, of course.'

What is clear is that Thomas went back to England owning a copy that he was now free to distribute. It has been alleged that not only has Thomas never spoken about how he obtained the rights to the photo but even forbidden his former employees from talking about it. Whatever the truth, Thomas was now able to sell the licence on the photograph, which became one of the defining sports images of the 20th century.

The picture was first used in England on page three in the late edition of the *London Evening Standard* two days later. Under the headline 'Caught in the Act', the paper published a full-page black-and-white image that they claimed was 'irrefutable proof' of the handball. They credited the picture to the *El Heraldo* newspaper in Mexico before explaining that 'Associated Press today completed long negotiations for the syndication of the picture'.

A closely cropped black-and-white image of the photo was used on page 25 of *The Sun* the next day. They described it as 'our picture' under the headline 'The final proof'.

In 2007, the entire Bob Thomas archive was purchased by Getty Images. To buy a licence for the photograph now, which is not included in the standard Getty subscription, will cost you a minimum of £150 for a low-resolution image.

Speaking about the forgotten Ojeda to *El Heraldo* in 2020, his son Juan Carlos said, 'My father was very dedicated. He said that what he liked most was being sent to football. Whenever he took a good photo, he knew it, he had that gift, that feeling.'[16]

Certainly there are few more recognisable photographs in the world. The image holds endless fascination. The two outstanding players in their respective teams leaping in tandem, rising above their own shadows cast on the pitch in their matching Puma King boots, with their captain's armbands visible. Maradona's jump seems almost other-worldly, with his legs splayed, rising above a man seven inches taller than him. His ribs show through his shiny blue-striped shirt, emphasising a man at the peak of his physical fitness. 'I didn't have an ounce of fat – and how strong my legs are,' Maradona recalled.

In contrast to the dynamic Argentine, Shilton appears leaden-footed in his dull grey kit, barely off the ground. Even today on social media, the goalkeeper remains a prisoner of this image, perceived to have been outjumped by a smaller man. The truth is, he was never close enough to the ball to jump for it. The ball was played back diagonally and Maradona anticipated the play better, jumping across the front of Shilton, even though the angle of the photograph makes it appear they are almost face to face.

The one other player in the image is caught on the very edge of the frame. Jorge Burruchaga – someone who would earn the reputation as Maradona's lieutenant on the pitch – is by his side here. His eyes are transfixed on Maradona, as much an onlooker upon history as every one of the hundreds of fans captured in the shot.

One of those may well have been Peter Robinson, sitting in the main tribune. Educated at the Royal College of Art, Robinson wanted to be a documentary photographer, having little interest in sport and even less in team games like football. He began shooting at matches as a means to earn money, earning a shilling for each shot printed in

---

16 https://heraldodemexico.com.mx/deportes/2020/11/26/la-mano-de-dios-el-engano-que-un-fotografo-mexicano-revelo-al-mundo-229482.html

a new publication called *Soccer Review* during the 1965/66 season. He hoped to earn enough from his temporary job to eventually shoot the sort of images he yearned to.

Given free rein, the money kept coming and the opportunity to work at the 1966 World Cup presented itself to the young photographer who had developed a talent for capturing memorable, eye-catching images. Fifty years later he was still making his name as one of the world's leading sports photographers.

Aged 42 at the time of the 1986 World Cup, Robinson was employed by FIFA's marketing arm ISL as their official photographer, together with a Madrid-based colleague. Unlike the other cameramen at the tournament, Robinson's media pass allowed him to access any part of the stadium, either pitch-side or in the stands.

Instructed to make sure all his pictures captured the advertising boards of the multinationals who had bankrolled the tournament through ISL, Robinson positioned himself on the same side of the stadium as the primary television camera facing the row of uninterrupted hoardings. Robinson was therefore in no position to capture a clear image of Maradona's first goal as he had made the decision to be close to the Argentina coach Bilardo, standing in front of his dugout, at the start of the second half.

Yet as Maradona set off on the run that would end with him scoring the 'Goal of the Century', Robinson followed him from the opposite edge of the pitch with his 400mm-long lens, shooting all the time on to Fujifilm, the official sponsor of the World Cup.

When Maradona ran to the corner, Robinson carried on snapping as the Argentina captain celebrated in front of England fans standing behind two Union Jack flags, one emblazoned with the name of 'Oxford United'. Other photographers took pictures of this scene but only Robinson captured Maradona walking back alone, pumping his fists, overshadowed by one England fan standing on the seats behind him and therefore elevated above the rest of the masses.

The grass is slightly out of focus, appearing as a green haze at the bottom of the picture, forcing the attention on to the protagonists.

The supporter, bare-chested and wearing sunglasses, is captured sticking his middle finger up at Maradona in a perfect demonstration of everything the game meant to both sides. The England fan was Mark Woodroffe, who together with his best friend Nick were sitting at the front of the stand. Having paid around £10 each for their seats to the Paraguay match, they found the same touts demanding more money for the quarter-final but managed to haggle them down into paying the same price.

As Maradona ran to the corner, Woodroffe was separated from the celebrating Argentina players only by a moat filled with armed Mexican troops on standby to counter any hint of hooliganism. Woodroffe alleges that Maradona stuck his middle finger up at the England fans before turning away, which is why he responded in kind. At least four supporters in the image were offering Maradona the full panoply of one-finger, two-finger and closed fist gestures they felt he deserved, but only Woodroffe is caught by the photographer so clearly in the act.

With supreme irony, the angle of the photograph captures the gesticulating Woodroffe directly above the Sport Billy cartoon character created by ISL to represent fair play at the tournament. He told me, 'Maradona retreated after a hail of spit landed on him from the surrounding England fans.'

Robinson reveals that 'the 400mm-long lens compressed the perspective, so they look as if they are on top of each other. It's one I like most out of the whole day I think.' Described by *The Athletic* in April 2022 as 'arguably the world's greatest living soccer photographer', Robinson himself prefers the shot in black and white, as he says the colours of the other fans confused the image.

Higher up in the main stand, Juha Tamminen was sitting in the designated press box. The Finn had travelled at his own expense, hoping to be accredited as a written journalist. 'When I applied it was about a year or so before, it didn't cross my mind that I could go as a photographer.'

Now, strict controls over broadcast rights and the live streaming of games prevent any written journalist using a camera in a World Cup press box once a match has begun. Yet, long before social networks made it commonplace, Tamminen was a multimedia journalist, having bought himself a new Canon A-1 camera. He told me, 'I bought the big lens during the winter and in Mexico started taking photos from the press box when I noticed that Kodak was giving free film to photographers.'

As Maradona began his dribble from inside his own half for the second goal, Tamminen was ideally place to follow him, shooting frame after frame as he bore down on the England goal. Taking three frames per second, his pictures show Maradona at different stages of his dribble, including the split second before he poked the ball into the net as Terry Butcher made a desperate lunge to knock him off balance.

On the ITV commentary, Martin Tyler, upon viewing the various replays of the second goal, intimated that 'in fact the final touch might even have come off the defender ... Terry Butcher trying to make up the ground, tackled and got a toe to it', a theory that many people ran with based on the speed with which the ball hit the net and the fact that Maradona rarely used his right foot to score.

Tamminen's final shot of the dribble conclusively proves that it was Maradona, not Butcher, who scored the goal. The Argentina captain using his right leg to shield the ball from Butcher, whose leg is nowhere near it. Maradona's left foot is poised to add the finishing touch to the greatest dribble ever seen at this level of the game.

Tamminen told me that image was the most widely distributed photograph he took at the game and his personal favourite. It is one Maradona liked too, after Tamminen presented the family with a book of his photographs from the World Cup. 'I handed it to his brothers in 1987 at the Maradona home in Buenos Aires. They definitely kept the book on the shelf. [Maradona's agent] Fernando Signorini once told me that he had seen the book there.'

The Other No.10

Speaking to *ESTO* the day before the 1986 World Cup quarter-final, Jorge Valdano said that Gary Lineker (spelled Linecker in the paper) is 'the only player in this World Cup who knows how to take advantage of all the opportunities to score goals. Linecker (sic) is so opportunistic that his companions do not introduce him to their respective wives, since he takes advantage of them all.'

In the official report of the FIFA World Cup Mexico 1986 released after the tournament, it was said that 'Gary Lineker was selected by the English manager although he is not a typical British centre forward. His way of playing is rather based on quickness and agility than on strength and dynamism.'

During England's opening game against Portugal, that sharpness had brought Lineker into goalscoring positions but he had missed the chances presented to him. Going into the World Cup, Lineker had not scored an international goal in 1986. His strike partner Mark Hateley was the man in form, scoring three times in England's two preceding warm-up games against Mexico and Canada as well as one in an unofficial friendly against South Korea. As Bobby Robson admitted, 'Mark had arrived in Mexico as my number-one centre-forward.'

When Bobby Robson dropped Hateley from the team rather than Lineker after both had failed to score in England's opening two games, the AC Milan striker believed he had been singled out. In his autobiography *Top Mark!* he said that 'to some extent, I felt that I had carried the can for those two poor results and I found that hard to take. I thought I had played okay; I had made chances for other people, which has always been part of my game, but I hadn't been able to score myself so I was left out even though I had not too many scoring chances.'

The AC Milan striker wanted to let the manager know how he felt about the decision. 'I was annoyed and I told Bobby Robson. I just told him how let down I felt. I'd gone there as the main striker, scored the goals in the two warm-up matches and then, when things started to go a little bit wrong, I was out. I still think I could have played a part in the rest of the competition and I told him that, too. Not that it made the slightest bit of difference: Bobby listened but he wasn't going to do anything, was he?'

The PFA Footballer of the Year and the top scorer in the English top flight after scoring 40 goals for Everton, Lineker seemed unable to cut it at the highest level. He admits to suffering from 'imposter syndrome' during the early part of his career, which even lasted beyond the 1986 World Cup and into his first season at FC Barcelona. 'I kept thinking I was blagging it and getting away with it.'

In the *Sunday Times* on the eve of the make-or-break match against Poland, Brian Glanville wrote that 'of Lineker, it seems plainer than ever that he is a talented club player who cannot take the great step up to international football'.

Yet, in the space of 180 minutes, Gary Winston Lineker had propelled himself from nowhere to the top of the World Cup goalscoring charts alongside Emilio Butragueño of Spain by the end of the Round of 16.

Now in his 60s, Lineker's quickness and agility is still apparent, today demonstrated more through his words on television and social media. However, the only reason those words carry any weight now is due to the goals he scored during 12 life-changing days in Mexico.

He maintains that the first goal he scored at the tournament against Poland was the most important of his entire career. 'We went into that game with only one point from the first two games, getting loads of abuse at home. I thought Bobby Robson would leave me out because I'd gone about five games without a goal but he stuck with me and brought in Beardsley and we hit it off. I scored a hat-trick within half an hour and it changed my life.'

Bobby Robson had included Beardsley in his squad ahead of 1982 World Cup veteran Trevor Francis, primarily to serve as Lineker's back-up. Three months before the tournament, with Hateley one of five strikers injured, Beardsley had been drafted in as a late replacement to start away to the Soviet Union in Tbilisi. Alongside Lineker, he excelled, creating the game's only goal for Waddle as England became the first away team to score and win a game in the country during the 1980s. Robson remembered how well the Lineker-Beardsley partnership worked and kept it up his sleeve.

Speaking on the *Design Museum* podcast, Lineker explained why the partnership worked for him: 'Now Peter Beardsley, he's obviously not a big striker. He's not flicking on and all that, he was actually more of a number ten. So, I played up front on my own. And I really, really liked it. People say, well, you know, it's much better isn't it, having someone alongside you? Well, not if you're a goalscorer that scores. I hear it all the time in punditry, people saying, "Don't get enough bodies in the box, don't get enough bodies in the box." And I used to think exactly the opposite. I don't like many bodies in the box because the more bodies in the box the less space there is.

'So as a striker, you gamble on space. If you're playing up front with another striker, he's in the box. Therefore there's a defender with him, and then they say the midfielders are in there and suddenly there's eight to ten people and there's not the space. But Beardsley came in and suddenly there was loads of space.'[17]

After scoring on his first international start for England against the Republic of Ireland in March 1985, Lineker's only other goals had come in 5-0 wins over the United States (2) and Turkey (3). Going

---

17   https://designmuseum.org/exhibitions/podcast-gary-lineker-in-conversation-with-tim-marlow

into the pivotal group game against Poland in Monterrey, he had not scored an international goal since October 1985.

A month earlier, the new Republic of Ireland manager Jack Charlton admitted, 'He has yet to produce his best form when playing for England, although personally I don't feel that there he is being used in the right way. He's a forward runner – all his best work and goals have come from situations where he was able to run on to the ball – and that's the way he should be allowed to play for England. He needs room to be able to use his marvellous pace. He's not a target man and shouldn't be used as one.'

Struggling for confidence ahead of the game against Poland, Lineker phoned his mother from Mexico and pleaded to her, 'Mum, please change my luck.' She reassured him by saying, 'I do feel, Gary, that you will score, not just one, two. I know it's going to be two, I really feel it.'[18] She was wrong.

As well as Beardsley, it took the introduction of two of his Everton colleagues in midfield, Trevor Steven and Peter Reid, along with Steve Hodge, to liberate Lineker and provide him with the ammunition to fire England into the knockout stages with the country's first hat-trick at the tournament since Geoff Hurst in the 1966 World Cup Final.

Each of Lineker's three goals against Poland were scored within the six-yard box, with Beardsley not even in the penalty area. 'The first goal was basically a striker's goal. I moved the ball across and it went to the right. Gary Stevens crossed it and I just took a chance on where it might go, and it did, so I scored. And life was different after that.'

Two more in the 3-0 win over Paraguay had moved Lineker level with Hurst as England's all-time leading goalscorer at a World Cup. During the course of the season, Lineker had now scored a total of 48 goals for club and country. Bobby Robson said ahead of the quarter-

---

18   https://www.youtube.com/watch?si=XsZBmhvmChfbO7kR&v=_
pieVLPOZFs&feature=youtu.be

final that 'Argentina will be as concerned about our number ten as we are about theirs'.

For Lineker, the start to the World Cup must have brought back memories of his first few weeks at Everton the previous summer. Having joined the reigning league champions from Leicester City for a club record fee of £800,000, he was seen as a direct replacement for the fans' favourite Andy Gray. Lineker failed to score in any of his first four games for Everton.

His club team-mate Peter Reid told me, 'He didn't have a great start. I remember back in the day, when we used to have a bath, I said, "Links, some pressure on you now?" He said, "I keep getting there and missing. They'll go in, if I keep getting there." I thought then – wow, what a confident lad you are. After the first two games at the World Cup, there was massive pressure on Gary Lineker – and I mean massive. He was getting plenty of criticism. And then, just like he did for Everton, when the chances came against Poland, he stuck them away, and he kept sticking them away.

'A lot of people say a lot of things about him, but I tell you what, mentally as a footballer, very, very strong, besides being a great finisher, and a good player. Did he change? Not for me, no. He's always had that belief that he'd score goals. I didn't see a difference at all, I've just seen the same guy, that same confidence and, whether he was scoring goals or not, he had a belief that, yeah, you go through a spell, but if you get there and you're missing, sooner or later it will go in.'

Trevor Steven concurred: 'Gary and I were room-mates at Everton. Gary never changed at all. He was always cool, calm and collected. He was sort of mid-range as far as volume was concerned, sort of sat in the midfield of the characters and personalities. I sat at the bottom end! He was great at his job. I got to know his game extremely well obviously, playing at Everton with him. He was probably good at four things, but he did them excellently. Let's say there's a sort of range of skills in football, it could be seven or eight things. Gary stuck to his four. His four were world-class at the time.

'He showed that in the World Cup. He was doing the same thing for Everton on a weekly basis. Same kind of movement, anticipation, bravery, determination to win. That really took him on to the next levels.'

Lineker eventually enjoyed what would be the most prolific goalscoring season of his career, winning the English Golden Boot with 30 league goals among a total of 40 from 57 games in all competitions.

The player who would later win his first major trophies with FC Barcelona and Tottenham Hotspur still looks back fondly on his time at Goodison Park. 'It was one year, but it was an incredible year. It was the best team I ever played for.'

However, all his goals for Everton had not brought him any silverware. After winning the Charity Shield in his first official game for Everton, they had finished as runners-up to Liverpool in the First Division title race and also lost the FA Cup Final to them after Lineker had given his team a first-half lead.

Everton had led the league going into the final three matches, and retaining the title was in their own hands going into a midweek match away to relegation-threatened Oxford United at the Manor Ground in April. Lineker spurned three 'gilt-edged' opportunities at the start of the second half. Les Phillips scored at the other end, which left Liverpool, who won the same night, only needing to take three points in their final game away at Chelsea to wrestle the title back from their Merseyside neighbours.

The *Liverpool Echo* reported that Lineker 'stood alone by the gates of the Oxford United car park last night – disconsolate, drained, his thoughts a million miles away from the bustle and activity going on all around him'.

It later transpired that Lineker's misfortune that night in Oxford was down to a missing pair of seemingly charmed boots. He had worn the same set of Adidas boots since just before Christmas. Costing £70, Lineker went on a New Year scoring streak using the new Copa Mundial (World Cup) boots until they started to wear out.

Nowadays, most players wear a new pair of football boots in every single game – often personalised and match-specific – but battered and repaired several times, Lineker believed these particular boots had brought him good fortune. 'We played Oxford away and we arrived there. They used to carry the boots in like a skip, like an old bin, and they got all the boots out and mine weren't in there. I had to borrow a pair and can't remember whose they were but they were like a size and a half too big and we ended up losing 1-0.'

Speaking to *The Sun*, Lineker said he had asked an Adidas representative to have the boots repaired and, while they were away, he failed to score in three successive matches and damaged his hamstring.

Whatever the truth, Lineker was reunited with the 'magic boots' for the last two games of the league season, scoring a hat-trick against Southampton and two against West Ham United. In terms of the championship race, it was all to no avail as player-manager Kenny Dalglish scored the decisive winner at Stamford Bridge to seal a 16th league title for Liverpool.

The worn-out boots also went to Mexico, by which time they were beginning to fall apart. Lineker said, 'I don't believe in giving up good things so I decided to hold on to them for as long as I could.'[19] The seams on the goalscoring toe ends were beginning to go and the sides of the right one were starting to split. Yet patched up from game to game, Lineker hoped the magic that had brought him 40 goals for Everton in all competitions would eventually bring him more good fortune in an England shirt, having not scored for his country since the previous October.

So important were the boots to Lineker that the *News of the World* reported that, should England defeat Argentina, they would be flown back to London where Adidas had a cobbler on hand to repair them. They would then be immediately flown back to

---

19   https://www.youtube.com/watch?si=XsZBmhvmChfbO7kR&v=_
     pieVLPOZFs&feature=youtu.be

Mexico City for the semi-final scheduled to be played just three days later.

The *Daily Star* upped the ante, stating that it was prepared to foot the bill of flying Lineker's personal cobbler out to Mexico. Their front-page leader claimed that Carl Kuehl, 21, from Poynton, Cheshire 'has already packed his bags'. Kuehl said, 'I know the boots better than anyone and if they are in need of repair I would consider it an honour to fly out and mend them.'

Lineker had nearly missed the tournament entirely after damaging his wrist in England's final warm-up match away to Canada in Vancouver. After colliding with centre-back Randy Mitchell, Lineker fell on his hand and he heard his wrist crack. 'It was the most pain I'd ever been in, in all of my life, it was just excruciating.'

A broken wrist would have ruled him out of the tournament but fortunately the X-rays revealed that he had suffered a badly sprained ligament. He recalls that 'for two hours I was convinced I wouldn't play in the World Cup. But once the hospital told me it wasn't broken that was it, I was determined to play.' He was able to train wearing a soft cast on his left arm that had to be approved by FIFA.

Speaking to the *High Performance* podcast in 2022, Lineker admitted that he played the entire tournament in pain. 'They were trying different splints on and stuff. In the end, I had this one, it was fairly useless but it meant I could play. I was in so much pain in '86 from just running, just running. The wind against my hand when I was running was absolutely agony. Let alone when falling over and stuff, but I was so determined to play. This was the World Cup, you do everything.'[20]

Going into the quarter-final, his strapped-up arm had been held up five times in celebration of a goal in England's last two matches, which led the *Manchester Evening News* to label him 'the one-armed bandit of the competition'. Questioned about the possibility of winning the Golden Boot, Lineker confessed, 'It's a dream of

---

20   https://www.thehighperformancepodcast.com/hp-podcast/garylineker

everybody probably to be the top goalscorer in the World Cup. I'd be lying if I said I didn't have that dream as well.'

Gary Lineker's 21-year-old 'sweetheart' Michelle Cockayne was pictured in the *Sunday Mirror* on the day of the game wearing an England shirt and shorts under the banner 'what a striker'. She confessed that her telephone was ringing non-stop since Lineker's hat-trick against Poland, and the only way she could speak to *Today* newspaper's Sue Ryan for an exclusive interview was to take it off the hook for an hour.

They were the very definition of childhood sweethearts, having first met as toddlers, as their grandparents were close friends in Leicestershire. The pair had been dating for four years. Cockayne, then aged 17, admitted, 'When I first met him I hated him. I knew he'd had lady friends and I thought he was a womaniser just because he was a footballer.'

Cockayne was poised to board the charter flight to Mexico City with other friends and family to join the squad should they reach the semi-final. Watching the England matches from her parents' home in Leicester, she confidently stated that 'my bags are already packed, I'll be biting my nails throughout the game … We are quite different – he is very easy-going, very calm. He keeps his worries to himself.'

Lineker himself said, 'It's a great incentive for us to get through. We've been missing the girls, though I think if they were out here now they might distract us from our football. But it will be terrific if they're all here to see us in the semi-final … and hopefully the final next Sunday.'

The pair's wedding was booked for 5 July, the Saturday after the World Cup Final, and they had reportedly spent £150,000 converting a barn into their new dream home. 'A winner's medal will be the perfect wedding present,' claimed Lineker.

Cockayne admitted that even though they spoke every day, the subject of their upcoming nuptials was never mentioned. 'People keep asking me if I feel bitter having to organise it on my own. Of course I don't. Even if he was here, he wouldn't have done anything. Men never do, do they?'[21]

If England defeated Argentina, guaranteeing them two more matches in Mexico, it was unlikely that Lineker would have enough time to visit a barbers before the wedding. Cockayne revealed to the *Daily Express* that Lineker never had his hair cut when he was on a scoring run and always ate scrambled eggs on the day of a match.

Lineker also phoned his mum, Margaret, in the Leicestershire village of Broughton Astley, before every big game. She told *The Sun*, 'When Gary was eight he said that one day he would play for England. That's almost every schoolboy's dream, but in his case, it has come true.'

His 47-year-old father, Barry, a greengrocer in Leicester, appeared on ITV's *Central News* while working on his market stall the day after the Paraguay match. Wearing a Leicester City scarf, he said, 'We'll settle for one,' when asked how many goals his son would score against Argentina.

He also spoke to the *Sunday Mirror* in an interview that was published on the day of the game. He confessed, 'I've been a football nut all my life but for Gary to be called a hero – well it's unbelievable. It's like Roy of the Rovers, something out of a comic. You won't find a prouder dad anywhere in the world.'

Barry Lineker had put money on his son, at odds of 16/1, to win the Golden Boot awarded to the top goalscorer at the World Cup. He said, 'I've never known him so bubbly, chattering away, the words keep tumbling out. He is keyed up and ready for the match and that's a very good sign, believe me. He sounds full of goals.'

His son already had his own newspaper column, writing exclusively for the *News of the World* during the tournament. On the day of the game he labelled Maradona as one of 'my greatest

---

21 https://www.youtube.com/watch?si=XsZBmhvmChfbO7kR&v=_
   pieVLPOZFs&feature=youtu.be

heroes', admitting he had sat 'in front of my TV admiring his skills in the last World Cup in Spain'.

On the ITV coverage, the broadcast used head-to-head portraits of Maradona and Lineker on their commercial breaks. Ahead of the game, Jim Rosenthal asked Lineker about people back home suggesting he had now become as big a star as Maradona. Lineker demurred at the comparison: 'Well I hope so after today, but no, Maradona's probably the best player in the world at the moment. There's no doubt about that.'

In the Argentinian camp, the press asked how their defenders planned on stopping England's new golden boy. Sweeper José Luis Brown said Argentina would use a tactic they had working on throughout the tournament. 'We have always used the offside law, and that is precisely what we will do tomorrow.'

The feeling was that José Cuciuffo would be chosen to shadow Lineker. The defender said, 'I've done well marking top players like Uruguay's Enzo Francescoli and feel confident I can do the same with Lineker if that's what the coach wants me to do.' Already booked in the tournament, Cuciuffo did not believe the threat of suspension would hinder him in stopping Lineker: 'If it meant preventing a goal against Argentina, I would risk getting another yellow card.'

In the event, Cuciuffo would be asked to mark Beardsley, the linkman between the attack and midfield. It was the regular stopper Ruggeri who was given the task of following Lineker. Bilardo offered Ruggeri $1,500 if he could stop Lineker from scoring a goal. He could not.

Lineker's goal against Argentina ultimately earned him the Golden Boot outright. In an age before assists were used as a tie breaker, had he not scored against Argentina he would have shared the award with Maradona (five goals, five assists), Careca of Brazil (five goals, two assists) and Emilio Butragueño (five goals, one assist). Today, if Lineker had not scored that sixth goal, with no assists at the tournament he would have finished fourth in the Golden Boot rankings.

For Lineker to win the Golden Boot was also notable for the fact that he became the first-ever winner of the award to finish as outright top scorer without his team playing the maximum quota of games at the tournament by reaching at least the semi-finals. His feat was only matched 28 years later by Colombian James Rodríguez, who was also eliminated at the quarter-final stage.

Russia's Oleg Salenko is the only Golden Boot winner to play in fewer games at the tournament than Lineker since 1986. His six goals in just three group stage games remain the best ratio of goals per game since 1958, although, like the only other quarter-finalists to finish as World Cup top scorer – Flórián Albert of Hungary and Valentin Ivanov of the Soviet Union, both in 1962 – they shared the award with other players, unlike Lineker and Rodríguez.

Before the Paraguay match, Lineker had taken a call from Barcelona, who were keen to sign him after the World Cup. Speaking to him in his room, Steve Hodge insisted that he couldn't turn down an opportunity like that. Lineker later revealed he signed for Barcelona a few days after arriving back in England from the World Cup following a phone call with Everton manager Howard Kendall.

Trevor Steven told me that Lineker's Everton team-mates were unaware he was on the verge of leaving the club. 'There was no intention or thought of Gary leaving Everton, because he'd had the best season that he'd ever had. He'd scored more goals than he had got anywhere near in previous seasons.'

In fact, the *News or the World* had first reported of Barcelona's interest in Lineker back in April. Speaking to me years later, his long-term agent Jon Holmes confirmed that this was accurate. Holmes had taken a call from Kendall informing him of Barcelona's approach shortly before Everton travelled to play Watford on 15 April. Kendall told Holmes that, although he did not want to lose the services of his leading striker, he felt, having always wanted to work abroad himself, he could not deny Lineker the once-in-a-lifetime opportunity to represent FC Barcelona and the chance to play in Europe, which was denied to all English teams, indefinitely banned from entering European club competitions following the Heysel Stadium disaster.

Holmes first talked to Lineker about the possibility of a move in April: 'I spoke to him after the Watford game and then it sort of progressed through the end of the season and then the World Cup.'

Yet, speaking to *Shoot!* magazine ahead of the end of the season in May, Lineker insisted that the FA Cup Final would not be his last appearance for Everton. 'It is flattering to be linked with the great European clubs, but I have a four-year contract with Everton and intend to fulfil every year. I'm not looking to go anywhere.'

On 6 June, the day England played Morocco, Holmes, who was playing golf at the time, was told that Barcelona vice-president Joan Gaspart had been back in touch with Kendall. With England preparing for their decisive match against Poland, the family decided not to inform Lineker until after his life-changing hat-trick. When Cockayne told her fiancé of Barcelona's offer, his words to her were, 'Leave it to Jon, I'll talk when we've finished here.'[22]

Now Barcelona just needed Lineker's signature to beat off a clutch of Italian clubs who were ready to offer a lot more money to secure the services of the World Cup's leading goalscorer. During the tournament, Holmes travelled to Spain with an accountant to discuss the personal terms of the transfer and in particular how to get Lineker's potential earnings out of the country at a time of strict currency control.

Speaking a few years later, the then-Barcelona head coach Terry Venables admitted that the deal had been set in motion even before the tournament had begun after they considered that their other target, Liverpool striker Ian Rush, was too expensive. It was a version corroborated by Kendall in his autobiography *Love Affairs and Marriage.*

---

22   https://www.youtube.com/watch?si=XsZBmhvmChfbO7kR&v=_
     pieVLPOZFs&feature=youtu.be

'We had done the negotiation actually just before the World Cup,' said Venables, 'and we got the price of £2.4 million, which at that time we thought was a good one. Then with him being the highest goalscorer in the World Cup, I'm sure if we'd have left it any longer, the price would have been higher.'

The previous summer, Leicester City had valued Lineker at £1.25m, with Everton initially offering £400,000. A transfer tribunal settled on a figure halfway in between and a clause was inserted guaranteeing Leicester a third of any profit Everton made through his future sale, which meant they eventually received more for Lineker than they initially asked for in 1985.

'To be fair to Everton,' said Venables, 'they stuck on the price that we had negotiated and they played the game. We felt all round, I think, both clubs felt it was a good deal.' Without Lineker, Everton regained the English league championship they had lost to Liverpool the season before. Lineker never won a league title in his entire career.

The Officials

ooking back on the match in his *World Cup Diary*, Bobby Robson said he did not feel any bitterness towards Diego Maradona. 'If I feel any anger at all, it is directed towards the FIFA Committee that selected a Tunisian referee and a Costa Rican linesman for a potentially explosive match.'

The last time England played Argentina at the World Cup finals in 1966, the choice of referee was to prove a bone of contention that still rankles in South America today. In a tournament already heavily weighted in favour of Europe – ten of the 16 finalists were from the continent – a staggering total of 19 of the 25 referees appointed were also European, including five from the UK.

None of the four South American referees officiated a match beyond the group phase. After Brazil were eliminated in the first round following a shocking acquiescence by English and German referees of the physical treatment handed out to Pelé in particular, the continent's fears about a predetermined outcome for the tournament were heightened.

The two remaining South American nations, Argentina and Uruguay, were drawn to play England and West Germany, respectively. FIFA, then under the control of an English president, Stanley Rous, appointed a West German, Rudolf Kreitlein, to take charge of England's game, and an Englishman, John Finney, to referee the West German match.

An Argentine, captain Antonio Rattin, and two Uruguayans were sent off by those European referees. The merits of those decisions were lost when England and West Germany went on to meet in the World Cup Final, ensuring a European winner. For many in South America, the refereeing appointments had been a fait accompli. Rattin later said, 'It was clear that the referee played with an England shirt on.'

After England had prevailed against the ten-man Argentinians thanks to Geoff Hurst's late header, Argentina's midfielder Ermindo Onega spat in the face of FIFA vice-president, Harry Cavan from Northern Ireland, earning himself a three-match ban. Twenty years later, Cavan, also head of the Irish FA, was now a senior vice-president at FIFA and in charge of the Referee Committee for the 1986 World Cup. Facing another potentially explosive quarter-final encounter between England and Argentina, he felt the need for the appointment of a 'strong official' for the game, suggesting an Eastern European.

Fearing a repeat of 1966, Argentina understandably objected to the appointment of any European referee. England were reticent to have a South American in charge. Therefore, a compromise had to be achieved and FIFA was forced to look outside the two historically dominant continents for a match official.

From their initial pool of 36 referees, each of whom took charge of one of the first round group matches, that left a pool of just 11 from outside Europe and South America. Two were English-speaking – Australian Chris Bambridge and David Socha from the United States – but the countries' close ties to England probably ruled them out. Three more were Spanish-speaking – Berny Ulloa from Costa Rica, who had already taken charge of Argentina's match against Bulgaria, Antonio Márquez Ramírez of Mexico and Rómulo Méndez of Guatemala – all of whom may have garnered suspicions in England of favouring their fellow Latin Americans.

Also out of contention were Syria's Jamal Al Sharif, who had refereed England's previous match against Paraguay, with Saudi Arabia's Fallaj Al Shanar running the line. That left four candidates, three from Africa, one from Asia. It would be the first-ever time in

56 years of World Cup history that a referee from either continent had taken charge of any World Cup quarter-final match.

Ali Bin Nasser was born in March 1944. Aged 22, during his first year of training to be a referee he had watched the 1966 World Cup quarter-final between England and Argentina, dreaming that one day he would be in charge of a match like that, while remembering how the European officials had struggled to maintain order.

He joined the international list in 1975, and by the time of the 1986 World Cup the 42-year-old was at the peak of his career. In an age before fully professional referees, English newspapers reported that Bin Nasser (or Bennaceur) was a computer scientist in Tunis.

The quarter-final at Estadio Azteca was not the largest crowd he had officiated in front of during his career, or even in 1986. Three months earlier he had refereed in front of 120,000 fans at the Africa Cup of Nations Final between hosts Egypt and holders Cameroon at the Cairo International Stadium. It was Bin Nasser's second successive final of the continent's premiere tournament, the first referee to be selected twice. Speaking to me from Tunis, he believed that going into the 1986 World Cup, his first, that he was a more experienced referee than many of his colleagues. 'It's a lot harder to be a referee in Africa than on the world stage.'

He was also appointed to referee at the 1985 FIFA World Youth Cup, handed the politically sensitive quarter-final match between the Soviet Union and China in Minsk. Ten months later he was put in charge of another potential quarter-final tinderbox. He told me that 'FIFA always considered me as a sort of "saviour" in many, many situations because I am an honest referee and I do the best I can.'

Bin Nasser admitted he spoke only French and Arabic but said there was no requirement at the time for referees to communicate with players on the pitch. 'In football, the only language we need to speak is from the whistle, the flags of my colleagues and the red and yellow cards. I don't speak English, but the two words I know are "advantage" and "play". They were the only two words you would hear me say during the game. That's how I refereed that game, and any game in which I don't speak the language.'

He had earlier taken charge of the group stage match between Poland and Portugal in Monterrey, showing two yellow cards. Just four days before the quarter-final, Bin Nasser had run the line in Querétaro during the Round of 16 match between Denmark and Spain. Bogdan Dochev, the linesman facing Maradona when he scored the notorious first goal against England, ran the opposite line.

Dochev was a former professional footballer in Bulgaria. A talented all-round athlete, he claimed he could run 100m in 11.11 seconds. A pacy winger, he initially represented the army club CSKA Sofia before playing for three years with Levski Sofia. At the end of his playing days he pursued a career in refereeing, joining the Bulgarian A list in 1970 and reaching the FIFA standard eight years later. In the meantime, Dochev had become a police inspector and, according to ITV commentator Gerry Harrison, was also a classical violinist with a love of ten-pin bowling.

In a 1984 UEFA Cup match at Old Trafford between Manchester United and Dundee United, Dochev failed to spot that Maurice Malpas had denied the home side a goal when he saved a goal-bound header from Gordon McQueen with both hands. Dochev only awarded a penalty after being forced to consult his linesman.

Before his failure to spot Maradona's handball made him a hero in Scotland, Dochev had become the scourge of Dundee United. He presided over their UEFA Cup exit in March 1982 to Radnički Niš with what the *Daily Record* labelled as a 'joke refereeing performance'. Reporter Wallace Moore called Dochev's handling of the game 'a disgrace' and alleged that the Bulgarian, who lived less than 100 miles across the border from Niš, favoured the Eastern Bloc side, awarding them 'the softest penalty I have seen in European football'. Earlier in 1984, Dundee United had also lost a European Cup first leg tie away to Rapid Wien with Dochev in charge.

The 1986 tournament was his second World Cup. In 1982, Dochev had refereed the group stage match between Italy and Cameroon in

Vigo before running the line during the epic second-phase game between Brazil and Italy in Barcelona, which was refereed by Israeli Abraham Klein.

Speaking to me from Tel Aviv, Klein told me he thought Dochev spoke some English – one of four languages required for FIFA officials at the time (English, French, Spanish or Russian). In Klein's opinion, Dochev was 'very, very good on the line'.

Klein, who also took charge of another World Cup classic, the 1970 epic between Brazil and England, told me he gave the officials working with him clear areas of delineation to avoid any confusion during matches. 'In my games, I told all my linesmen, "Don't interfere in the penalty area." I make the decision alone because I am closer to the action.'

In the dying moments of that game, Dino Zoff smothered a powerful header from Brazilian captain Óscar, which ran along the goal line. The Brazilians pleaded that the ball had crossed the line. Dochev was better placed than referee Klein to see whether a goal should be awarded, the correct call to play on was made, which eliminated Brazil from the tournament.

Now in Mexico, aged 50, Dochev's first involvement in the tournament had been to run the line in England's 1-0 defeat to Portugal in Monterrey. He also ran the line during Scotland's match against West Germany in Querétaro. On the opposite line that day was Alan Snoddy of Northern Ireland. On Dochev, the English-speaking official told me, 'I don't recall having any difficulties with our communication.'

The Bulgarian had then taken charge of an eventful group-stage match between Belgium and Paraguay in Toluca. His linesman that afternoon was Bin Nasser. Had Belgium won, it would have been them, rather than Paraguay, that England faced in the Round of 16. In the 19th minute of an inconsistent performance, Dochev missed a stamp by Belgian midfielder Enzo Scifo on Jorge Nuñez right in front of him. As the Paraguayan writhed in agony, Dochev appeared to send the stretcher bearers away before restarting the game with a drop-ball, handing possession to the South Americans even though Belgium had kicked the ball out of play to allow Nuñez to receive treatment.

During an over-physical match in which Dochev allowed several robust challenges to go unpunished and struggled to retain control, he also had to contend with a mass brawl involving almost every player early in the second half. Dochev showed a yellow card to one protagonist from each side.

With the Europeans leading 2-1, the referee correctly awarded them an indirect free kick for an obstruction on Jan Ceulemans, signalling to that effect by clearly raising his arm. When Enzo Scifo curled the free kick straight into the net, Dochev stood by his initial call and ruled the goal out. However, he created confusion by restarting the game with a free kick rather than a goal kick, suggesting he had disallowed the goal for an offside flagged by Bin Nasser.

Paraguay quickly equalised to finish ahead of Belgium in Group B, but there was still time for Dochev to antagonise them, too. Seven minutes before the end of the match, after being alerted by Bin Nasser's waving flag and speaking to fourth official Jorge Alberto Leanza, Dochev sent off the Paraguayan coach Cayetano Ré. It was the first time in World Cup history that a referee had sent a coach from the field of play.

Dochev had therefore shown himself unafraid to make big decisions. The Bulgarian and Bin Nasser shook hands at the end of the game but their performance raised questions about their ability to work as an effective refereeing team. Nevertheless, they were soon appointed to work together for the third time in two weeks in the quarter-final. It was four days before Dochev's birthday.

With the Cold War still raging, the selection of a European linesman from behind the Iron Curtain was more acceptable for Argentina. Likewise, for England, the choice of the Spanish-speaking Costa Rican Berny Ulloa as the other linesman was preferable to an official from South America. A second African, Malian Idrissa Traoré, was selected as the reserve official.

The match passed without major incident on the pitch during the first half but two minutes after the restart, an Argentina free kick was headed out for a corner by Kenny Sansom under pressure from Ruggeri. Referee Bin Nasser pointed for a goal kick, while Dochev flagged for offside. Neither was correct in their decision. Peter Shilton was left perplexed about how to restart the game, eventually taking a free kick rather than a goal kick when it should have been a corner to Argentina. Within minutes, the inability of the Tunisian referee and Bulgarian linesman to communicate with each other would have more fateful consequences for the England goalkeeper.

Speaking to me 36 years later, Bin Nasser recalled that 'FIFA's instruction before the tournament was that if you did not see an incident clearly, you should take the opinion of your colleague if he was in a better position.' After the disputed first goal, Bin Nasser was chased by Fenwick, who was appealing vehemently for handball, gesticulating clearly to that effect. Bin Nasser looked towards Dochev, only to see him running towards the halfway line. Bin Nasser backpedalled through the centre circle as Fenwick confronted him, his eyes fixed on his linesman, who didn't indicate any offence.

Bin Nasser admitted to me, 'I didn't see the goal but I was moving to the centre backwards and I was looking at my colleague the whole time. When he met me at the halfway line, then it was a goal. He had a better view than me at that time.'

At 32, Alan Snoddy was the youngest referee at the tournament. Having taken charge of Morocco versus Portugal in the group stage he had been a linesman at the previous evening's quarter-final between Mexico and West Germany in Monterrey. After flying back to the capital, where all the referees were based throughout the tournament, he took the opportunity to watch the third quarter-final live at the Azteca. He told me, 'It was normal for the referees to attend games in Mexico City when they did not have a game or were not travelling. I was there with a small group of other referees with tickets provided by FIFA.'

Sat together in the stadium and watching from the stands, neither Snoddy nor any of the other FIFA-appointed officials spotted Maradona's sleight of hand. Snoddy admitted, 'At that moment we did not see the handball.'

Looking back, Dochev said Bin Nasser was in the wrong position on the field, in line with Shilton and Maradona. Having reviewed photographic stills of the incident, Snoddy told me, 'In my opinion Bin Nasser is in a normal and expected position to have a good view of the incident.'

Speaking to the Bulgarian newspaper *Sport* four years before his death in 2017, Dochev said, 'Even now the incident runs through my mind like a film. It was no accident that I stood statically on the touchline. I couldn't wave the flag and show Bin Nasser that the goal was illegal.'[23]

Snoddy feels that if Dochev saw the handball, it was up to him to alert the referee. 'In 1986 we did not have the radio communication systems or electronic flags that are common now. This meant eye-to-eye contact/body language was important. I don't know the full facts but for the teamwork between the officials to be effective – and if the linesman saw clearly the offence – then he should flag.'

The television footage also contradicts Dochev. After just a momentary glance at Bin Nasser, he is running back to the halfway line. Dochev continued to jog back to the centre, never looking back at the celebrating Argentines behind him, so much so that he outpaced the protesting Shilton, who attempted in vain to get his attention.

'The ghost of this match will probably haunt me to the grave,' said Dochev. After the 1986 World Cup quarter-final, he never officiated at another match, removed from the list of referees by the Bulgarian Football Union after 16 seasons.

---

23   https://temasport.com/bogdan-dochev-vidjah-bozhijata-rka-na/

'Refereeing was different then,' claimed Dochev, 'the rules were different. Linesmen didn't have the powers they have now to disallow goals, call fouls for cards, etc. I had no right to influence the leader. All power on the field was concentrated in the hands of the head referee. Bin Nasser knew only his native French. I speak German and Spanish. As soon as he signals that everything is fine, what can I do? It wasn't until he started walking with his back to the centre that I started too.'

Dochev never forgave Bin Nasser and Maradona for ending his career, scribbling 'Maradona is my gravedigger' on the back of a photo of him a few weeks after the game. 'I am adamant about something else. A European referee would absolutely never have awarded the goal.

If the three officials in the quarter-finals were made up of elite referees, there would have been no such blunder. Perhaps things in the match would have developed in a completely different way. Diego Maradona ruined my life. He is a brilliant footballer but a small man. He is low in height and as a person too.'

Dochev admitted to not feeling 'an iota of guilt' for the incident. 'After the match, no one asked me for an explanation. It wasn't until much later that I was interrogated.'

The other linesman, Ulloa, said the refereeing trio congratulated themselves at the end of the match. 'We hugged each other at the end, happy because we felt that everything had gone very well for us.'

At the end of the World Cup, Dochev even received a letter from FIFA President João Havelange expressing his heartfelt thanks for his contribution to the tournament. 'The letter of thanks from FIFA exonerates me 100 per cent.'

Nonetheless, Dochev was not forgiven in his own country. He explained that 'a real hysteria broke out in our country and an intolerable atmosphere was created. They accused me of being a national traitor. I heard the worst insults not from foreigners, but from Bulgarians.' To date, no Bulgarian has since taken charge of a match at the FIFA World Cup finals.

Bogdan Dochev died in May 2017, aged 81. His wife Emily and daughter Elena were among just 20 people who attended his funeral. Speaking to *The Sun* a year later, Emily Docheva lamented that 'after the World Cup our life was ruined. Bogdan withdrew into himself and friends never said hello to me again. It wasn't a Hand of God for us, it was a kick in the teeth. The referee said "you don't have to do any work – it will be all my calls". I'll never forgive that referee and I'll never forgive Diego Maradona.'

After blowing the final whistle, Bin Nasser chased the ball that Gary Stevens had clipped into the Argentinian penalty area in frustration. He handed it to Dochev on the pitch. The Bulgarian is pictured shaking hands with Maradona as the Argentina captain leaves the pitch chased by a group of photographers.

Bin Nasser told me, 'FIFA gave very strict instructions to the referees regarding the match ball, the referee got to keep the ball. When we went into the changing rooms, I got my colleagues to sign it for me so I could keep it as a souvenir of the game. I was very pleased to keep it. That was the pinnacle of my career.'

In October 2022, Bin Nasser put the ball he claimed up for auction, setting a valuation of £2.5 million. So what if Maradona had asked him for the ball after his man-of-the-match performance? Bin Nasser told me, 'I kept it for 36 years and four months so, to answer your question, I would not have given him the ball, as FIFA instructed me to keep the ball.'

The officials remained ensconced at the Azteca for an hour and a half after the end of the match. In the facility split between a reception, a changing room and a toilet, they were visited by the FIFA commissary for the match, the German President of the DFB, Hermann Neuberger.

The refereeing team were unaware of the furore being generated by the first goal. All four officials signed the match ball, which Bin Nasser took home.

In his official referee's report submitted to FIFA, Bin Nasser reported nothing out of the ordinary other than spelling the first name of England's No.10 as 'Garry'. He recorded that the only two cautions were handed out for 'jeu incorrect' (incorrect play) to Fenvick (sic) and Batista.

Asked to rate the attitude of team A (Argentina) and team B (England), he rates both as 'Bonne' (Good). In a section left for 'incidents' in which 'the referee must state the reasons and circumstances of any incident connected with the match', Bin Nasser writes 'Non'. The same word is written under the section reserved for 'Possible Remarks'. The report is stamped, presumably by Neuberger, with the German word 'EINGETRAGEN' (registered).

Both Neuberger and Cavan were required to assess the performance of the match officials immediately after the game. Neuberger gave Bin Nasser a score of 9 out of 10 in every category – except 'Performance of his Duties' where he was given an 8.5 – creating a weighted average mark of 8.9. Cavan rated Bin Nasser as an 8 out of 10 in every category except for 'Fitness', where he scored a 7. His average mark for Bin Nasser was 7.8. Both officials gave the match a medium degree of difficulty (+0.5), which was then added to the referee's marks to give Bin Nasser an overall score of 9.4 and 8.3, respectively, from the two FIFA assessors at the game.

Both Neuberger and Cavan also rated each linesman as 'good' on a four-point scale, offering no other comments on their performances. Indeed, in the section reserved for 'Other Observations', Cavan was more concerned with the fact that he was forced to take a minibus back to the FIFA hotel as 'car "blocked in" a considerable distance from VIP entrance', adding the requirement that those looking after the stadium parking 'must be better next time'.

Ulloa said the officials remained unaware of the doubts surrounding the first goal until later that afternoon. 'We took a shower and went to the hotel, and when we got to the lobby people started telling us "Maradona scored with his hand" and showing us replays.'

For calling into question Bin Nasser's suitability for the game, controversial French commentator Thierry Roland quipped to his colleague live on air, 'Don't you think they could have picked someone else rather than a Tunisian referee for such a big game?' He was subsequently threatened with legal action by the Tunisian ambassador in Paris, Hedi Mabrouk, who called the comments 'vindictive and slanderous words', adding that 'nobody can attack the dignity of Tunisians without receiving, from our part, the reaction that it merits'.

Roland eventually apologised to Bin Nasser, saying, 'I'm no racist, my son's babysitter is Tunisian.' In Mexican newspaper, *ESTO*, celebrity writer Shanik Berman remarked on Bin Nasser that 'his refereeing was blacker than the colour of his skin'. On the appointment of the Tunisian for the game, Bobby Robson was more diplomatic after the match: 'I have my opinions, but it doesn't matter. The World Cup is in the hands of FIFA and is best left like that.'

The next day, Bin Nasser spoke to the English press who went to his hotel. According to the *Daily Mail*, he sipped a coffee and expressed his sympathy that England had gone out of the World Cup, while explaining in French that he could not have done anything differently. 'I had to make the decision at the time. I was the man on the spot. I have not watched any of the replays or looked at the papers. The referee is the man who must make up his own mind and stick by his decision. That is all there is. It is part of the game.'

However, former international referee Clive Thomas – himself no stranger to World Cup controversy, having disallowed a late Brazilian winner against Sweden in 1978 by calling time on the match while a corner was in mid-air, was scathing in his criticism of Bin Nasser. Writing in a 1988 book, *In the Eye of the Whistle*, reviewing the refereeing standards at the 1986 World Cup, Thomas questioned whether Bin Nasser should ever have been put in charge of a game at such an elevated level: 'He is quite inevitably limited in his experience of controlling big matches and quality players when compared with South American and European referees. If neither referee nor linesman saw the goal clearly, then I have to query their expertise. Anybody who has refereed even a park game on a Sunday morning is aware that an attacker, in order to gain advantage over a defender or goalkeeper when a cross comes in, is likely to jump with arm raised alongside his head.'

In giving him an overall rating of 'D' for the game, the book concluded that 'it would have been logical to consult with the linesman who was in a good position to see the play. This was a serious breakdown in referee-linesman coordination … The referee used his cards well but the [first] goal by Maradona was inexcusable.'

Bin Nasser never refereed a match at the World Cup finals again but, unlike Dochev, his career did not end at the Estadio Azteca. He went to the 1988 Africa Cup of Nations, taking charge of one match between Côte d'Ivoire and Zaïre in Casablanca. A year later, FIFA appointed the experienced Tunisian for another politically charged match, the potentially explosive World Cup qualifying play-off second leg between North African neighbours Egypt and Algeria.

After the first leg in Algeria had ended goalless, Bin Nasser was once again the man in the middle before another six-figure crowd for a match at the Cairo International Stadium. He was once more a lucky omen for Egypt as a single Hossam Hassan goal settled the tie and qualified the Pharaohs for their first World Cup finals since 1934. There they would go out to England in Sardinia.

Having turned 45 in 1989, the maximum age for an international referee at the time, he was not considered for the 1990 World Cup finals. The 40-year-old Neji Jouini was instead Tunisia's refereeing representative in Italy and again four years later in the United States.

After Gary Lineker scored in the 1986 World Cup quarter-final to pull a goal back for England, Bin Nasser longed for the game to go to extra time so he could enjoy another half an hour. Bin Nasser claimed that Bobby Robson came to him after the game and said, 'You did a good job but the linesman was irresponsible.'

Aside from the controversial first goal, Bin Nasser told me his performance during the rest of the match illustrated his competence as a referee at the highest level. 'That will tell you how ready I was for the game and how clear my conscience was. I didn't actually know the first goal was scored with the hand.'

The FIFA media officer in 1986, Guido Tognoni, concurred. He told me that the appointment of Bin Nasser was 'a special tribute to African refereeing because in those days not many of them were of the level to lead a match like Argentina against England – but he did a good job, except in this one moment'.

The Day of Destiny

In England, the final day of the Glastonbury Festival was taking place. On the Pyramid Stage, Gil Scott-Heron headlined alongside Level 42, Madness, Simply Red and The Housemartins. An estimated 100,000 people attended the three-day event for which only 65,000 tickets were sold costing £17 each.

Thousands of people gained illegal entry by clambering through hedges and fences, and 130 were arrested by police, mainly for the misuse of recreational drugs. Michael Eavis, the owner of Worthy Farm on which he organised the festival, despaired that 'there are too many people here and too many problems. In all honesty I do not think we can cope with so many people. I do not think there will be a festival next year.'

Preparations were underway at Wimbledon for the 100th edition of the All England Championship beginning the next day. The defending champions were a teenage Boris Becker and a 29-year-old Martina Navratilova, who warmed up by winning a fifth successive Eastbourne title the day before. Both Becker and Navratilova would retain their Wimbledon titles.

Just six months older than Navratilova, former French Open champion Sue Barker was two years into her retirement from the sport. In the morning's *Sunday Mirror* she released the first in a series of exclusive 'tell-all' exposés in which she revealed 'the truth about tennis'.

Elsewhere, the newspapers were dominated by the impending nuptials of Queen Elizabeth's second son, the 26-year-old Prince

Andrew – now fourth in line to the throne – to Sarah Ferguson. The wedding was due to take place in a month's time on 23 July at Westminster Abbey.

On Merseyside, the evening services at the Church of St Luke the Evangelist, on the corner of Goodison Park, were brought forward. As four Everton players prepared to take the field for England against Argentina, the decision was made to allow parishioners to get home in time for the match. Vicar Julian Charley said, 'People live and breathe soccer around here. We didn't have much choice.'

At the Estadio Azteca in Mexico City, the biggest security operation of the World Cup got underway at the crack of dawn. An estimated 10,000 soldiers began to congregate on the stadium concourse. They made up half of almost 20,000 security personnel gathered for the game, two for every fan that had actually travelled from the two competing nations.

The Argentina players were first up on Sunday, 22 June 1986, awaking at around 7.30am. Not usually a morning person, Maradona was the first to rise. 'Even though I always sleep like a baby, I had woken up earlier than ever. I wanted the game to start. I wanted to go out there and play and put an end to all the talk.'

Not all of the players' rooms had a bathroom so it became a ritual during the tournament for Maradona to shave outside, something his father used to do when he went fishing. Maradona's dad 'Don Diego' would be at the Estadio Azteca that afternoon.

The squad then showered and had breakfast, which was more like a pre-match lunch. Valdano recalled that 10 of the 11 players drank Coca-Cola with their food.[24] Maradona would insist that his personal masseuse, Salvatore Carmando, an employee of Napoli, prepare him a bowl of pasta, something he had become accustomed to eating since playing in Italy.

---

24 https://www.elgrafico.com.ar/articulo/%C2%A1habla-memoria!/4944/la-historia-de-la-camiseta-azul-contra-los-ingleses

The England players woke up at 8am. They had breakfast 30 minutes later before leaving for the stadium at 9am. The streets were relatively empty as the squad were driven to the venue of their most important football match in 16 years.

The England entourage made the 15km journey from the Holiday Inn to the Estadio Azteca accompanied on their silver DINA (a hybrid of the Mexican state-owned DIesel NAcional) coach by four, fully-armed plain-clothes security men, in addition to the usual cavalcade of police cars and motorcycle outriders.

The FA had requested the only coach with tables, to enable the squad to play cards on the journey. There were eight places for those that chose to pass the time playing Cincinnati Poker, such as Glenn Hoddle, Kenny Sansom and the two goalkeepers, Peter Shilton and Chris Woods. The third-choice goalkeeper Gary Bailey had brought along a 'boom box' to the tournament and was in charge of the music played on the bus. Before the advent of mp3s, or even compact discs, cassette tapes were the only way to take your own music with you.

The suffocating police presence, omnipresent wherever the team travelled since the start of the tournament in Mexico, shielded the team bus from the outside world. As the coach passed through crossroads, gun-toting policeman blocked off the through roads to facilitate the team's journey.

Earlier in the tournament, the tape of Whitney Houston's eponymous first album had been played to the extent that manager Bobby Robson said that he had learned all the lyrics to her songs. By now, however, Bailey told me he chose to play the tape of a Scottish rock band to help the team focus on the job in hand: 'I thought nice, vibey music would add to the excitement of the World Cup, so I played the full Simple Minds album – *Once Upon a Time* – that had just come out.'

However, it was track number four of the playlist that had become the unofficial anthem for the squad as they recovered from the dismal start to the tournament. Released as a single in September

1985, 'Alive and Kicking' had peaked at No.7 in the UK charts but, as Bailey said, 'It was ideal to set the mood.'

Terry Butcher told me, 'It got you in the right frame of mind. Then the players would all speak, play cards. Some players would read a book, I liked to read a book sometimes. It was quite comforting, music, before a game because it takes you away to a place and you forget about the importance of a game and the millions watching. It take you away, which is what you want at that stage.'

As Glaswegian Jim Kerr sang 'you lift me up, like the sweetest cup I'd share with you …' the England players on board knew they were now three Azteca wins from lifting the ultimate cup in sport.

With the squad staying closer to the stadium, the Argentina bus was not due to leave until 9.30am. However, so eager were the players to get going that they were ready to set off half an hour early, 'lined up like soldiers', according to Maradona. Knowing he would return to prepare for another match in the tournament, it had become a ritual for the captain to mark their departure from the training camp with the words 'see you later'.

The Argentina squad made the shorter journey from the Club América training facility. The same two motorcycle outriders – named Jesús and Tobías – escorted their DINA bus to the Azteca. On board, the so-called troublemakers sitting in the middle of the coach – Almirón, Islas, Olarticoechea, Tapia, Zelada and Maradona – led the team in singing along to their usual playlist consisting of Valeria Lynch's 'Cada dia Mas', Sergio Denis's 'Gigante Chiquito', Bonnie Tyler's 'Total Eclipse of the Heart' and the theme tune from the *Rocky* film.

On a Sunday morning, fans who walked to the stadium from the city centre would have seen children dressed in white coming out of churches, having been to First Communion as hordes of bare-chested men descended upon the Colossus of Santa Úrsula.

Peppering the vast concourse surrounding the Estadio Azteca were huge inflatables promoting some of the official sponsors of the 1986 World Cup – such as Coca-Cola, Fujifilm and Camel Cigarettes

– dwarfing the gathering crowds. The name of another sponsor, Bata, was written on a polka-dot football suspended on strings above the esplanade.

There were no official souvenir stands. Traders laid out their wares on blankets in the vast parking lots outside the stadium. Pins, horns, sombreros and flags were available. Seat cushions with the 'Mexico '86' logo were also on sale, necessary to protect backsides on the concrete steps of the stadium, which the vast majority of the crowd would discover were their allocated seats.

Life-size cutouts of the 1986 World Cup mascot Pique – a green chilli-wearing a sombrero – were erected by Fujifilm for people to put their face through for souvenir photos. For anyone requiring a pre-match snack, tacos, tortas (cakes) and sandwiches were all available from the stadium vendors for under the equivalent of a pound.

Inside the ground, licensed traders wearing the red-and-yellow tabards of the official FIFA sponsors – Camel and Coca-Cola – carried huge trays of up to 30 beers, which they manoeuvred over the steep steps to anyone who called them over.

Travelling from a country where the sale of alcohol within football stadiums was prohibited, the England fans found it novel that here beer-sellers were fighting for their custom. The fans entertained themselves by racing the traders to see who would get to them first. 'I'll be honest with you,' England fan Paddy Buckley told me, 'at times you'd put your hand up for a drink just to see them climbing over everybody. It didn't matter who were in between you and them, they'd race somebody else from a different direction coming to you. It were a spectacle to watch them. It's a wonder they didn't go flying all the time. We never saw that, in fact, we never saw one dropped.'

Selling at around 50p each, the beer was still priced five times in excess of what was being charged in the local bars. Buckley told me, 'it didn't stop many people wanting a drink'.

From the concrete exterior skeleton of the Estadio Azteca, hung the flags of all the FIFA member nations; 121 countries had entered the qualification stages, which had begun in 1984. Argentina and

England were now two of six teams remaining who could win the 13th FIFA World Cup.

The England bus arrived at the ground and was driven down under the stadium out of the increasing strength of the Mexican sunshine into the artificial lighting of the subterranean concourse.

Outside the Estadio Azteca, a young England fan sporting a headband spoke to ITV News, explaining that any animosity between the supporters would be one-sided. 'There'll be tension from their side because they lost the war, we won it, so there won't be no tension on our side. We are the kings. We are the champions of the world.'

On the roof of the stadium, the flags of Argentina and England had been hoisted up either side of the banners of FIFA and the host nation, Mexico. Fans heading up the ramps to the upper tiers walked over fractures in the concrete caused by the earthquake in the city nine months earlier.

Joe O'Connell and his wife Anne came out of the vomitory at the top of the stadium and were instantly staggered by the view. 'My wife is afraid of heights,' Joe told me. 'When she came out of the opening and looked down, she just froze. She just sat down on the floor. It was a major thing to get her to move, to get her to stand up and to come out into the seating area. The stadium was quite steep, it was fantastic, it was just unbelievable to see the size of the stadium. All my wife had to do was to crawl up the steps to the seats. She was terrified, she was so terrified, she couldn't stand up beside the seat because she would get this feeling that she'd fall down. It was one of those things that prayed on her mind.'

The Times reported that four England fans entered the seating area and unfurled a banner that they displayed behind the goal Peter Shilton would be defending in the first half. It read 'Make Love, Not War'.

Earlier in the year, *Today* newspaper was launched amid much fanfare and offering the first full colour pages in a British national. Having appointed him as their first football correspondent, Patrick Barclay was in Mexico to cover England at the tournament. Speaking to me a year before he passed away aged 77, Barclay recalls being posted high up in the stands of the Estadio Azteca. Equipped with one of the first portable computers used in journalism, a Tandy that could display up to five lines of text, Barclay was situated on a long wooden table with only a standard dial-up phone for company.

The Tandy could connect to the receiver of the phone with what Barclay recalls as 'a suction device'. Once connected it could dial through to the newspaper's front desk in London, read the report and convert each character into a sound beep, which then could be sent down the line and turned back into a story using a similar contraption at the other end.

American journalist Barry Wilner was a writer and editor for the Associated Press. He remembers that the media presence at the Azteca that morning was larger than at the other matches at the tournament. Attending the first of nine World Cups, Wilner told me what set covering this tournament apart: 'This is something I had not experienced previously at sporting events in the United States – so many media members were outwardly rooting for their country. That was true for nearly all of the nations, but particularly for England.'

Not all the journalists would have the luxury of a desk. Without assigned seating, the media were left to claim whatever place they could in the oversubscribed press box. Those who arrived late had to report on the World Cup quarter-final sitting on the same concrete steps as the majority of the spectators.

First out on the pitch, the England players once more voiced their concern about the bumpy surface, which they described as a 'cabbage patch'. Instead of the heavy roller the surface required, half an hour before kick-off a single groundsman pushing a Ransomes lawnmower, manufactured close to Robson's former home of Ipswich, made a final futile attempt to level the surface.

Another concern for the England players was the mounting heat. Speaking to me from Perth, Australia, Gary Andrew Stevens told me, 'Certainly the heat on that day was vicious. We were trying to get as much fluid as we could. There was no drinks break. They used to fill little plastic bags with water and throw them on the pitch.' He joked, 'I think once or twice I ignored the ball and went after the water bag! I'm over in Perth, and we cancel training sessions and football matches because of the temperatures. So it would be interesting to know medically what sort of rules and regulations there would be now, whether or not that game would have been played at 12 noon.'

Butcher took time to notice the many St George Crosses and Union Jack flags that were already mounted around the vast concrete bowl. 'The England fans are brilliant wherever you go, they have their flags with where they're from and all that sort of thing. That's really lovely to see from an England player's point of view because there's a story behind their journey and how they got out here and all sort of things. It's brilliant, it unites the country – the fans with the players – it's what I felt.'

The superstitious Lineker, remembering he had spoken to the England fans through the ITV cameras before the Paraguay match, sought out Jim Rosenthal once again to repeat the pre-match process that had led to him scoring two goals in the stadium four days previously. Given instructions by Rosenthal on exactly what to say, Lineker still managed to get his words slightly wrong. 'Here we are at the Aztec, we're going to give it all we've got. Be sure and join us, here on ITV, after the break,' he said.

Also speaking to ITV Sport, captain Shilton said, 'I think everyone's in a good mood. Of course, there's a bit of tension there but not too much. Hopefully just enough to put a bit of edge on us.'

Bobby Robson was asked by Rosenthal if he believed that England would still be in the World Cup at the end of the match. Robson took a deep breath. 'Well, I mean … who knows? Yes, we're confident, we're going to give it the go. We're going to it everything we've got and let's hope that that will do the trick. The players know what it means to everybody back home. They know what it means to them. So we're doing it for everybody.'

In the ITV studio, the panel picked up on Robson's anxiety. Jimmy Greaves said, 'Well he is a very unsure manager, isn't he? He always has been. I remember when he was manager of Ipswich and they had a really great side. Bill Shankly said to him, "When are you going to tell your side you can win the league championship?" Because Bobby was always a little bit "well, I don't know" and a little bit unsure. That can at times reflect through the team, and I think at times Bobby – we all tend to look at the manager – but the manager needs help and let's hope he's got one or two there that are helping him.' Referring to a well-known men's hair colouring product of the time, Greaves added, 'I think he forgot to put the old Grecian 2000 on as well today, it looks as though he missed out on that.'

Kevin Keegan later quipped that the nerves had got to him: 'I was in the toilet as well, I think I had a touch of the Bobby Robsons.'

When the Argentina players entered the underground changing room at the Azteca Stadium, defender José Cuciuffo placed a statue of Our Lady of Luján on top of the players' lockers. During the Falklands War, Argentinian soldiers had taken similar icons with them on their ships for good luck. Now she was offered as divine protection against the English once again.

A more substantive protection was provided by the bandages that Salvador Carmando applied around Maradona's ankles as strapping. After putting on his shin pads and socks, Carmando applied the bandages tightly to act 'like a cast' above his trademark Puma King boots. Goalkeeper Pumpido went out on to the pitch alone to inspect the goalmouth he would be defending.

It was all part of the many rituals which the Argentina squad had repeated at every game they had played once they started winning in Mexico. None was more odd than Maradona creating a figure on the ground using a shirt, socks and some boots, which no one was allowed to walk over.

As the England players got ready in their changing room, Lineker recalls how different players dealt with the magnitude of the occasion. 'I was pretty calm before the game, just getting my thoughts together, others were different. You get people who head to the toilets, some who go off to throw up in the toilets with nerves, you know, plenty of those. Then there's people who want to rally the troops. Terry Butcher, crikey, he used to give it the old "CAGED TIGERS!"' The defender was exhorting himself and others in preparation for what he believed was 'the biggest match of his life', punching the air and banging people on the shoulders.

Butcher remembers how he used to motivate his team-mates, shouting at them, 'We're snarling, we're snapping, we're ripping them to shreds. Come on, this is England, this is what you play for. The Three Lions. Get out there. Caged Tigers, Caged Tigers.'

In contrast, Glenn Hoddle listened to music on his Walkman. Captain Peter Shilton also kept himself to himself, according to Peter Reid, who told me, 'We're all different, I was quite vociferous.'

Steve Hodge went out on his own to warm up on some astroturf under the stadium, knocking balls against a wall. His former Nottingham Forest team-mate Viv Anderson, a spectator at the tournament so far, came up to him and said, 'Can you believe it? You're playing in a World Cup quarter-final. I've been to two World Cups and haven't kicked a ball yet.'

Having made his senior England debut against the Soviet Union in Tbilisi just 88 days earlier, this was only Hodge's eighth international cap, five of those appearances had come at the 1986 World Cup. Anderson first played for England in 1978 and never played at the World Cup finals.

Before the England players left the dressing room, manager Bobby Robson's last words were, 'We're England. We play our way!' Some of the players shouted, 'No regrets,' and 'Don't let it pass you by!' As they walked out into the tunnel leading out on to the pitch, their opponents were already there waiting for them.

Speaking on the 2002 documentary *The Hand of God*, Peter Beardsley recalled Bobby Robson's last words: 'He was just so positive. "We can go and win. We're England," and he always said that "we don't need to worry about the opposition", which is great. As a player, that's what you want. When you go out on the football field, wherever it may be, you want to feel positive.'

Argentina were first into the tunnel, limbering up as they waited to go out on to the pitch. Valdano and Enrique looked out into the stands for friends and family. Their substitutes and coaches stood among the starting 11.

The England substitutes, led out by coach Don Howe, were out first on to the pitch ahead of the two starting teams. Tottenham's Gary Stevens walked alongside Bryan Robson, who was wearing an England tracksuit and holding a camera hung around his neck. Stevens told me about how the atmosphere compared with the game against Paraguay four days earlier: 'It felt more intense, it felt more hyped-up.' A pensive-looking Bobby Robson strode up the ramp behind them and into the midday sunshine.

Five members of the England squad not included in the 16 – Anderson, Bailey, Dixon, Hateley and Martin – headed up to a box reserved by ITV in the middle tier of the stadium to watch the match from behind the goal that England were defending in the first half. The sixth non-playing member of the squad was captain Bryan Robson. Photographer Bob Thomas had provided him with a camera to use during the match and himself took one of Robson smiling wistfully as the two teams lined up for the national anthems. Thomas told me, 'Robson was curious to look through it. I don't think he took many photographs with it.'

The country's best footballer took his place on the end of the England dugout, reduced to taking pictures of what should have been the biggest match of his career. He told me, 'Bobby Robson, he was the one that wanted me to sit on the bench because he wanted me to be in the dressing room before the game and at half-time. That was great because you feel a little bit part of it even though I knew I wasn't going to be able to play any role in the semi-finals onwards if we had beat Argentina.'

The 22 players who started the game lined up side by side, waiting to come out. Unlike four days earlier against Paraguay when they were the designated home team, England walked out on the near side of the pitch, to the left of their opponents. Argentina would maintain their position as 'Team A', walking out on to the Azteca on the right of the two teams in the semi-final and final. Of the nine matches played at the Estadio Azteca during the 1986 World Cup, only host nation Mexico would win a game playing as 'Team B'.

At the head of the tunnel, Diego Maradona looked back down the ramp to acknowledge one member of the England team with a wink and a thumbs-up. Fourth in the line behind Shilton, Sansom and Stevens, Hoddle recalled, 'I looked at Diego, he looked at me and we just nodded at each other because we'd played together in that testimonial game at White Hart Lane. So there was this connection before the game.'

Uncapped before 1986, Peter Beardsley was making only his sixth start for the senior England team. Given the choice, he would have opted to come out on to the pitch last but ceded to the seniority of two others who also shared the same foible – Lineker and Butcher. On such a huge stage he was nonetheless able to fulfil his other superstition by walking out carrying a football. Aside from the three match officials, Beardsley was alone in carrying an Adidas Azteca, the official ball of the 13th FIFA World Cup, on to the field of play.

Lineker, a player who never suffered from nerves and thrived on the big occasion, admitted that this game felt different. 'It was just a truly memorable occasion, and one, I think, where for the first time there was that real tingling, heart-thumping moments before as you walked out.'

In their two previous winning matches, Hodge had walked out sixth in the England line behind Steven and ahead of first Fenwick, against Poland, and Fenwick's replacement Alvin Martin against Paraguay. Now, with Fenwick restored, the order was changed, with the centre-back walking out sixth ahead of Hodge. Both men would have pivotal roles to play in the two goals England conceded.

As he crossed the touchline on to the field of play, Maradona hopped on his right foot five times and crossed himself. When they arrived at the halfway line, Maradona turned around to look at the seating behind him to try to locate where his father Don Diego was sitting.

The Argentinian national anthem was played first. With the players electing not to sing the lyrics, Burruchaga and Olarticoechea chewed gum. Only Valdano look relaxed, smiling and puffing out his chest. The television pictures panned down the line but the hymn ended before the camera reached captain Maradona. José Luis Brown claimed that as the final notes died away, Maradona turned to his team-mates and screamed, 'Come on, come on! These sons of bitches killed our kids, our friends, our neighbours. We cannot lose!'

Four days earlier when lining up ahead of their Round of 16 match against Paraguay, the England players had turned left as 'God Save the Queen' was played. Perhaps thinking they were looking towards their homeland as the Irish team often do during their anthem, they were actually facing south rather than east. As the designated away team, they this time lined up on the left side of the refereeing team. On this occasion they looked straight ahead to the main west tribune, the television cameras catching their expressions as it panned along the line of 11 players.

All except captain Shilton and Butcher, at the other end of the line, stood with their hands behind their backs. Only Stevens, Hoddle, Steven, Fenwick and Hodge appeared to sing any of the words. Hoddle repeatedly used the Umbro sweatband on his left wrist to wipe away beads of perspiration from his face. Maradona and Pumpido glared at their opponents with disdain from across the halfway line.

Following the national anthems and team photographs, the England players ran into the centre circle to raise their arms in acknowledgement of the crowd. It was a gesture met with whistles from the predominately Mexican audience. The England team withdrew to do their final stretches in their own half. In a gesture of friendship, each Argentina player then ran up to one of their opponents to present them with a blue-and-white pennant.

As the players warmed up in opposite halves of the pitch, several of the England players attempted to snatch a glimpse of the Argentina captain. Maradona moved towards the halfway line and began juggling the ball, kicking it ten metres into the air each time, 'which is impossible to do', according to John Barnes. After doing this ten times, Maradona caught the ball, looked at the English players and walked back into his own half.

Just before the game began, Maradona walked across the centre circle towards the No.10 in the England team and shook his hand. Lineker never knew if it was the ultimate gesture of respect or an attempt at intimidation.

In the wilting midday heat approaching 30°C, referee Bin Nasser and his linesmen stood in the only shade on the pitch provided by the stadium architecture, the spider shadow created by the spiralling public address system that had come to be the trademark of games at the Estadio Azteca during the 1986 World Cup.

Terry Butcher went round to all his England colleagues to give them encouragement. Years later he told me how he attempted to block out the pressure and magnitude of the occasion: 'When you go out for the game, I'm in a zone, I'm not sort of there. I'm just concentrating on getting the first touch. The first thing you do, you do well. If you do that, it sets you up for the game. You're thinking about what you've got to do and how you've got to play. I'm in another world. It's hard to explain. There's 100,000 people screaming and shouting and all that sort of thing, it's a hell of a noise, but it's not. It's just background. You might as well not be there, you could be on a park, anywhere, playing football. You just get on with it.'

A fired-up Maradona went through a vigorous set of stretches before pumping his fists and yelling at Ruggeri, 'Come on, these sons of bitches don't touch it, they don't touch it!'

Despite Maradona's wishes, it was England who kicked off the match. Peter Reid crossed himself in the centre circle as Peter Beardsley rolled the ball to Gary Lineker to begin the game underneath the unforgiving sun at high noon in the Mexican capital. England retained possession for the first 47 seconds during, which every player except Steven and Shilton touched the ball.

The First Half

As the game kicked off, Martin Tyler on ITV prophetically said, 'Winning isn't everything in sport, but trying to win certainly is.' Looking back on it, he recalled, 'My memory of the game is that England were a bit overawed to start with. I thought it at the time, and I still think, that England were a little passive.'

Héctor Enrique committed the first foul within the opening minute, a lunging tackle on Hodge. As he whistled for the foul, referee Bin Nasser raced forward to get in between the players to stop any potential flashpoint escalating. It was a recurring theme of his performance.

Seven minutes into the game, Reid, playing an intelligent give and go with Sansom, was clattered once more on his suspect ankle by the left corner flag as sweeper Brown came across to win the ball cleanly. The Everton midfielder quickly recovered and soon nicked the ball away from Maradona as he picked up pace for the first time in midfield.

Indeed, Reid was probably England's best player in the first half, working industriously, always maintaining possession with his short passes and even attempting to run beyond the ball on several occasions, demonstrating his indefatigable style in the suffocating atmosphere.

In the ninth minute, England lost possession in the attacking third and Butcher committed himself forward to press Burruchaga and Cuciuffo, who both tricked their way around him. Once the ball went past Butcher, Maradona attacked the space he left. Fed by Valdano's impudent flick into the air, Maradona controlled the ball effortlessly on his chest and side-stepped Sansom in one move without the ball touching the ground. Picking up pace, he hurtled inside and, feeling exposed, Fenwick jumped in and caught Maradona with a strong scissors tackle, sending him flying into the air. Referee Bin Nasser came racing over with his yellow card already brandished in what appeared to be a statement booking.

Fenwick admitted to me, 'I went for him. I tried to go through him and I thought that early in the game I might get away with it, so I took the gamble.' It did not pay off and ultimately impaired everything else he did in the game. It was Fenwick's third booking in four games at the World Cup, which is, to date, still a record for an England player at the tournament.

An angry Maradona arose after initially clutching his left ankle and shouted at Fenwick, who was quickly retreating away from the scene of the crime. 'Maradona said to me as we were walking away from it, "This is football, not rugby," in English, which surprised me, so I just laughed at him.'

Bin Nasser wisely put his arm across Maradona and put himself between the Argentina captain and the English defenders to prevent any confrontation. Fenwick said to me, 'The tackle that I went through with, I hardly clipped him and he took a dive, got me a yellow card. That was exactly what he wanted from us.'

With the benefit of hindsight and knowing what was to come in the match, Maradona certainly regarded the incident as 'a sign, a good sign. Because later on I would make another run with the ball like that and Fenwick would be one of the guys in my way. And I believe that yellow card taught him a lesson.'

On ITV, the commentators considered the consequences of the challenge. Tyler revealed that the FA were uncertain whether a third yellow card would lead to another automatic suspension for the defender. David Pleat's concerns were more immediate: 'Certainly it means that for the rest of the game Fenwick will be under great pressure and need to show a lot of restraint, and I'm not sure that's a natural characteristic of his.'

At half-time, former England captain Kevin Keegan said, 'I think it was a silly one. He wasn't really going anywhere too dangerous and he really lunged in. That's the sort of tackle you expect from a midfield player, not from a defender.'

In that one thrust, the template for the game was established. As soon as Maradona gained possession, wherever that may be on the field, Argentina's attack ignited into life as their players rushed to support him, and England's shape was consequently stretched to contain it.

Fenwick told me, 'There was a lot of tension around the match. That tension, I think, showed within the game, the first half was poor. The one person that was different class, that didn't seem to have any fears at all was Diego Maradona. Their other ten players, including the keeper, as soon as they won it, they gave it to Maradona and let him get on with it. That's exactly what their game plan was.'

Trevor Steven explained it to me like this: 'The magnet for them was Maradona. Their team would manoeuvre around him. Whereas we weren't getting on the ball as much, we were more spread, trying to find opportunity, trying to spread them. We just weren't able to do it on the day.'

For the first time, Maradona now had a chance to test Shilton with a free kick in a similar position to which he had struck the crossbar during the Round of 16 match against Uruguay six days earlier. Hoddle, Lineker, Steven and Reid lined up in the four-man wall. Maradona hit the ball at Lineker and it went up in a parabola into the air, much as it would four years later during England's World Cup semi-final from Andreas Brehme's free kick.

Four years younger than he would be in Turin, Shilton read the flight and backpedalled to push the ball double-handed over the crossbar. It was to prove the only shot on target in the first half and one of the few touches Lineker had until late in the game.

After the ball was cleared from the resulting corner, Olarticoechea broke forward and was this time cleanly slide-tackled by Fenwick. Maradona picked up the loose ball, drove around Stevens and produced one of his trademark whipped crosses, which Sexton had forewarned England about. Butcher did well to lean into Ruggeri as he jumped, so his header under pressure went harmlessly wide.

England responded with their first opportunity of the game. Butcher fed Hoddle in the centre circle with 11 Argentina players behind the ball. Hoddle hit a hopeful right-footed pass into an area down the right channel of the penalty area for Beardsley to chase. The ball was running through to Pumpido, who unexpectedly slipped on the suspect Azteca turf, his left foot giving way under him. The ball hit his knee and ran out to the left side of the area where Beardsley beat him to it, running away from the goal. The forward produced the shuffle that would, in the years to come, become famous to all Liverpool fans, but in 1986 was as fresh as any trick Maradona could muster, sending Pumpido sprawling once more in the wrong direction. Beardsley turned on to his weaker left foot and, with the goalkeeper throwing himself at him feet first, shot for goal.

The ball hit the side-netting but, even if it had been on target, Olarticoechea had, not for the last time in the match, run back to cover the open goal. Lineker, closely shadowed by the taller Ruggeri in the six-yard area, put his hands on his head then generously applauded his strike partner's effort. Beardsley acknowledged that he had seen him. It was as close as England got to a goal in the first half.

Shortly afterwards, Trevor Steven had his first chance to take on his marker Olarticoechea. Despite a feint, his attempt to run to the outside of the right-footed midfielder was met with a firm challenge and Argentina quickly regained possession. Even though Olarticoechea had featured in every game in Mexico, Steven admitted to me that he had not been told anything about his potential marker, in the absence of the suspended Garré. 'I didn't even know who I was playing against, I did not have a clue. I wasn't told it was a right-footed left-back. We didn't even have that kind of information back then. It was get on, play your game.'

For Hoddle, England had lost the tactical battle: 'The ineffectiveness of the England side in the first half was the result of stifling tactics by Argentina. They had changed their team, deploying a defensive midfielder [Enrique] in place of an attacker [Pasculli]. The tactics worked, we played into their hands.'

Speaking on the FIFA film, *When the World Watched*, Valdano explained how Argentina's new formation also increased the unpredictability of their attack. 'The two big innovations were the full-backs being midfielders and the forwards were not strikers. Our starting positions were often very deep and marking players who change position is not the same as those who just stay forward. That gave us the ability of launching very big surprises.'

Pleat voiced the concerns of a watching nation at the ease with which Argentina attacked, demonstrating a flair for the unorthodox. 'They try the unusual things in the last 40 yards of the field – back-heels, little side-flicks – they're not frightened to be inventive.'

As if perturbed by the slight against English players, Beardsley then demonstrated again why Maradona later described him as 'a player I really admired'. In his own third of the field, he eased the pressure on England by winning a free kick from Batista with a sharp Cruyff turn as he was closed down by three Argentina players.

In the 18th minute, Maradona escaped down the right followed by Butcher, who watched the ball carefully to dispossess him for a corner. From it, Maradona played a short ball along the ground to the onrushing Olarticoechea, whose shot was charged down by Steven. The ball broke to Beardsley, who led a promising England counter-attack. With Lineker's marker, Ruggeri, and Brown up for the corner, the England striker had space for the first time on the right, one on one with Cuciuffo. Beardsley instead fed Steven on the left, who played it back for Hoddle. By the time he played a poor ball into the centre, the Argentinians had regrouped and Brown chested the ball clear. Lineker would not have such freedom again in the first half.

In the 22nd minute, Lineker, chasing a hopeful lofted pass by Steven down the right touchline, headed it back towards the centre to no one in particular. It was his first clear touch of the ball since kicking off the game, illustrating how tightly shackled Ruggeri had him.

The game meandered aimlessly for the next ten minutes with each side's parry nullified by a sharp challenge or a foul. Steven told me of his exasperation at the way the game was going: 'It was a funny game because it had no pattern to it. There was a coming together or players all over the field all the time. The only time there was anything constructive happening was when Maradona had the ball. He elevated the game. If he wasn't playing? We would have won if he wasn't playing, simply. They very much matched us in the group of players that they were. Maradona was just the difference on the day.'

On the half-hour, an unorthodox backheel by Maradona on the left touchline found Valdano. His right-footed centre was collected bravely by Shilton as Giusti charged into him with his foot up, knocking the England captain over. Desperate again to diffuse any aggravation, referee Bin Nasser slipped over in his haste to intervene. Despite Fenwick's attempt to provoke Giusti, the Argentina midfielder quickly raised both his arms in a show of contrition to Shilton, who accepted his apology and shook his hand.

Shortly afterwards, the Mexican wave started to go around the Estadio Azteca as the crowd attempted to lift a match that had fallen flat. 'It was just a slow game,' Steven told me. 'We were struggling to get the ball into any advanced position, covering a lot of ground. We were always wary of Maradona getting on the ball. There was no doubt that he had an effect in the way that we played. He also had pace and, to be fair to our midfield, centrally, we didn't have pace. We just didn't have it with Hoddle and Peter Reid. Hodgey and myself were quicker players, but we couldn't get on the ball as much as we wanted. I found it an extremely frustrating football match.'

Fenwick hit an aimless pass forward that was returned first time by Giusti to Burruchaga. The midfielder fed Maradona in space, who began once more to dribble at pace. Shadowed by Hoddle, he ran to the right across the Spurs man, and away from the outrushing Fenwick. Hodge came in quickly from his blind side to nudge him off balance with an attempted challenge that sent Maradona stumbling head first into Sansom's chest ahead of him.

Having picked up a yellow card during the previous match against Paraguay, Hodge feared a second booking would rule him out of a potential World Cup semi-final. He made sure he picked Maradona up, something he was taught by Brian Clough coming through the ranks at Nottingham Forest. He immediately apologised, which was accepted by Maradona while nursing his own head.

The prospect of another free shot at Shilton got him to his feet. Bin Nasser tapped Maradona on the shoulder to ensure he knew not to take the kick until the referee had blown his whistle. Maradona told him to get the five-man England wall back the requisite ten yards. This the referee did, and Maradona's clipped free kick sent Shilton scrambling across his goal, diving full length. The ball went just past the near post and the England captain could say he had the shot covered. As Emlyn Hughes put it at half-time, 'He wouldn't have got to it had it gone in the top corner, that's for sure.' Such was the curl on the ball that Maradona admitted he should have aimed the free kick for the centre of the goal.

Tyler recounted to me how four years later he was mesmerised by watching Maradona practising taking free kicks. 'In 1990, I stood behind the goal he was taking free kicks into prior to the World Cup Final in Italy. It was astonishing. I tried to read which way it was going to go, I had no chance. Just a short back-lift, hardly any run-up. It was just a bit of shooting practice for him but it was a great experience to watch that.'

A minute later, Hoddle was beaten to a challenge by a more determined Enrique. Giusti charged forward, cutting inside Butcher before making the most of a challenge from Hodge, who gave away another free kick in a shooting position for Maradona. A visibly annoyed Hodge accused Giusti of diving, gesticulating to that effect towards the referee and his floored opponent. Valdano attempted to provoke Hodge further by pinching his nose as he began to form the English defensive wall. Hodge reacted by pushing him aside.

This time from a wider position, the Argentina captain's free kick shot ballooned off the wall for a corner kick. He went to take the ensuing corner, which resulted in a moment of comedy off the pitch. Hemmed in by the photographers tight to the touchline, Maradona could not find the angle to make his run-up for the inswinging corner. According to the Costa Rican linesman, Maradona told him, 'Ulloa, these idiots are in my way, can you move them?' As Ulloa turned around to ask the photographers to move, a frustrated Maradona knocked over the corner flag to clear a path to the ball, sending the pole and red flag flying.

Like a parent admonishing a naughty child, Ulloa insisted Maradona replace the flag before he was allowed to take the kick. Maradona replaced the pole but this was insufficient for Ulloa, who wanted the flag repaired completely. Maradona told him to 'quit breaking my balls'. Exasperated, Maradona held out his hands, retrieved the flag and flippantly balanced it on top of he pole. Ulloa once more pulled rank and asked him to put it back on properly. Maradona muttered 'fuck it'.

Now seeing the funny side of the farce, the world's most expensive player was then forced to thread the nylon flag over the post and asked Ulloa if he was 'satisfied', which led to an approving nod from the linesman. With ominous prescience, commentator Martin Tyler quipped on ITV, 'Well he can do most things, a bit of handiwork is not beyond him.'

After all that, with a photographer leaning back out of the way to make room for the corner taker, Maradona's far-post corner was caught expertly at full stretch by Shilton. 'He's surely the best in the world,' eulogised Tyler.

Maradona was nonetheless beginning to concern the England defence more and more, his ability to run with the ball all the more remarkable to the other players who were struggling to get the ball moving on the poor playing surface.

'The pitch as well was poor,' Steven told me. 'The grass was long. It would throw up divots. It wasn't really a pitch on which you would think you could run with the ball effectively. To be honest, it was difficult. Of course, Maradona could because he just had that capacity. I suppose with that surface, the South Americans would play on that kind of surface regularly but for us it was a bit slow and slowed our game down. We needed Hoddle to get on the ball a lot so he could feed balls through to Beardsley, feed balls through to Lineker or bring us into the game.

'It was just a tough game for all of us to stamp any kind of authority over a period of time. There were flashes of it, but not continuous. It was likewise for them; the only things they ever really produced came through Maradona.'

When Ruggeri outjumped Lineker and headed an England free kick down to him midway inside his own half, Maradona set off at full pace, twisting Hoddle inside-out before he could get close enough to challenge him. Going outside Fenwick, who slipped, Maradona's shot was blocked by Stevens and ricocheted across the goalmouth. Stretched by the pace of the counter-attack, Hodge miscued his clearance and needlessly conceded another corner.

Stevens told me that after coming across Maradona a few times, he began to appreciate 'how quick he was over five or ten metres. I think that's something he wasn't necessarily given that much credit for. Like all the brilliant players, he seemed to appreciate which foot your weight was on and go the other way. He could almost beat you from three or four metres away. That gift of knowing which way you should go – I say gift, but obviously it's practised – and just a sporting genius.'

Butcher had not yet fulfilled his pre-match promise to 'kick' Maradona. 'Well, it's easier said than done!' he told me. 'You can't get near him. Honestly, he's so aware of where you were. If you did get near him to kick him, or try and kick him, he'd ride it. He was a very clever player. Obviously he's had to deal with a lot of people trying to stop him, by any means, and trying to be physical with him. I think he learned a lot from the World Cup in 1982 as well, having been kicked off the park, a little bit like Pelé was in 1966.'

After Fenwick sent a long ball straight into touch, Argentina instigated another attack, breaking through England's press on the right flank. Olarticoechea ran the ball forward for Maradona to collect in space in midfield. He laid the ball to Cuciuffo to his right and ran forward, only to be floored by Fenwick's outstretched arm.

Fenwick described the incident to me: 'He went to play a one-two around us. Like you can in football, I got my body in the way, I put my arms out and made sure he couldn't get by me and he tried to make as though I'd hit him the second time, which wasn't right. I just blocked him off, basically.'

To all intents and purposes it appeared like an off-the-ball elbow to the face, not unlike the one Lineker suffered against Paraguay that left the England striker clutching his windpipe. On that occasion BBC co-commentator, Jimmy Hill, had been outraged: 'Lineker – abused, brutally, deliberately and cynically by the South Americans,' he fumed.

Now, four days later, Hill sang a different tune. Watching a replay, he accused Maradona of running into the back of Fenwick. 'He's the best player in the world and by no means the worst actor by the look of it. You can't foul a man who's behind you.' On ITV, Tyler was more honest: 'The abrasive nature of Terry Fenwick, I think it's fair to say, caused the problem. He's playing a dangerous game.'

At half-time, Jimmy Greaves said, 'He's very lucky here the referee was looking the other way. He turns and he does give him a clump.' Keegan added, 'That for me is just stupidity. After a yellow card to go and do something like that off the ball, the player is not in a dangerous position … Incredible. He's lucky to be on still but the referee hasn't got eyes in the back of his head.'

In *Touched By God*, Maradona absolved Fenwick of any fault for the incident: 'The English guy did bump into me, it's true, but it wasn't intentional: he was turning just as I was getting up. That's why I don't blame him for it.'

Already booked, Fenwick escaped any further censure as the referee, following the play, failed to see what had happened. The footage on *Hero*, the official film of the 1986 FIFA World Cup, was focused on Maradona rather than the ball. It brilliantly captures how the many faces of the crowd were also turned away from the incident.

Holding the left side of his jaw, Maradona struggled to get to his feet. The referee called for treatment to be administered, waving away Butcher's complaints about time-wasting, by gesticulating that Maradona had caught one in the eye.

Maradona later cheekily suggested the fact that the referee failed to rule in his favour on this occasion was eventually evened up. 'If not seeing this one means not seeing that other one later on, all the better.'

Once the customary splash of water and rub-down had revived him, Maradona confronted Fenwick, wagging the finger of his right hand and gesturing as if to show an elbow had been thrown. Speaking to the Press Association, Fenwick said, 'I didn't say two words to him but he was chatting to me from start to finish.'

What is clear is, had VAR existed, England would have been down to ten men for the second half. It would not be the last incident from which Fenwick would be fortunate to see out the game. Had he been sent off, England did not have another central defender on the substitutes' bench to come on in his position.

On the touchline, a tense Bobby Robson fidgeted uncomfortably as England failed to make any impression going forward. He relentlessly manipulated a piece of paper between the fingers of his outstretched hands as he sat hunched over in the dugout.

In the final minute of the half, Reid hustled Burruchaga out of possession and cleverly won a free kick in the centre of the Argentina half. It was the first opportunity England had earned to play a set piece into the opposition penalty area.

Waddle revealed to me that England had worked on a specific free kick in training ahead of the game: 'We'd watched them, obviously, and the first free kick, they'd always run out for offside. We'd worked with Kenny Sansom running over the ball, keep running when everyone came out and Kenny gets in.'

As planned, Sansom rolled the ball to Hoddle, who chipped it over the advancing defence. It was a perfectly executed manoeuvre but for Hodge, who instinctively went towards the ball instead of running back and moving out of the way with the other forwards.

Sansom recalled, 'We practised the move on the day before, but it all went wrong in the match because Hodge forgot to run out with the rest of the England players and was caught offside.'

Dochev correctly raised his flag as Hodge collided with a frustrated Sansom. Bin Nasser blew for half-time before the game could be restarted. Less than a minute of injury time had been played.

Sansom vented his anger over the failure of the training ground move to Reid as they left the field together. 'Bobby Robson went mad with him at half-time,' revealed Sansom, 'and he just sat there and said, "Sorry lads, I forgot." There was nothing you could say to that! That was Hodge. If the boss asked us to wear blue tracksuits, he'd turn up in red.'

A pensive-looking Bobby Robson walked briskly off the pitch unaccompanied. Behind him, Bryan Robson stopped to take a photo of the coaching staff. The manager felt, 'Though we had hustled, worked hard and chased, we had to find a way of playing more in their half while keeping our defence intact. We had four at the back marking two and I felt that was where we could bring the ball out far more, especially through Gary Stevens.'

In the BBC studio, future England manager Terry Venables concurred but proposed a different tactical solution: 'We're showing far, far too much respect for them. Hoddle is defending with everybody else. I think we've got to risk Hoddle, leave him between the defence and the front players. Therefore, they'll be worried about him and stay back. He will give them problems and we will have more space to play in. If we're just going to rely on a counter-attack, we'll wait and wait, and we might win 1-0 but, on the other hand, they might get a break when we've given them too much respect.'

On BBC Radio 2, former England manager Ron Greenwood advocated a tactical substitution to give the team a greater attacking edge: 'What we want more is a bit more construction from midfield to get up to the front players and it might mean even that possibly a wider person might give us that opportunity.'

At home in England, the Central Electricity Generating Board reported a surge of 1,200 megawatts in three minutes as the television viewing audience of millions throughout the country collectively flicked on their kettles for a half-time brew. England had become the first side in the tournament to prevent Argentina scoring a first-half goal against them.

On the ITV panel, Kevin Keegan said, 'What's disappointed me slightly is the fact that we said, alright we know Maradona's a world-class player, but we've got our strengths. Now at the moment, our strengths – whatever you feel they are, whatever anybody at home feels they are – they're not coming through.'

Fellow pundit Mick Channon labelled the surface 'diabolical'. Kevin Keegan added, 'I can't believe they can't do just a bit more with it. They know it's bad, everyone who's played on it said it's bad and still it's bad. They can water it, roll it. I'm sure they can do something with it.'

When asked by Brian Moore how England could defeat Argentina, Jimmy Greaves said with a familiar glint in his eye, 'What we've got to do is, Beardsley and Lineker, along with Steven and Hodge, have got to adopt a Harrier-type attitude and go at them with the old motto "who dares wins!" Brian.'

The fact that Argentina had enjoyed the better of the first half was not necessarily a decisive factor at this World Cup. Perhaps the three most impressive teams in the group phase – Brazil, Denmark and the Soviet Union – had been eliminated in the knockout stages after dominating their opponents in the first half.

England were hoping they had similarly drawn Argentina's sting. In the dressing room at half-time, substitute Stevens said, 'I think the feeling was we were pretty pleased with the situation. Maradona hadn't done anything to really hurt us so far. Again, because of the heat out there, when we came in at half-time, we had these big troughs of ice water and towels in the iced water. It was a case of wringing them out and dropping them over people's shoulders and over their heads to try and bring their body temperature down a little bit.'

Trevor Steven told me, 'It was scorching hot. I had the cold towels on at half-time, feet up on the benches trying to really conserve as much energy as we possibly could.' Everton's Gary Stevens recalls players standing in the draughts of the changing rooms, rehydrating and swallowing their prescribed salt tablets.

One person who would definitely need the extra electrolytes was Peter Beardsley. Chris Woods told me, 'One thing I do remember, I think Peter Beardsley, he would never have a drink at half-time. In this day and age, I think the sports science people would go ballistic!'

Butcher said to me, 'I went in at half-time disappointed because we hadn't performed anywhere near what we could do. They hadn't really set the world alight by playing brilliant football anyway. It was stalemate, the teams had sort of cancelled each other out. I think there was a little bit of anger at half-time. We've got to step up a little bit because we weren't great. It didn't feel like us. I think possibly the importance of the occasion was the winner in the first half rather than anything else. We all felt if we could get out there second half and play the way we can play, we've got a chance.'

Fenwick told me, 'The game itself in the first half, I felt was very frustrating because both teams were looking to stop each other rather than play. We had such good players, but we were trying to frustrate the opposition and we weren't allowing ourselves to play.'

Reid agreed, sharing his opinions in the changing room, 'We hadn't played particularly well up to that stage but it was still 0-0 and I sat there believing that we could win if went at them a bit more. Argentina had played their best football of the competition but they still hadn't broken us down. We knew we could do better.'

Hoddle suggested to his central defenders how England could improve in the second half: 'Peter Reid and I wanted the ball in midfield. We were becoming frustrated by the lack of service, and I spoke to Terry Butcher and Terry Fenwick, asking for the simple pass to Peter or myself. We kept on needlessly, foolishly conceding possession with our long-ball strategy. It simply wasn't working.'

However, Steven told me the coaching staff never suggested any alteration of England's tactics. 'I don't think there was any particular thing said, we were just hoping the intensity of the game would lessen, purely because of the altitude. The games were starting to pile up then, so you expected there to be a bit of a fall-off. There were no specifics other than let's get to what we were doing against the previous teams where the balance worked well, but it wasn't working particularly well for us, the way the game went.'

As the teams came out for the second half, Bryan Robson was stopped by Jim Rosenthal working for ITV. He was asked about the mood in the dressing room: 'It's quite good Jim, we know that we're doing quite well. We're containing them, but what I think, what it is now, the front two have had a hard game. We haven't got good service to them so it's up to the back four, the back four has maybe got to step up a bit and come out now and again and let's bring the ball forward and get closer to the front people so then we could play from there.'

When asked by Rosenthal if England were happy that the game was still goalless, Robson retorted, 'Well not really, I mean we're out to win the game. But I think the first half, it's been quite solid. They haven't really looked like as if they'd score so we're just hoping they step up a little bit more so then we look as if we're going to score.'

In the ITV studio, Keegan lamented, 'It is tailor-made made for Bryan Robson this game. Someone to go from midfield without the ball and get in there where it hurts, and we haven't gambled yet. And I'd like to see us not stupidly gamble, but just take a risk because a faint heart never won a fair lady.'

A year earlier at the Copa Ciudad de la México, Robson and his coaching staff recognised that his team were most vulnerable to the heat and altitude of the country's capital in the first 15–20 minutes of the second half as the players struggled to get back into the flow of the game after sitting down at the interval. It would prove to be the fatal period during this World Cup for not only England but Argentina's subsequent opponents. In the semi-finals, both of Maradona's goals against Belgium were scored in the opening 18 minutes of the second half. Argentina also scored 11 minutes into the second half in the final against West Germany.

In the Argentina changing room, Maradona was also frustrated: 'Being in control of the game wasn't enough. At half-time I said, "Boys, boys! Not one step back, not a single step back!" I felt like we were playing too defensively, and I didn't like that.'

It wasn't just the Argentina players who refused to concede any ground. As Valdano and Maradona waited in the centre circle to restart the game, a white dove flew from the end Argentina were defending towards the centre of the Azteca. As the symbol of peace evacuated Pumpido's goal at the south end of the stadium – and unseen on the live television footage – fighting broke out in the lower tier between a group of Argentina and England supporters.

Two England fans held up a Union Jack with 'NEWCASTLE' written across it, it in an area mostly populated by Argentinian supporters. Angry at their presence, the South Americans began pushing the England fan closest to them and attempting to whip them with their own Argentina flag.

The Argentines then made a grab for the Union Jack, eventually pulling it away from them. The two England fans, backed up by some others close to them, reacted. One threw his beer at the Argentines before running punches and kicks were thrown by both sides as the area around them was swiftly vacated.

The England fans were driven out of that sector of the stadium by the mainly bare-chested Argentinian supporters. One of them was a man called Raúl Héctor Gámez, nicknamed 'Pistola'. Gámez was a leader of the Vélez Sarsfield *barra brava* who had served six months in prison for attacking the police. In 2007, he told *El Gráfico*, 'We fought with a clean fist, without weapons, without drugs and alcohol.' Nevertheless, recounting the day to Mexican sports newspaper *Récord* in 2014, Gámez admits to his own 'bad behaviour'. 'I was with friends that day. I didn't go with the hooligans. I don't want to act like a good guy, but I didn't travel with them. I'm embarrassed about that. I don't want my grandchildren to find out. I got into a fist-fight. There were a lot of Englishmen and that's how it went. They hit me quite a bit.'

Ten years later, the man filmed attacking Englishmen in the Estadio Azteca would be voted in as the chairman of Vélez Sarsfield, his image as a no-nonsense hard-man encapsulated by the punches and kicks he threw in defence of his country's honour. It was a position he held on three separate occasions for a club he literally fought to defend.

Eventually Mexican police, an official in a grey suit and, remarkably, a man with a television camera intervened to stand in between the rival fans as scores of riot police gathered in the moat just in front in the incident. A blond England fan stared into a television camera and muttered, 'We'll see you outside.'

The ITV News reporter Paul Davies told *News at Ten* that 'violence was isolated, but in many cases, the English fans were provoked'. In Mexican newspaper *ESTO* the next day, columnist Shanik Berman also had sympathy with what she called 'the poor English people who wanted to wave their flag and say God save the Queen'. 'Shame on the Argentinians who went to the Argentina-England game because just as the players were in a state of confusion on the field and what hit them hardest was the sun, in the stands the atmosphere was cloudier than chocolate water.'

German Hermann Neuberger, acting as FIFA commissary at the game, noted in his match report under the subheading 'Attitude of Spectators' that 'small groups of troublemakers (English and Argentinian) tried to start quarrels but quick intervention minimised this'.

Under the same section in his post-match report, head of the FIFA Refereeing Committee, Harry Cavan noted that the attitude of the spectators was 'generally very good but there was some crowd disturbance' calling them 'local scuffles'.

As this particular scuffle died down, a different sort of punch at the other end of the ground elicited a roar around the stadium. Pumpido turned to celebrate, pumping his fists in front of the supporters who had just been throwing theirs around. Hundreds of photographers had been drawn to the wrong end of the pitch and missed one of the most infamous moments of sporting history.

The Hand of Fate

Two minutes before the first goal in the match, an Argentinian clearance was bouncing towards the centre circle where Diego Maradona went to challenge Terry Fenwick in the air. The England defender went in aggressively, leading with a straight arm outstretched and caught Maradona on the temple.

A quarter of an hour later, Fenwick went in with Maradona with similar intent and forced him to leave the pitch. Had he connected with Maradona in the same way at this point, the Argentina captain would not have been able to start and finish the move that broke the deadlock. Instead, Maradona just momentarily held his head before carrying on upfield towards the England goal.

Fenwick told me that, despite his repeated attempts to rough him up, Diego Maradona was not someone to be intimidated physically. 'Wherever he went in the world, somebody, like myself, was targeted to go and sort him out. What people didn't realise was you couldn't do that. He wouldn't give in to anybody.'

Speaking on the 2016 ITV documentary *The Hand of God*, Glenn Hoddle – one of just three England players who clearly saw Maradona handle the ball past Peter Shilton – said of the incident that shaped the game, 'If you watch that from behind the goal, he has done that before. You watch his head, don't watch his arm, watch his head. As he does it, he flicks his head. He's done that before.'

In July 1984, Diego Maradona joined SS Napoli from FC Barcelona for a world record transfer fee of £6.9m ($10.5m). The scenes of him being introduced to 75,000 Napoli fans at Stadio San Paolo have been immortalised in the mesmeric opening of the Asif Kapadia film *Maradona* released in 2019.

Ahead of the new Italian league season, Maradona's home debut for the southern Italian side came in a glamorous friendly match in August against his old local rivals from Buenos Aires, River Plate. Napoli still owed River Plate money for the 1982 transfer of another Argentina international, Ramón Díaz. The visiting side included Maradona's Argentina team-mates Héctor Enrique and Julio Olarticoechea.

Half an hour into the game, a ball came into the River Plate penalty area from the right side at head height. The 5ft 5in Maradona beat the 6ft 2in goalkeeper Carlos Gay to the ball to score. Italian referee Pietro D'Elia disallowed the goal. Argentinian newspaper *El Gráfico* remarked that 'Maradona's goal after 30 minutes, annulled due to an obvious slap'.

Almost a year later, in the penultimate Serie A match of Maradona's first season in Italy, Napoli travelled north to play Udinese in a mid-table clash at the Stadio Friuli. Maradona had given Napoli the lead with a stunning free kick but Udinese had hit back to lead the game going into the final stages. With two minutes remaining, a long, hopeful forward pass was headed goalwards by Daniel Bertoni. The ball looped over the goalkeeper and hit the underside of the crossbar, crashed down and out. Following up, Maradona reached the ball before the goalkeeper but the bounce was too high for him. In a flash he raised his right arm behind and above his head to slam the ball into the net. The goal stood, earning Napoli a 2-2 draw.

The opposite No.10 in the Udinese side was the great Brazilian star Zico. He allegedly said to Maradona, 'You're cheating if you don't say you scored with your hand.' The Argentine claimed he responded by shaking his opponent's hand and saying, 'Nice to meet you Zico. My name's Diego Armando Cheating Maradona.'

Another year on in the Estadio Azteca and Maradona had perfected his repertoire. Collecting the ball from Olarticoechea at walking pace five minutes into the second half, Maradona dropped his shoulder to sidestep Hoddle, who slipped forward on the loose surface. Fenwick rushed out of the back line to confront him, but picking up pace Maradona veered right, in between him and Reid. Running into traffic, he was now confronted by Butcher and Sansom, and chose to lay the ball off in the hope of a one-two, stabbing it wide to Valdano with the outside of his left foot. The Real Madrid striker failed to read Maradona's intentions and miscontrolled the ball, which looped up off his foot.

In his 2008 autobiography *To Cap it All*, Sansom revealed that the English defence had been working on using a tactic soon to be employed by his club side Arsenal on a regular basis under their new manager George Graham. 'Maradona picked up the ball and then ran at our defence, looking to play a one-two. We had been practising the day before and told to race forward in a situation like this to push Maradona into the offside position.' However, one man had followed Valdano and got himself behind the line of the England back four – Mr Forgetful. Tucking in to cover, Steve Hodge got his body in between the opponent and the ball and was in position to snuff out the attack.

As Maradona laid the ball off to the right, Burruchaga had run beyond the English line on the left edge of the area. Although clearly not interfering with play under the modern law, according to the stricter interpretation of the day, he could have been judged marginally offside by the linesman Dochev. Hodge raised his arm to appeal to that effect.

In his desperation to retrieve possession as the ball popped up off his boot, Valdano put his left arm across Hodge, leaning on him and possibly inhibiting his movement, but only after Hodge had chosen to volley the ball back to Shilton rather than clear it into touch. It was a decision that changed the course of World Cup history.

Sansom believes that 'had Steve not flicked the ball back to Shilton but run in the other direction with the rest of us, Maradona would have been offside and a goal would not have been possible – hand or no hand'.

'I had a good left foot,' insisted Hodge on the *Hand of God* documentary. 'It came at a nice height and I flicked it back and I caught the contact spot on. I had no hesitation in my brain saying that could be a problem. In those days, the keeper comes out, catches the ball and off we go.'

Speaking in *Peter Shilton – My Autobiography*, the goalkeeper admitted that until Hodge played the ball, he was not anticipating a threat to his goal. 'Whenever play unfolded around the edge of the penalty area, I always knew if there was danger or not. I'd been a professional goalkeeper for twenty-one years. In addition to working tirelessly on my craft, I had evolved a sixth sense, so I knew whether to hit my toes or not. When Maradona chipped the ball towards the angle of my penalty area I was relaxed.'

As Hodge flicked the ball back, Maradona was still running forward in the hope of a return pass. In contrast, Shilton was not expecting a back-pass. Standing in his six-yard area, the England goalkeeper was caught fatally flat-footed. Shilton admitted that 'my brain immediately went into action – red alert'.

BBC Sport's co-commentator Jimmy Hill later made the observation that 'if there is a slight weakness in the England captain's goalkeeping skills, it is that he's not maybe as quick off his line than other goalkeepers tend to be'.

Shilton's manager at Southampton at the time, Lawrie McMenemy, was also working for the BBC as a pundit during the World Cup and had just returned back to London from Mexico in time for the quarter-final.

Speaking four years later on the documentary, *Peter Shilton – Born to Save*, McMenemy explained how his now former goalkeeper worked in training. 'Peter does a lot of work from a short distance, reflex saves. People are hammering a football at him from five and six yards and he stays on his line and he's continually diving for it. He's done this for 30 years, and if you watch him closely in his games there's many an occasion when you think, *Where's the goalkeeper, why didn't he come off his line?*[25]

Four years later in the 1990 World Cup quarter-final, with the match against Cameroon deep into extra time, a ball was similarly skied high into the six-yard area by an England midfielder, this time Trevor Steven. Shilton stayed rooted to the line as the 6ft 1in forward François Omam-Biyik leapt to head the ball goalwards. On that occasion Shilton made the right choice and dived left to catch the shot. This time with no other defenders between Maradona and the goal, Shilton had to make a decision.

As a teenager, Shilton worked on what he perceived to be the weaknesses in his goalkeeping armoury. One of those was punching the ball. As a young keeper, he admits that he often flapped at high balls, later reasoning that it was because he had failed to get his feet in the correct position and ended up overstretching. Watching major fights he noticed that boxers similarly mistimed their punches by over-reaching. The best ones were delivered when the boxer moved close to their opponent. He therefore bought himself a punch bag, spending hours moving his feet close to the bag and executing short, sharp thrusts to clear an imaginary ball.

In his autobiography, Shilton came to the conclusion that different situations of this type demanded different solutions: 'If the cross was coming from wide or from the byline, I discovered it was best to get one fist to the ball, and I practised punching to both the left and right. A two-fisted punch was most effective when the ball was delivered straight at me from deep.'

At almost exactly the same moment in the match against Paraguay – five minutes into the second half – Shilton had taken a goal kick that was headed straight back towards his area. A Paraguayan forward, Buenaventura Ferreira, chased the ball and jumped for it with his arm extended. Having run forward to take

---

25 https://www.youtube.com/watch?si=XsZBmhvmChfbO7kR&v=_pieVLPOZFs&feature=youtu.be

the initial kick, Shilton's momentum was already going forward. He made the decision to go for the ball as it came down close to the edge of the 18-yard line. As he had practised, the England captain jumped for the ball with both arms, getting to it momentarily ahead of Ferreira and punching clear despite a heavy challenge from the smaller forward.

Now in the sixth minute of the second half, a similar situation presented itself. Maradona was four inches smaller than Ferreira but on this occasion Shilton did not have any forward momentum. A straight ball looped towards him, and this time he went for it with just one fist.

'He's never really been a goalkeeper to take a chance,' admitted McMenemy. 'So if a goalkeeper comes off his line, he's got to get it. I think with Peter, if there's an element of doubt, he won't come. That's why he works ever so hard, when he stays on his line to make those reflex saves and I think personally he's the best in the business at that.'

Shilton said of Maradona, 'He was actually running into the area at full pelt, I was obviously having to move from a standing start. Something told me I might just get there before him, that's why I went for it. Otherwise I'd have just stood and tried to react to his header.

'It's a split-second thing that you do. I think the pictures prove I would have just beaten him, I'd got my arm over his head. I was always stretching for it, I was always chasing the ball and I just sort of dived at the last minute to try and get my arm over his head and he knew that, that's why he touched it, otherwise he'd have just flicked it with his head and knocked it in anyway.'

The ball was dropping to a point eight yards out from England's goal. Shilton said, 'I never left my goal area unless I was certain that I would win the ball. I knew I had to leave my line to win this ball and, what's more, I knew I would win it.'

As the ball hung in the air, Glenn Hoddle remembers what he felt: 'As a professional, I'm thinking, *You've got a chance here Pete, not only a chance to punch the ball, but to wipe Maradona out*, if you get my point.'

It is a question Shilton has had to deal with continually in the four decades since. In his autobiography, he explained why that was not an option: 'It wasn't my style to go through a forward, although I did do unwittingly on occasions when the player arrived so late I hadn't seen him. In over-reaching for the ball, and given Maradona's position, even if that had been my intention, it would have been physically impossible.'

Maradona was quicker to sense the opportunity. From jogging in hope, he quickly transitioned into a sprint, and in five short steps he got himself under the flight of the ball, in his words 'leapfrogging' up off his right foot. 'Even I don't know how I managed to jump so high.'

Shilton always felt the ball was his. 'As I took off from the ground, I wasn't so much reaching for the ball as over-reaching, but I knew I was going to make contact. It was my ball and flung out my right arm, ready to punch it clear. I was really stretching so I knew I wasn't going to achieve the ideal height and distance, but it was good enough to avert danger.'

Hoddle saw things differently. 'I'm thinking Peter – the timing of it – he's getting there, but he's getting there a tad late. His fist is about to punch the ball and suddenly Maradona – I see his hand – come and flick the ball first. He just beats Peter's fist with the side of his fist.'

Shilton did not see Maradona handle the ball but, as he punched thin air, he stumbled over and fell to hear the roar of the crowd. In the goalkeeper's estimation, it was impossible for Maradona to have headed the ball and, upon seeing him jump up to celebrate, Shilton quickly deduced that the only explanation was that he must have used his hand.

Maradona admitted, 'At just 1.65m tall, I was never going to beat Shilton in the air. So I put my fist up, and I put my head just behind it and Shilton came out with both hands. So Shilton shouted, "Handball, handball."'

As the ball bounced into the net, 'with a little sigh of apology' in the words of Bryon Butler, Burruchaga and Olarticoechea turned away from the action rather than celebrating as if expecting that the goal would be disallowed. Maradona sprung up with arms raised and began to jog sheepishly towards the sideline. He twice turned his head towards the referee, who pointed towards the centre circle for a goal, before Maradona actually began to celebrate.

'When I saw the linesman running to the centre circle,' recalled Maradona, 'I shouted [to my team-mates], "Come on celebrate, put your arms around me, it's a goal," because if we doubted it, then the linesman and referee would doubt it to, and they'd have disallowed it.'

Olarticoechea, Cuciuffo and Batista were the first to congratulate Maradona on the goal. Batista, who was one of the few Argentines who reacted by raising his arms in celebration, asked Maradona, 'You knocked it in with your hand, right? Did you use your hand?' Maradona replied, 'Shut the fuck up and keep on celebrating.'

Speaking to CNN, Burruchaga said, 'When I was approaching him, I realised it because everyone had a surprised face and we celebrated the goal with surprise. At that point, Diego asked us to hug him because he obviously knew what he had done.'[26]

As he walked back to the halfway line, Maradona attempted to maintain the deception of him heading the ball. He felt his head searching for the pain created by an imaginary impact. Immediately after the game, he would claim to journalists he had a bump on his head from the collision.

In the England dugout, manager Robson remained seated during the incident and admitted to initially feeling calm before a dreaded realisation sunk in as the referee failed to act. 'At that moment, I didn't worry. I remember turning to Don Howe, my assistant: "Hey Don, I think he hasn't seen this. I think he's going to give a goal."'

On the BBC, commentator Barry Davies did not realise that Maradona had handled the ball, initially believing England were appealing for offside. Maradona had indeed run beyond the line

---

26 https://cnnespanol.cnn.com/video/diego-maradona-mano-de-dios-1986-argentina-mexico-mundial-inglaterra-malvinas-deportes-cnnee-pkg

of England's defence but the fact that Hodge played the ball back meant he could not have been offside. Picking up on the protests of the England players, and the first of three television replays, Davies asked the millions watching back at home, '… or was it a use of the hand that England are complaining about?' Davies said to me, 'I just didn't see what had happened, to be honest.'

On his return to England to begin commentary on the Wimbledon Championships starting the next day, Davies admitted he was constantly reminded of his faux pas. 'I got taken to task by one or two people for the "offside" comments, which they were perfectly entitled to do, because it was a huge mistake on my part.'

On ITV, Martin Tyler was quicker to appreciate what had happened. 'England claim that it was put in with the hand. Shilton is so incensed that he's come all the way to argue with the referee.' It was a claim Tyler became certain of upon watching the repeated playbacks. 'It was a miscued attempted clearance, and Maradona handled it in … Clearly, put in with the hand.'

Tyler revealed to me that his words were more driven by the reaction of the England captain than anything he had actually seen on the monitors. 'I'll tell you why I was sure, or pretty sure anyway – Peter Shilton chased the ref. I'd commentated on Peter and known Peter, he didn't do that sort of thing lightly. That was my clue.'

Despite leading the protests, the England captain did not speak to the referee. Talking to the BBC after the game, Shilton admitted, 'I couldn't believe it when the referee didn't see it – even the linesman. I looked across and he was in position. I didn't say anything because I couldn't get near him. He just ran off.'

A rule change instigated in time for the 1990 World Cup stipulated that deliberate handball become a yellow card offence. There, in the second group game, Maradona also got away with a match-altering handball that saved a goal from being scored by the Soviet Union.

In 1986, deliberate handball was not a bookable offence. In the group stage match between Brazil and Spain in Guadalajara, the

Selecão captain Edinho punched a ball into the Spanish goal, which was spotted by Australian referee Chris Bambridge. A free kick was awarded but no further action was taken. Seen in those terms, Maradona had nothing to lose by punching the ball into the goal.

The player closest to the action was Everton's Gary Stevens, who was almost perfectly in line with Shilton and Maradona. 'I couldn't see,' he tells me. 'All I could see was the head movement and on the other side of Maradona's head was the hand.'

Nonetheless, his instant reaction was to hold out his arm outstretched. He admits that was 'what you do in football, I guess. I realised something had happened. You don't get the rest of the outfield players all running around clapping their hands and gesticulating there was a handball. With them all doing that within a few seconds, I realised that's what has happened so, yeah, I started to do the same to copy them, but I didn't actually see it there and then on the pitch. I thought he'd outjumped Shilton.'

Kenny Sansom was next to Stevens: 'I didn't see the handball for the first goal. I saw Peter Shilton run to the referee and thought *What's that all about?* Some of the lads were asking for offside, some were saying it was a handball but I didn't really know what had happened until later.'

One man who definitely saw what had occurred was Fenwick. He told me, 'I was right there, right underneath Shilts when he went up to punch it. Maradona put his hand out – handball.'

After momentarily glancing at Dochev to see whether he had raised his flag, Fenwick sprinted forward towards the referee. 'I chased the referee back to the halfway line, telling him, "Handball, handball, come on, this goal can't stand."'

As demonstratively as possible for a man who did not speak the same language as the referee, Fenwick began pounding the palm of his right hand before throwing it forward to imitate what he had witnessed.

'He went for his pocket,' Fenwick told me, 'and I thought, *Oh god, this could be another yellow or red card,* so I quickly got out the way.

Obviously, looking back on this over the years, the referee wasn't in the best position to see it clearly, I was.'

On the opposite side of the pitch, right-midfielder Trevor Steven was 20 yards away from the incident. Upon the ball looping up into the penalty area, he was so confident that Shilton would clear the danger that he turned around and began to run forward. He told me, 'When it went up in the air and Peter was coming out, your natural instinct is to look for space because he's going to punch this and where's he likely to punch it? So I was looking around for space, and in that split second Maradona put his arm up there and punched the ball in. So when I turned around, the ball was bobbling into the net. Others were appealing, so I did that almost in a reaction to what others were doing. Not knowing why I was putting my hand up really, just copying the team ethic.'

Watching high up in the south stand, the unused members of the England squad were staring into the afternoon sun. Alvin Martin told me, 'There was something not right about the flight of the ball and then we saw Shilts remonstrating. We knew something was wrong but we weren't near a monitor like they've got now.'

In the moment, only Mark Hateley instantly thought that Maradona had punched the ball. Together with Kerry Dixon, they rushed over to catch the live action replay on the one television screen in the ITV box but the pictures were inconclusive. In his autobiography, Hateley was in no doubt as to who was culpable: 'Looking back now, and taking away the fact that Maradona punched the ball into the net, I still have to blame Peter Shilton. There was this little fellow going up for a ball in the box with his arm raised and Shilts allowed him the time and space to get the ball past him and into the net. Shilton should have flattened him. He shouldn't have given Maradona the chance to cheat England that day.'

Despite heated discussions among the squad members, no one in the box situated high in the stands could be sure of what had happened. 'Everybody had got to make their minds up in that split second at that moment,' said Martin. 'We just knew there was something not right but we didn't know he handled it.'

Hoddle, who Maradona went past at the start of the move, saw the handball clearly. Standing closest to the referee as Maradona put the ball in the net, he immediately turned to Bin Nasser with his right arm raised, yelling for a handball. Bin Nasser ran backwards towards the halfway line with his eyes fixed on Dochev. 'Peter [Shilton], myself and Terry Fenwick started to chase the referee back,' recalls Hoddle, 'but my stomach was churning because I knew, as much we could say it was handball, he was not going to change his mind. I remember this sickening feeling inside as I watched the Argentinians celebrating. It didn't feel real. The incident destroyed us. But my grievances don't lie with Maradona. I feel cheated by the officials. At least one of them should have seen such a blatant handball. That was the most horrific and horrible feeling I've ever, ever had on a football pitch, I've got to say, because it just felt so unjust that the referee and the linesman didn't see it.'

Speaking on the *Aldo Meets* podcast, Peter Beardsley said, 'I didn't see him punch the ball, but I knew by Peter Shilton's reaction. He knew when he was right. I can picture Bobby Robson going up and down [in the dugout], knowing it's going to go against us.'[27]

Close to the halfway line, Lineker had not seen Maradona punch the ball but also picked up on the gesticulations of his team-mates. As he prepared to restart the game, strike partner Beardsley said to him, 'He's punched it in the net.' Lineker made one final plea to Bin Nasser. 'Please referee, handball!' to which the official replied, 'Please play.'

Looking back, Lineker said, 'I quickly assumed it was handball. I looked at the linesman, he looked like he was going to give something. I think he actually saw it but wasn't brave enough to give it, for whatever reasons. The referee clearly hadn't seen it, and if you haven't seen it, you can't give it.'

—

27   https://www.youtube.com/watch?si=XsZBmhvmChfbO7kR&v=_
pieVLPOZFs&feature=youtu.be

Among the England substitutes, Gary Andrew Stevens confessed that the dugouts at the Azteca were below the pitch, meaning those sitting on the bench were at eye level with the playing surface. The curvature of the pitch meant that Stevens could only see the ankles of those at the opposite end.

Chris Woods concurred: 'From where we were, you couldn't actually see that Maradona had handballed it. It looked like he'd headed it. It was only when Shilts come running out saying he'd handled it that we thought there was something wrong.'

Watching on the Argentina bench, Pedro Pasculli confessed as to having no inkling of what his room-mate had done. Speaking to *The Guardian* in 2019, he said, 'Maradona's reaction to the goal was a normal celebration; he just ran to the corner and the team ran after him. We didn't know what he'd done until he told us all at full-time. We were all laughing. Even if it was unfortunate for the English, it wasn't something a normal person would think of doing.'

As he walked back to the halfway line, Maradona acknowledged his father sitting in the stand by brandishing the part of his body with which he had scored. He later admitted in his autobiography *El Diego*, 'I was a bit stupid because I was celebrating with my left fist outstretched and watching what the linesman was up to out of the corner of my eye. The ref could have cottoned on to that and suspected something was up.'

High up in the press stand, Barclay recalls his initial reaction, shouting out, 'What a fucking great header!' Without television monitors in the media area, mandatory now for a major tournament, the journalists could only debate among themselves about what had just happened.

Michael Calvin was on the far right of the press box towards the opposite end of the pitch to which Maradona scored: 'We were sort of there doing a sort of shrug, *What on Earth had happened there?* From the guys at the other end of the press box, there was this sort of semaphore going on, where they started pounding their fists into the palm of their hand. That's how we worked it out.'

During an injury break, Diego Maradona offers Steve Hodge some refreshment – very soon after he would give him something much more valuable

'I was just delighted for even those fifteen minutes against Argentina' John Barnes takes on the Argentina defence as he becomes the first black footballer to represent England at the FIFA World Cup finals

Óscar Ruggeri (far left) watches $1,500 slip through his fingers as Gary Lineker scores the goal which earned him the Golden Boot and ensured his place in World Cup history

La nuca de Dios – straining every sinew, Olarticoechea somehow appears underneath Gary Lineker to deny the England striker the goal which would have taken the tie to extra time – 'we have to find that little bit extra that the shirt and the World Cup demands of you'

Maradona kisses the jersey he would soon give away. Behind him cameraman Tony Coggans captures his every move for Hero – The Official Film of the 13th FIFA World Cup

After failing to spot Maradona's handball goal, Bulgarian referee Bogdan Dochev shakes the hand of the man he would later call his 'gravedigger'

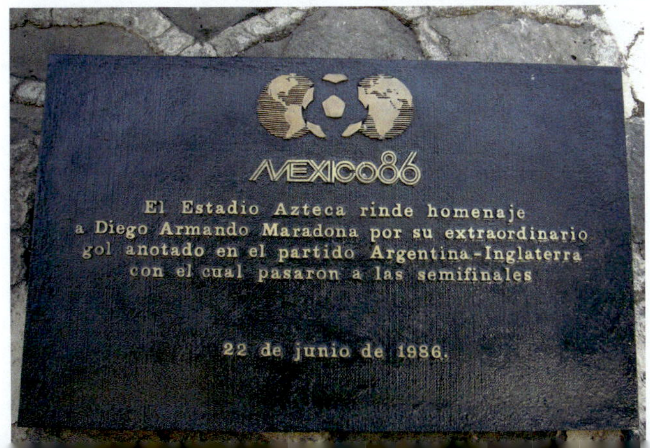

The plaque at the entrance of the Estadio Azteca which pays homage to the 'extraordinary goal' scored by Diego Maradona in the 1986 World Cup quarter-final. It was unveiled within a week of the game ahead of the final. (Credit: Asif Burhan)

Diego Maradona's shirt from the second half of the 1986 World Cup quarter-final is displayed at Sotheby's in London. The scoreboard display pays homage to the distinctive dot matrix display at the Estadio Azteca (Credit: Asif Burhan)

The Adidas Azteca ball which Diego Maradona punched past Peter Shilton at Wembley Stadium where it was put on auction by Ali Bin Nasser, the referee who failed to spot the handball. (Credit: Asif Burhan)

'I can't help looking back and thinking, it might just have made me' - Gary Andrew Stevens shows me his shirts from the 1986 World Cup quarter-final as he wonders how his life could have been different if he had been asked to man-mark Maradona (Credit: Asif Burhan)

Together with Sports Memorabilia Specialist, Ted Alabaster, holding the jersey Peter Shilton wore during the 1986 World Cup quarter-final. It was auctioned ahead of the 2026 World Cup by the anonymous shirt collector who purchased it from him (©: BUDDS.COM)

Sitting in front of Barclay, it took a phone call from Tony Smith of the Press Association back to England to confirm the truth – Maradona had put the ball past Shilton with his left hand. As the match restarted, Bobby Robson sat in the dugout, scowling at the unfairness of the decision, shaking his head in frustration.

Reid was one of the few players who definitely saw Maradona's handball. Rather than immediately protest, he went to gather the ball from the back of the net. On *Hero*, the official film of the 1986 FIFA World Cup, he is later pictured snarling at Bin Nasser. I asked him what he said to the referee. He laughed, '"It was fucking handball!" He didn't get my Scouse accent.'

Reid later admitted to me that he now admired the way Maradona had deceived the officials. 'He was clever, the way he did it was so, so clever. Even his cheating was clever. You've got to say that.'

Sat at the far end of the stadium, England fan Jono Vernon-Powell was watching at the front of the middle tier behind the opposite goal. Like many others in the ground, he too picked up on the reaction of the ones who were protesting on the pitch. 'We knew something was wrong because we were high enough up to see all the players. All the England players reacted the same and literally ran to the referee. At the time we had no idea exactly what it was. Of course, there was no social media or internet in those days and things like that. It wasn't really until after the game that we understood it was the "Hand of God" goal. The TV images weren't that conclusive. What sealed it was that famous photograph that appeared in the press the next day. There was a feeling of injustice, more after the game, when you saw what had happened.'

A quarter of an hour after the handball with the match still ongoing, BBC television viewers were shown a new angle of the incident during a stoppage in the play, which was filmed by their own cameraman stationed behind the goal line at the end at which Maradona scored. The one person who could not see the images was the man commentating on the pictures. Barry Davies recalled that 'the replays that were shown, I was talked through them by people in London, they were supplied by the BBC. That was quite difficult too.'

Davies revealed to me that he was describing the most significant sporting moment of the year to millions of people around the UK on blind faith: 'There was somebody in my ear from the VT area in Shepherd's Bush saying, "He's going up for the ball now … the hand is touching the ball now." They saw it clearly on the replays. It was clear on the replays.'

The replay was slowed down and paused at the vital moment to show, as much as technology allowed in those days, Maradona's left hand raised as it touched the ball and clear daylight between that and his head, which he later claimed to have used.

Speaking to the *Daily Mirror* the following week, Pelé exonerated Shilton from any blame, at the same time condemning Maradona, stating, 'That was a fraud. Shilton was overconfident, yes, in assuming he would out-jump the small man and catch the ball without trouble. … but he can't be blamed for someone else's crime.'

In the ITV studio, former England captain Kevin Keegan, one of Maradona's heroes growing up, said, 'It's an old con trick that all pros do and they never get away with it. He's got away with it on the biggest stage in the world, which is a shame.'

Fifteen years later, speaking to Guy Oliver on the *History of Football* documentary in 2001, Maradona had these words for his opposing captain that afternoon: 'Shilton, you think you're the hero, the phenomenon. If a ball crossed just over the line, and you swept it away without the referee seeing it, would you go and tell him it was a goal?'[28]

---

28 https://www.youtube.com/watch?si=fkHkbplkbZK1vAGC&v=mxbML7QTI-8&feature=youtu.be

The Cosmic Kite

As much as Geoff Hurst's final goal in the 1966 World Cup Final is synonymous with Kenneth Wolstenholme's 'some people are on the pitch' commentary, so for many in Argentina the actions of Diego Maradona in the 55th minute of the match are forever interlinked with the commentary of a Uruguayan, Victor Hugo Morales, working for radio in Argentina.

'It's enough to make you cry, forgive me. Maradona, in an unforgettable run, in the play of all time. Cosmic kite! What planet are you from? Leaving in your wake so many Englishmen, so that the whole country is a clenched fist shouting for Argentina!'

Esteemed football journalist Brian Glanville was more circumspect in his description of the goal for his definitive book, *The Story of the World Cup*, calling it 'a goal so unusual, almost romantic, that it might have been scored by some schoolboy hero, or some remote Corinthian, from the days when dribbling was the vogue'.

BBC commentator Barry Davies describing the goal live to millions in the UK just said simply, 'Oh, you have to say that's magnificent! There is no debate about that goal, that was just pure football genius.'

Speaking to *When the World Watched*, Maradona explained, 'Top-class players do things others can't. When everything is unclear they can see lucidly. I liked to take on defenders, and take on one, take on another. This really fired me up.'

The 12 left-footed touches with which Diego Maradona took the ball a total of 51 metres from his own half, beyond five Englishmen to score the goal that ultimately won the match are the most analysed and venerated in the history of football.

Maradona believes those unforgettable ten seconds, which forever defined his sporting genius, could not possibly have occurred against any other of the leading football nations. 'English players are probably the most noble in the world, there's no doubt about that. Don't get me wrong, they tackle hard. They are not soft, but they always go after the ball. When they have no chance to get it, then that's it for them. That's something we South Americans don't understand. I always say England allowed me to score the best goal of my life.'

Hoddle believed that the duplicity of the first goal had rendered England punch-drunk and open to what proved to be the knockout blow. 'I think there was a shock going through us as a team, for two, three, maybe four minutes. We were talking, the ones who hadn't seen it, we've quickly said it was handball. We've got this deflation.'

Steven told me, 'I think if the handball hadn't gone in, the game over the next 10, 15 minutes would have been completely different as to what it was. If we would have got through that whilst we were at 0-0, I think we would have become favourites to win. The key moment of them getting the lift and us getting the sort of punch on the chin, we were dazed. Maradona took full advantage of that. A brilliant footballer, a brilliant football mind. He could smell uncertainty, he could smell opportunity. He had the ability to capitalise on that.'

Speaking to the *Daily Mail* in 2020, Peter Shilton said, 'It was a great goal but we were in no doubt – without the first goal he would not have scored the second.' Fenwick agreed, 'This was the biggest game of our lives – quarter-final of a World Cup. There was immense pressure on the game. We were just broken down mentally from the Hand of God goal.'

A picture taken from the opposite end of the stadium just as Maradona is about to put the ball in the net illustrates what Fenwick is saying. With the exception of Trevor Steven and Gary Lineker, the image captures the nine other England players almost in a straight line from front to back, pulled apart by a once-in-a-lifetime set of circumstances.

Fenwick told me, 'We were all over the place. When you look at it, there was no structure to the team. Everything that we work on, on a daily basis, on the training ground to keep everything tight and tough, to give the opposition no lift, because of the Hand of God goal, we were in a mess. We were all over the shop. I can't remember getting any direction from the bench. I can't remember anybody sharing any information to pull us back together again.'

An Italian journalist speaking to Brian Glanville after the match summed it up more succinctly: 'England were still in a state of shock, like a man who's just had his wallet stolen.'

Steven described it like this to me: 'You can imagine the noise of 115,000 people, you can't hear yourself think. Communication is extremely difficult at that point. Naturally a goal increases energy in a team by 5 per cent and it can decrease a team by 5 per cent. All of a sudden it became a 10 per cent difference between us and them in the next few moments as we were trying to deal with going 1-0 down, but also the nature of the goal. It was so unfair but what could we do? Whilst we were coming to terms with that, that's when Maradona produced what he produced with his run. That was in all the timing, really. Our heads had gone a little bit.'

Comedian Jim Davidson later remarked on the Saint and Greavsie World Cup show, 'You know why he scored that goal don't you? Why he dribbled past? Because our lads was marking his hands.'

The passage of play began with England in possession. Looking to force the game, Reid spread the ball wide to left-back Sansom. Faced by Maradona, Sansom fed the ball forward to Beardsley, who was coming off his marker Cuciuffo, before racing past him on the overlap. Beardsley neatly touched the ball off to Hoddle, who looked to find Sansom. Hoddle's pass was misdirected and intercepted easily by Giusti, who passed forward to Enrique. The England midfielder was then floored by a reckless late challenge by Ruggeri. Argentina had already gained possession but the foul might have been given.

Hoddle admitted he had not realised he had been brought down at the start of the move until recent years. 'Someone said to me, it shouldn't have happened because there was a foul on me. It was 50/50 with the referee whether it would have been given as a foul.' Five yards away and facing the incident, Bin Nasser held out both his arms and waved play on by gesturing for Hoddle to get up.

Héctor Enrique poked the ball into Maradona with the outside of his right foot at pace. Maradona's first touch was away from his body, taking the ball out of the reach of Beardsley, who was trying to close him down. The Newcastle United striker stabbed his left foot at the ball but his boot brushed the ball without changing its direction.

Beardsley recalls, 'I was lucky, I was the first one. He didn't actually beat me, he turned away from me. As he left me on the halfway line, then left Reidy, you think, *He's going to score here*, honestly. I was thinking, *We're in trouble*, definitely. I couldn't have brought him down, I was nowhere near him, and I really mean that. He spins away from me and Peter Reid. I was very clever, and what I mean by that is, I knew I couldn't catch him, but if you look at Peter Reid trying to chase him now, he looks like a muppet!'

Maradona had turned towards the onrushing Reid but, anticipating his arrival, rolled it back towards himself, performing a sharp 180-degree pirouette. The more obvious move for a left-footed player would have been to cut inside again and turn on to his stronger side into the centre circle. However, with Sansom and Hodge both committed upfield, Maradona went in the opposite direction down England's fatally exposed left flank. In the words of Bryon Butler on BBC Radio 2: 'Maradona turns like a little eel and comes away from trouble.'

His next touch was to push the ball over the halfway line into the space on England's left vacated by Sansom's overlap, and to motor away from Reid from virtually a standing start. Speaking to the *Liverpool Echo* in the days after the game, Reid lamented that 'he turned me just inside their half and I thought he had a jet engine in him as he accelerated away. I just couldn't believe the speed at which he was moving.'

Hodge was also left trailing in Maradona's dust. He explained that, even at the age of 23, the conditions meant he had no more gears to go through. 'People said to me, "Why didn't you sprint back?" Well, it was an hour gone and if you're several thousand feet above sea level and you've made a run forward, trust me, you cannot get back. There was no air in my lungs.'

The man Reid had replaced in the team watched from the England bench as Maradona raced through the area of the pitch he commanded. Bryan Robson told me, 'Reidy and me are really good mates, we still go out together even now. Sometimes it comes up when we've had a couple of pints.'

The following August at Wembley, Robson captained a Football League side against a Rest of the World XI led by Maradona. Robson scored twice in a 3-0 victory but, more pertinently, in the 18th minute Maradona picked up the ball in his own half and ran at the opposition defence. Initially trailing him by ten yards, Robson eased through the gears before executing a perfectly timed sliding challenge that took the ball cleanly and left a perplexed-looking Maradona picking himself off the floor. So would the Goal of the Century have been prevented had Robson, rather than Reid, been in England's midfield?

'Look, you never know,' Robson told me. 'Maradona was a player who could do all sorts of things on a football pitch, he was really special. Whether you read him, that he was going to turn on the halfway line and then go away from Pete like he did, you know it's hypothetical whether it would have happened with me.' With a rye smile, he added, 'I think if he'd been running at our back four – I hadn't been booked in the earlier games – so I think he might have gone down!'

Butcher ran forward, leaving Burruchaga free, and attempted to show Maradona down the sideline. With the ball bouncing haphazardly on the uneven Azteca surface, Maradona took three quick touches to slow it down and get the ball under complete control before darting inside Butcher with a drop of the shoulder.

Steven told me, 'He was just brilliant at catching people flat-footed. For a split second he'd move the ball just at the moment you were squared up. He did that to Terry Butcher, coming in from the right-hand side, on to his left.'

Maradona sent Butcher the wrong way and cut inside the Ipswich Town defender, who swung out his right leg without committing himself totally to the tackle. It enabled him to spin round and chase back but it is a decision he regrets. I asked Butcher whether, if he had his time again, he would have taken Maradona out on the halfway line. 'Yes, without a shadow of a doubt. I've got no scruples about that. I think in the modern game now, he would have been taken out.'

Past one of the centre-backs, Maradona now hurtled towards the other, Terry Fenwick. The Queens Park Rangers defender, already on a yellow card, expected Maradona to move across him on to his stronger left foot and had his weight shifted in that direction. Fenwick told me, 'Over my career, we showed people inside. We showed them inside into more bodies. We were hoping to box him in. As he attacked me, he wanted to come to my right side and I tried to get my body in the way so he had to go to the left where Big Butch was coming back, hoping to push him that way and on to his right foot rather than his left.'

Maradona claimed, 'I had Jorge Valdano and Jorge Burruchaga in support, so I thought to myself – do I pass it, or do I go alone? Fenwick couldn't decide if he should cover me or Burruchaga. A defender in doubt, is a dead one.'

With the England defence pulled out of shape, Fenwick admitted to me that he felt fatally exposed: 'Kenny was further up the field, almost in a winger's position. Butch was playing left-back. When you look at the actual goal, I was in loads of space, too big. We were stretched all over the place. It was too much to give Diego Maradona.'

Fenwick too was rendered flat-footed as Maradona swayed to the defender's left. With all his weight on his right foot as Maradona raced past him, Fenwick was not really close enough to even knock him over. He could only offer a flailing arm in riposte, which brushed Maradona's thigh. The Argentina captain, now in full flow, breezed past him and bore down on the England goal.

Speaking to *World Cup Heroes and Villains*, Fenwick described his thought process: 'Really at the time, I thought I've got to take the guy out. I really felt that, but I'd been booked already. I wasn't quite sure where I was, I didn't know if I was inside the box or out. I tried to just put him off, I tried to put my left arm round but the guy's such a strong fellow, he just brushed us aside and he's gone on to finish the goal.'[29]

Waddle told me he felt the defender was inhibited by his earlier caution: 'Terry Fenwick, on a normal day, would have taken him out, but he was booked, so he couldn't do that. If it had been a different player, another player would have probably taken Maradona out. Let's be honest, he would have took him down.'

Fenwick admitted, 'People, whenever they bump into me, the first thing they ask is why didn't you take Maradona out? You know what I mean, I have nightmares about it. It's what happens at the time, and at the time, for all I wanted to take him out, I felt there was a red card on the way here. It's one of those decisions that I've got to live with.' He added, 'I couldn't bring him down, I was already on a yellow card. I tried to just force him back into an area. I was hoping Big Butch would come back in and maybe get a foot in.'

Speaking on BBC television, Fenwick's former manager Terry Venables said, 'He's come inside one, and then here, Fenwick should make him come across again, actually, but he's taken the short route.'

Following the run all the way, referee Bin Nasser told me he played his part in the goal: 'I gave him the advantage every time he was fouled. I was anticipating what he was going to do. Once he got

---

29 https://www.youtube.com/watch?si=XsZBmhvmChfbO7kR&v=_
    pieVLPOZFs&feature=youtu.be

in the penalty area, I was ready to make a huge decision to award a penalty kick if anyone fouled Maradona, but he kept going.'

Maradona now raced towards the England captain. Throughout his childhood, the methodical Shilton had spent hours creating diagrams, analysing the angles required to perfect his goalkeeping. 'Even as a small boy, I had a grasp of angles, lines and positioning. The subject fascinated me and this fascination was to become almost an obsession when I became a professional goalkeeper.'

Drawing on all this information and entering the third decade of his senior career, Shilton felt like he 'possessed certain knowledge that others didn't have'. He now attempted to force Maradona into shooting across him. 'I came off my line to narrow Maradona's vision of goal. He was moving the ball forward with his left foot and my position offered him a wide gap through which to fire off a shot.

'Terry Butcher was breathing down his neck. I would say that 99 per cent of players finding themselves in that situation would opt to shoot into the gap. I was expecting him to do that and was ready for him.'

However, Diego Maradona did not think like 99 per cent of players. Confronting Shilton, he opened up his body to fool the goalkeeper into thinking he would shoot into the far side of the goal before side-stepping him and leaving the England captain helpless on the ground.

In the days after the match, Maradona claimed in that split second he had remembered the last time he had played against England in 1980. Then, aged 19, he had in the first half of a friendly game at Wembley performed a similar slalom through the England defence and found himself one on one with the goalkeeper, which that night was Ray Clemence. On that occasion, he had poked the ball across the goalkeeper towards the far post and narrowly missed. When Maradona phoned home, his 11-year-old brother Hugo, known as *El Turco* (The Turk), told him he should have gone round Clemence and scored with his right foot.

In October 2017, Maradona was invited to the new Wembley Stadium, where he was introduced to England captain Harry Kane ahead of a Tottenham Hotspur game. After a brief meeting in the changing room, Maradona held on to Kane's hand and said in typically demonstrative fashion, 'Oh, and Harry, don't always go near post with your shots. Go across goal sometimes. You know why? Goalkeepers watch you on TV all the time. So next time … across.'

The implication was that a world-class striker needs sometimes to do the unexpected to catch goalkeepers out. Nine months later Kane emulated Lineker by winning the World Cup Golden Boot. In the heat of the battle three decades earlier, on the biggest possible stage, this is what Maradona had the foresight to do, making a fool of the world's best goalkeeper.

For many of the England players watching it this was the move that impressed them the most. In his 1986 autobiography, Kerry Dixon said of Shilton, 'He is the best goalkeeper I have ever come across in a one against one situation. He forces the striker to commit himself rather than the other way around, pitting his own confidence and nerve against the opposition. He stands firm, crouched low, ready to spring in any direction and his agility for a man of his size is incredible.'

Alvin Martin put it into perspective for me: 'We used to do drills with England where we would go one on one with goalkeepers. People like Chrissie Waddle, John Barnes, Glenn Hoddle, with just the keeper to beat. With Shilton, nobody could beat him. Nobody could beat him – we had great players – and that day at the end of a long run in searing heat, when the moment came, Maradona actually put Shilton on his backside. We couldn't do that, we used to try it regularly. Maradona was just on another level. It was just a moment when I thought nobody in this world could have stopped him.'

Shilton later said, 'I didn't realise that Stevens had got back really well and was covering that side of the goal, so Maradona did the only thing he could and switched it from his left to his right and put it in the narrow part of the goal.'

Stevens had one of the best views of the goal, running alongside Maradona as he attempted to shadow Valdano and Burruchaga who were both waiting to Maradona's left for the pass should he require them. The right-back told me, 'I was tracking, as he was going past player after player, I'm tracking. The expectation, of course, is at some point he is going to get tackled but he carried on, and carried on.'

Watching in the stands, Stevens's rival for the starting place at right-back felt that he personally could have done more in the same position. In his autobiography *First Among Unequals*, Viv Anderson said, 'I still say if I had been on the pitch against Argentina I would at least have anticipated and come across when Maradona went on his run for the second goal. If I had been there – who knows?'

Butcher had also tracked back and was closing Maradona down on his blind side as he went past Shilton and prepared to shoot. 'I'm thinking, *I can get this*, but I couldn't see the ball because his body positioning was such that he shielded me from the ball. So I just stuck out a left leg to try and hook the ball away.'

Stevens told me, 'That's where you just make your choice – okay, I do have to have a go now, he's gone past Shilton. The last little bit that he did, I've tried to kind of describe it as that last little bit of brilliance. You wait for clues as a defender. I was waiting for him to just pull his foot back and that would have given me a clue to slide in, and that's why I didn't slide in, because he just toe-poked it. He kind of toe-poked it rather than side-footed it and he didn't give me that clue. I always thought that was brilliant in itself.'

The last-ditch challenge by Butcher did take Maradona down but too late, his left toe had already dispatched the ball into the net for the greatest goal in the competition's history. Maradona only felt the pain of the challenge later in the changing rooms once the adrenaline of what he had accomplished wore off. 'When I looked at my ankle, I couldn't believe how screwed up it was.'

Butcher said, 'The next thing I see is the ball flying into the back of the net.' The defender slapped his legs in frustration as Maradona ran to the corner in celebration. Captain Peter Shilton consoled his centre-back with a pat on the head.

Still shadowed by his marker Ruggeri, Lineker watched the entire run from the centre circle. 'When I saw him go past defender after defender, I do remember thinking, after he finally stuck the ball in the net – and this is genuinely true – it was the one time in my career when I thought I ought to probably applaud, clap the goal from the opposition. 'I didn't, of course, because I'd probably have been sentenced to death on my return if I'd done otherwise, but it was: *Oh, my God, what have I just seen?* Of course, it was sickening to see the ball go in, because it meant we were 2-0 down, but I couldn't help, as a fellow football player and a lover of the game, to admire a goal of that brilliance. It was just truly extraordinary.'

In the dugout, Barnes also admits to being on the edge of his seat, restraining his excitement, as Maradona slalomed through the English defence. Sat next to Waddle on the bench, England's two left-footed dribblers looked at each other, struggling to hide their admiration for what they had just seen. Waddle simply said to me, 'What a goal that was. I always remember Ray Wilkins come running up the dugout to me and John Barnes sitting there and went "You will not see a better goal than that in your life."'

Watching from the executive box at the opposite end with the rest of the England squad, Viv Anderson was not so restrained: 'I remember getting up and just applauding because it was that good. To watch it develop live, in front of me, it was just sensational.'

Looking back on how Fenwick's career would later be defined by how he dealt with Maradona during the game, Martin told me that he still would have preferred to be involved. 'I'd rather have played. I'd rather I was one of the ones he's gone past. Absolutely. And believe you me, he would have. I've heard West Ham fans say if you would have played, he wouldn't have beat you. Look, I watched that game and I watched a man that day that was on a completely different level to any other man on the planet who was a footballer. He went past people as if they weren't there.'

Maradona raced to the right-hand corner flag, chased by Burruchaga and Batista, and leapt into the air. 'I really started screaming like a madman. I knew what I had done.'

This time there was no doubt among his team-mates about the legitimacy of the goal. Burruchaga grabbed Maradona by the face, telling him he was a son of a bitch. 'I saw the goal quite clearly because I was right along his left side the whole time. The best dribbling on a bad pitch, at a difficult point in the match and to finish it off as only he could.'

As Maradona was swamped by three of his celebrating team-mates, he was pushed back closer to the England fans. At least four of the supporters began gesticulating at him. In return, Burruchaga and Olarticoechea both pumped their fists at the crowd.

From behind the hoardings, Maradona was grabbed by Salvador Carmando – not permitted to sit on the Argentina bench – whose pasta had fuelled his epic run. The Italian planted a kiss on Maradona's head, something that would become a ritual before Napoli matches in the future.

At the opposite end of the pitch, Pumpido ran to the left edge of his area and performed a knee-slide in celebration. He covered his face in disbelief at what he had just seen before once again pumping his fists towards the supporters at the south end of the stadium. Facing the crowd, he slashed his arms across each other to indicate the match was won before putting his hands on his head in wonderment at what he had just witnessed.

Pasculli described the scenes on the Argentina bench: 'When Enrique gave him the ball inside our half and he started dribbling we all started to rise up on the bench, a little bit after the first player, then a little more after the second, more after the third, until we were all on our feet because we knew he was going for the goal. We were all going crazy on the bench, even Bilardo. Even the England supporters inside the stadium were applauding him. It was one of the best goals of the century.'

Bilardo claimed he did not celebrate the goal as he was too busy trying to prevent everyone else on the bench from going crazy.

Interviewed by FIFA TV in 2018, he admitted that he had made the players practise their goal celebrations in training to prevent the entire team running into one corner and potentially leaving them vulnerable to an immediate attack from the opposition's kick-off.

Speaking to *El Gráfico* in 2011, defender Brown said, 'We defenders couldn't go anywhere, otherwise Carlos would kill us. Just think that for us it was 100 metres there and 100 metres back. And at altitude we had to save our energy.'

Amid the delirium of perhaps the greatest goal ever scored at the World Cup, the ever-pragmatic Bilardo stood on the touchline waving midfielders Batista, Enrique and Olarticoechea – who had sprinted from their own half to celebrate at the corner flag – back into their own half.

Before heading back to the centre himself, Maradona sunk to his knees beside the corner flag looking back at the pitch he had graced. He covered his eyes with his clenched fists in disbelief at what he had just achieved. He was embraced by Valdano, who lifted him off the ground.

Maradona milked the acclaim of the stadium, walking back slowly, pumping his left fist at the crowd who worshipped him in return. He blew a single kiss to his father sitting in a box close to the halfway line. Maradona delayed the restart of the game to the extent that Bin Nasser had to twice wave him back into his own half so that England could kick off.

Immediately after the flash of brilliance in Mexico City, back home in England a lightning bolt struck an overhead electricity cable in the Horsham district of Sussex, causing a local blackout. Around 700 homes across four villages were unable to watch the last half an hour of the World Cup quarter-final. Their residents jammed the phone lines of the electricity board, but at that moment there seemed little chance of England prolonging their participation at the tournament.

Robson now threw caution to the wind. Waddle was brought on for the limping Reid in the 69th minute. The ball went out of play on the far side three times before fourth official Traoré attracted the attention of Bin Nasser to make the substitution. Two and a half minutes passed before Waddle got on the pitch. Waddle recalls that his instructions were 'to get some crosses in and get at the full-back and try and drive them back'.

When Reid was replaced, he wiped his face with his shirt and headed off the pitch, walking straight down the tunnel to receive treatment on his sore ankle. In the circumstances, with England needing to score twice, it was a substitution he was expecting. 'I had a fitness test before the game,' he told me. 'You're not daft as a footballer.' He returned soon after to sit in the English dugout in between the two men who might have started instead of him – Tottenham's Gary Stevens and Bryan Robson.

Up to that point, with Reid paired alongside Hoddle, England had attempted to play a short-passing game through their four-man midfield, but now with first Waddle, and later Barnes playing wide, Hodge dropped into Reid's central position and England looked to get the ball out to the flanks as soon as possible and utilise crosses into the box.

In the 66th minute, chasing a bouncing ball, Fenwick once more caught Maradona on the head with his arm, another offence that could have earned him a second yellow card, if not a red one. Enrique chased down the referee, alleging an elbow on the temple. As the play resumed, a dazed Maradona spent over two minutes receiving treatment off the pitch, lying back down on the grass after making an unsuccessful first attempt to get up. Fenwick believed he had finally put him out of the game.

The defender told me that this time he had intended to strike him: 'I caught him a beauty. I thought that's it, that's him done. I turned to have a look at the sidelines and he was warming up to come back on the field and I am thinking to myself, *What the hell have I got to do, to stop this guy?* He was just too much.'

Maradona returned to the action as Hoddle cleverly won a free kick from Batista on the edge of the Argentina area. Maradona joined the outside of a six-man wall and raised his elbow to the ball as it whistled by him. Hoddle was sure he had scored with a superb curling drive, raising his arms and turning away in celebration, before being 'astounded' as he was denied by a flying one-handed save at full stretch from Pumpido.

From the corner, Hoddle's kick was headed out to the right corner of the area. Waddle hit a devilish outswinging cross with the outside of his stronger left foot, which caught Pumpido in no-man's land but also eluded the England strikers. In his *World Cup Diary*, Bobby Robson called it 'one of the best crosses in the tournament'. On commentary, Barry Davies said more matter-of-factly, 'Actually it was rather a disappointing cross because there was nobody there for England.'

After saving Hoddle's free kick, Pumpido began to feel discomfort in the left elbow he landed on and started to signal to the bench for treatment, which he eventually received after a couple of minutes had passed. As the game was held up while he received a dose of magic spray, over a minute passed. Bin Nasser added just 55 seconds of injury time at the end of the game.

During the stoppage, Ruggeri picked several water bags out of the physio's medical bag and handed them out to his team-mates. Maradona was given too many and he whistled to the England player closest to him, Steve Hodge, motioning at him to ask if he would like one. Hodge accepted the bag and drunk the water. 'Perhaps he thought I was flagging and needed a drink,' he recalls, 'but it was kind and I did need it.' It would not be the last gift Maradona gave to Hodge that afternoon.

The Comeback

peaking to me, Bryan Robson recalls, 'The one thing when I look back at that game, I've got to say, when Bobby Robson made a couple of changes in the second half, I thought we came on really strongly and the boys were very unlucky not to take the game further because we really did play well in the second half.'

On the touchline Bobby Robson sent out John Barnes to warm up. Not used in the World Cup so far, or any of the preparatory matches, Barnes had not seen action in almost seven weeks since starting for Watford in a 5-1 win away to an already relegated Chelsea at Stamford Bridge.

Reid told me, 'John Barnes had to get on somewhere. We had many good players but I thought John Barnes was unlucky not getting more game time because I think he was one of the best that I played against or played with. Bobby Robson had to make changes and you know, in the end, we nearly got there.'

Robson had named Barnes among his five substitutes for the first two games at the World Cup and then again against Paraguay. In his diary, Robson admitted that he had made a mistake in not giving Barnes his first minutes at the tournament with England 3-0 up in the Round of 16, sending on Mark Hateley instead to replace Peter Beardsley.

Considering his sensational impact in the quarter-final, the 22-year-old Barnes did not feel hard done by that he was not given more of an opportunity at the tournament. He told me, 'I was just happy [to play at all] come the game against Argentina. Don't forget, I've not been on the pitch at all. So of course, I'm going to be disappointed because we're going out of the World Cup, we're losing 2-0 and I've not even been on the pitch. Viv Anderson has been to a couple of World Cups and never even been on as a substitute, so how can you feel part of it? So when Bobby Robson told me to get warmed up and it was apparent I was going to go on, I was just delighted for even those 15 minutes against Argentina.'

As Barnes got ready to come on, Fenwick, the scorer of a late headed equaliser in the 1982 FA Cup Final, wasted a good chance from a corner. Racing on to Hoddle's right-wing corner, he beat Brown in the air but sent a thumping header clear over the crossbar.

Bobby Robson instructed fourth official Traoré to hold up the No.17 on the touchline, sacrificing Trevor Steven. On the official documentation handed over to FIFA, the number initially written on the sheet to be taken off was that of Hodge, but this had been scribbled out and changed.

Speaking to me, Steven was honest enough to concede, 'I wasn't able to make an impression down the right-hand side, there was not enough ball coming out. Not really getting anywhere in a one-on-one situation. It was frustrating.'

When Barnes replaced Steven in the 75th minute of the match, he not only made his World Cup debut, he became the first black man to represent England at the FIFA World Cup, eight years after Anderson had become the first black footballer to play for the senior men's side.

'No I wasn't aware of that at all,' Barnes told me, 'and it didn't matter to me. I'm going to play in a World Cup. I was not a black player, I was a footballer. Me being a black player is for other people to look at. I'm not thinking, *I'm a black player so therefore, I'm playing here for a white team*. I'm playing with my team-mates. Regardless of whether I was the first black player or not, I'm just a player in the team. If people want to look at it that way … I didn't feel a lot of pressure from being a black footballer, I felt a lot of pressure from being a footballer who needs to help the team to win football matches.

'I'm playing for England in a World Cup quarter-final regardless of whether I'm black or not. My blackness never affected me or impacted me. I never thought about being a black footballer at all. Obviously, playing for England and there's racism being hurled at the team, or at me, then that's when you realise. In terms of the playing, the physical playing of it, I was never a black footballer, I was a footballer – who happened to be black.'

In 1980, Anderson had become the first black man to represent England at a major international tournament when he started the last group match at Euro 1980 in Naples, a 2-1 win over Spain. Two years later, he was selected for the 1982 World Cup squad but, aside from sitting on the substitute's bench against Kuwait, he was unused during the tournament.

Anderson also went to Mexico, and was named among the five substitutes against Paraguay but was again not called upon. While Barnes went on to become a regular starter by the time of the next World Cup in Italy, Anderson earned the dubious distinction of going to two tournaments and not seeing a single minute of action, a feat latter matched by Martin Keown in 1998 and 2002.

Barnes told me what Robson instructed him to do: 'Get at the full-back. Get on it, get at him, take him on, get some crosses in. That's what Gary Lineker likes. Of course, that's what I did. As a winger playing for England, that's what we were instructed. Obviously when Steve Hodge was on the field, he is more of a left-sided midfield player, not a winger to get down the line. So defensively, he was probably more of a midfield player than I was. But being 2-0 down, we had to attack. So Bobby Robson just said, "Every time you get the ball, attack the full-back and try and get crosses in."'

Although disappointed to be taken off, Steven knew Barnes's ability to run at defenders offered the team something new in attack: 'Towards the end of the game, people are tired now. Barnesy coming on and stripping past people, fresh as a daisy, was perfect for us.

It was a great tactical move from Bobby Robson really. Maybe an obvious one, but one that was effective and very nearly brought us back into the game.'

A minute later, Bilardo made his first and only change, taking off Jorge Burruchaga and bringing on Boca Juniors attacking midfielder Carlos Tapia for his first appearance since playing for 16 minutes in the opening match against South Korea.

With England now only playing two in central midfield, the game became more direct and stretched. From yet another Hoddle set piece on the right edge of the Argentina penalty area, Hodge made a clever pre-planned run out of the area and around the crowd down the left side, where he headed the free kick back into the danger area. The ball ricocheted up off the knee of the surprised Brown straight to Butcher on the edge of the six-yard box. He elected to head towards goal but from a standing start could not generate enough power or direction on his shot, so Pumpido caught the ball comfortably. A visibly frustrated Butcher resisted Brown's attempts to shake hands.

Pumpido kicked the ball straight out of play in the England half on the left side for a throw-in. As Sansom waited on the touchline for the ball to be retrieved by Butcher, he exchanged words with Dochev, gesturing handball by slapping one hand into the other. The linesman nodded sheepishly.

Moments later, after playing the ball forward, Sansom was caught on the hip by Enrique, who ran into him with a dangerously high straight-leg challenge. As the midfielder pleaded his ignorance to Bin Nasser, Sansom accused him of losing his head, after which angry words were exchanged.

As captain, Maradona ran in to point out to the referee that he had not spotted Fenwick's latest elbow to his head on the far side of the field. This distracted the referee from the fact that as Hoddle asked for the ball, Enrique threw it over him, wasting valuable seconds. Sansom continued to hurl insults at the Argentine. No action was taken. The two-footed Hoddle took the kick with his left but the Argentina players all ran out again, catching every England forward offside.

In the 80th minute, Bin Nasser awarded a free kick to England on the left corner of the Argentina penalty area for handball against Batista. Barnes ran over the ball and, as he continued his run, Hoddle attempted to slip him in around the side of the Argentina wall. The ball was poorly played and hit Batista, the crowd, hoping for another direct shot from Hoddle, howled its derision.

From the resultant England throw-in, Sansom launched a long missile into the penalty area. The ball was cleared and a bout of aerial pinball ensued. Hodge eventually brought the ball under control on the left side and fed Barnes behind him. Barnes took off, and with three taps of his right foot he moved the ball away from Enrique before two touches with his left took it past him. As Giusti closed in, another left-foot touch took the Watford winger to the byline from where he clipped a textbook cross into the six-yard area. Pumpido slipped as he backpedalled to meet the cross. The ball went over Ruggeri, and Lineker was behind him to head down into the unguarded net. The goal took him past Geoff Hurst to make him England's all-time top goalscorer at the World Cup finals, a position he still occupies today.

If Lineker had not scored, Fenwick was on hand to turn the ball in. Hodge went to retrieve the ball but Pumpido held on to it, resulting in a minor scuffle in the back of the net. It was the first goal Argentina had conceded from open play in over six hours of football at the World Cup.

After thanking Barnes for the assist, Lineker jogged back to the centre clapping his hands and shaking his fists at his team-mates, urging them to 'come on'. He slapped Butcher on the back after the defender came forward to shake his hand.

Straight from the kick-off, Maradona produced a piece of skill never seen before at the highest level. After going past Beardsley in the centre circle, he pulled off a double drag-back and 360-degree pirouette that left Butcher and Hoddle chasing shadows. Like the 'Cruyff Turn' in 1974, the piece of skill, known by some as a 'roulette', was named after Maradona but in fact was first pulled off by French striker Yves Mariot in the 1970s. It was later popularised and adapted by Zinedine Zidane. An 18-year-old Wayne Rooney even used it against Zidane in his first major tournament match at Euro 2004, but few have used it quite as decisively in such an important game as Maradona in this instance.

Running straight at the England defence again, Maradona this time prodded the ball wide to Tapia, who instantly returned it to him. As Sansom fell over, Maradona passed it back to Tapia, who cut inside Stevens and went through another challenge from Sansom. The substitute then hit a fierce drive that crashed against the inside of Shilton's near post and rebounded to safety out wide, where Barnes outwitted Valdano before returning the ball back to Shilton.

The goalkeeper threw the ball out to Waddle on the opposite side. The Tottenham Hotspur winger ran half the length of the pitch before cutting in and hitting a reverse pass to Lineker, who was incorrectly flagged offside. Pumpido beat him to the ball in any case.

The match was now stretched across the pitch. After Brown kicked the ball upfield, Giusti chased the bouncing ball, got it under control and cut inside Butcher. As he was challenged, Giusti released Valdano going through the centre. The Real Madrid forward ran away from Hoddle and pushed the ball wide of Fenwick. This time the Queens Park Rangers defender was not going to let the Argentine past, hacking him down 30 yards out. It was a clear and obvious yellow card offence for a player already booked. Bin Nasser waved away Maradona's justified protestations and only awarded a free kick. Valdano, who had ditched his shin pads, writhed in pain, rubbing his lower left leg.

Fenwick admitted to me that he was lucky to stay on the pitch: 'I was worried throughout. The referee, having given the Hand of God goal, I chased him to the halfway line. I'd been in his face. From that moment on, I could see he had an eye on me and that would have been a killer for the England team.'

As Valdano received a dose of magic spray from the Argentina physios, Butcher approached Bin Nasser, reminding him to add on the requisite stoppage time. The referee responded by attempting to wave Valdano on to the stretcher. The threat of being forced off the pitch sprung Valdano back to his feet. After a delay of 75 seconds, Maradona sent the ensuing free kick wide of the goal.

Hoddle then swung a majestic long pass from the centre circle just out of the reach of Ruggeri, and the ball fell at the feet of the onrushing Sansom, who did not anticipate the defender missing the ball. The left-back miscontrolled, and sweeper Brown cleared for a throw-in.

After Waddle ran into traffic, Tapia released Maradona with space to run into just over the halfway line. The indefatigable Hodge raced up behind him to dispossess him with a well-timed sliding challenge. The ball fell to Hoddle, who allowed Beardsley to take it off him to send a pass left to Barnes in acres of space on the left touchline.

Bilardo did have a specialist right-back at his disposal on his substitutes' bench. Néstor Clausen had started the tournament in that position in Argentina's first match against South Korea. According to Maradona, Clausen failed to adapt to the altitude as well as the man who replaced him in the team José Cuciuffo. Nevertheless, he remained an option on the bench. Bilardo still had the opportunity to make one more change and was urged by some in the Argentina dugout to bring Clausen on. Valdano claims he told Bilardo that Giusti did not know how to defend against Barnes. He responded by saying that if he didn't know, then he would have to learn.

As Dave Sexton had suggested in his scouting report, England had belatedly found the weakness in Argentina's defensive armoury. Reuters' journalist Rex Gowar told me, when speaking about the game, 'Bilardo later complained he hadn't had enough time to practise defending corners or tight centres from the wings, a fear borne out in the final when West

Germany recovered to make it 2-2 with both goals resulting from corners from the left.'

Faced by Enrique this time, Barnes executed a couple of step-overs before drifting past his marker and clipping another perfect far-post cross over goalkeeper Pumpido. For the first time in the match Bobby Robson jumped out of the seat in his dugout as Lineker headed it almost on the goal line, but from nowhere Olarticoechea appeared, diving under him to deflect the ball away with the back of his neck. As critical to their victory as 'la mano de Dios', in Argentina it was celebrated as 'la nuca de Dios', the nape of God.

'You put that scenario together ten times, Gary Lineker would score nine out of ten,' said Viv Anderson watching behind that goal. 'I thought it was in and I couldn't believe he missed because it was at the end we were at.'

Still to this day, Lineker cannot understand how he failed to score. His agent Jon Holmes told me upon returning to England that the first thing he remembers them doing is repeatedly watching the video of the incident to work out how the ball did not go in.

Lineker later said, 'Olarticoechea somehow has shot up from underneath my legs as I've headed it, it's hit the back of his head and spun out. I've seen it on video a million times to see exactly how he did it. It's incredible.'[30]

As Lineker writhed in agony in the goal, Olarticoechea leaned on the goalpost with a wry smile on his face. He later recalled, 'It may be one of the greatest plays of my life, of my career. Luckily I anticipated it and got there first, because it was exactly the same play that led to their goal. Lineker is in front of me waiting for the cross. He is about to yell "Goal!" and I appeared. We have to find that little bit extra that the shirt and the World Cup demands of you.'

As the defender unexpectedly challenged Lineker in mid-air, the England striker's legs whiplashed against the goalpost. He got

---

30   https://www.youtube.com/watch?si=XsZBmhvmChfbO7kR&v=_
   pieVLPOZFs&feature=youtu.be

up slowly and was hobbling about gingerly as the game restarted. England had made both their permitted substitutions so, had the match gone into extra time, Lineker would have been forced to play on.

Lineker later admitted, 'Not many people know if we'd got through to the semi-finals, I wouldn't have played anyway. I hit the post following through that and twisted my knee ligaments, which probably would have ruled me out of the semi and final.'[31]

That would be England's last chance. Argentina thereafter played for time. Enrique ran the ball into the corner in injury time and was eventually dispossessed after wasting valuable seconds. The ball was eventually returned to Shilton who belted it upfield, but Bin Nasser blew the final whistle as Ruggeri headed the ball out.

Just 55 seconds of injury time had been allowed. In today's game, the three substitutions by themselves would have necessitated 90 seconds of stoppage time to be played. Bobby Robson latter complained that 'we did not even get the injury time that the Argentinian time-wasting demanded'.

Surprisingly for a World Cup played in such demanding conditions, only one goal at the finals was scored in stoppage time – Rudi Völler's breakaway strike in the semi-final between West Germany and France. The feeling at the time was that FIFA had instructed referees not to play injury time as, for the 1986 World Cup, live coverage was only possible by satellite transmission, which was pre-booked for specific time periods. Excessive additional time would be an unnecessary expense for all those involved.

Matches at the 1986 World Cup were allotted an average of just 1.6 minutes of stoppage time. Since 1966, this was the lowest amount of injury time played except for the 1978 tournament (1.5 minutes per game), another World Cup dependent on satellite coverage for live transmission. This compares to the average of 11.6 minutes of

---

31   https://www.youtube.com/watch?si=XsZBmhvmChfbO7kR&v=_
     pieVLPOZFs&feature=youtu.be

stoppage time played per match at the 2022 World Cup in Qatar. Not surprisingly, 12.6 per cent of all goals at that tournament were scored after the 90th minute of play.

As Ruggeri raced forward with his arms aloft to hug his room-mate Trobbiani, Argentina's goalkeeper Nery Pumpido and José Luis Brown sank to their knees in the penalty area in a mutual embrace. The other defensive players in the team – Cuciuffo, Batista, Olarticoechea and the suspended Garré – joined their huddle of celebration.

The substituted Burruchaga hugged his coach Bilardo, who punched the air. Maradona, on the halfway line, ran to the dugouts punching both fists in the air in celebration. He was engulfed by members of the coaching staff leaping upon him.

His opposite number Lineker strode straight towards the tunnel, walking past Maradona, who he stopped to shake hands with. The two No.10s patted each other on the shoulder. Behind him, Hoddle also offered to shake Maradona's hand even though he was one of the few England players who had seen how he had scored the first goal. Even in the heat of battle, Hoddle did not bear any grudge towards the man who had cheated him out of what would prove to be his last opportunity to win the World Cup. He recalls, 'We embraced. It was a gesture of friendship, and of immediate forgiveness. I wished him good luck for the rest of the competition.' Maradona responded with the word 'bueno'.

As he left the pitch, Lineker briefly applauded the England fans sitting behind the tunnel as he walked down the ramp into the changing rooms. Fenwick hung his head and trudged off, running his hand through his hair. 'I was so disappointed that we'd been knocked out of the World Cup, didn't turn back, didn't shake anybody's hand.'

Wilkins approached goalkeeper Shilton for his view of the disputed first goal. The captain approached the referee, jabbing his finger at a man who spoke no English. Bobby Robson walked down the touchline before turning back to shake hands with and put a consoling arm around a crestfallen Bryan Robson.

Four years later, Bryan Robson's World Cup in 1990 was also curtailed by injury in the second group game. On that occasion he would fly home from Italy. As he left the Azteca that afternoon, little did he know that he would never again be part of a knockout match at the World Cup finals. 'I was so disappointed that I was one of the first from the dugout to go into the dressing room. When you haven't played, I didn't see the reason to shake players' hands and everything. I just wanted to get into the dressing room and out the way.'

After being substituted, Steven also walked straight off the pitch from the dugout, swapping shirts with another substitute Carlos Tapia. 'I think it was such a shattering moment to experience. All of the conversation was only about one thing, the handball. It was only about that.'

The Argentina players, shadowed by a phalanx of photographers, gathered in the centre circle to salute the crowd, raising both arms in the direction of the stand where Maradona's father Don Diego was sitting. The captain broke away, moving closer to his dad, pumping his fists in the air and blowing kisses into the crowd.

As the Argentina players celebrated extravagantly behind him, Bobby Robson stopped to speak to Jim Rosenthal live on ITV, who inevitably asked him about the disputed first goal. 'It looked a bit dubious, the second one is a miracle, a marvellous goal. We've gone out to a very good team. I think we've done as much as we could. We were so near, and in football that can be so far away.'

When asked to sum up what England had achieved during the World Cup, Robson was decisive: 'Oh, respectability. I think the players can go home with their heads held high. No one can criticise them, they've made terrific sacrifices. They've worked like trojans. They've given it all they could do. What more can you ask of human beings? They've been a terrific bunch of players and if anybody is sorry at home and a bit disappointed, come in the dressing room, come on with me in the dressing room.'

A deflated Bobby Robson then spoke to BBC pitch-side reporter Kevin Cosgrove: 'We've lost to a very good team, because they compressed the situation in midfield all in the first half when maybe we couldn't really get our game going together. As a result we lost the supply to the two front players, the sort of service they wanted anyway. You've got to hand that to the Argentinians.

'We did all we could in the last half-hour, we stuck the two wingers on, and had a right go at them. John Barnes did good work, and how Gary Lineker has missed with five minutes to go on a similar cross – well it doesn't defeat me – but it was just a very, very near miss. If it had gone in, who knows, we would have been still in there playing. It was the only way back for us. We had to just throw caution to the wind. At this stage, in the World Cup, you may as well lose 3-0 as 2-0 so we did the right thing with the two wingers and we nearly made it.'

When the Argentina players eventually headed down the ramp leading to the dressing room, Brown, Pumpido and Ruggeri ran the gauntlet of ire from the England fans sitting directly above the exit, some throwing plastic cups at them. A young supporter in an England replica shirt at the front of the lower tier repeatedly thrust his upper body forward in an attempt to project his spit at the players. In response, a laughing Ruggeri lifted his arms in celebration as Pumpido brandished the badge on his shirt at him and uttered the words 'son of a bitch'. Brown simply raised his middle fingers.

On commentary, Victor Hugo Morales perhaps spoke for a nation when he proclaimed, 'Argentina has won against England. Against England! I am going to say this only one time and may God forgive me because it is not a low blow ... this is for all the kids who can't scream this victory.'

Speaking on the FIFA film, *When We Won the World Cup*, 30 years later, Valdano said, 'We can ask ourselves how losing a war can be counterbalanced by winning a football match ... but it can.'

The Swap

At the last World Cup in Mexico 16 years earlier, the world's media captured the most famous shirt swap in the history of the game. World Cup winners Bobby Moore and Pelé stripped to the waist and exchanged sweat-soaked jerseys after an epic confrontation between England and Brazil in Guadalajara.

The England captain was pictured leaving the field wearing the iconic yellow shirt of his opponent but by 1986 the English FA had discouraged its representatives from doing the same. Glenn Hoddle said, 'We were told by the FA that they didn't particularly like changing the shirts on the pitch, they wanted it to be done down the tunnel or in the dressing rooms. With some physiques it might have been better not to do that and see that!'

Ahead of the tournament, the FA had allocated each player with 14 sets of shirts with the World Cup inscription. For each of the seven potential games, England could play, they were given two – one to keep, one to swap.

At the final whistle, Hoddle headed straight off the pitch after shaking hands with Maradona. 'I was absolutely devastated with the way we had gone out. I've got to be honest, the last thing on this planet was the thought of changing a shirt with one of their players – whether it was Maradona or not. I was distraught and I think most of the team were.'

Nonetheless, by the time he got to the tunnel, Hoddle did exchange shirts with one of the Argentina players he encountered. In *Shoot!* magazine, he proudly displayed the No.2 shirt he had taken home with him to Harlow, worn by Sergio Batista, the man who had shadowed him for much of the game. He claimed, 'I'm not sure I would have wanted Maradona's after his goal cheated England.'

In his autobiography, *The Man with Maradona's Shirt*, Steve Hodge recalled playing for Nottingham Forest in the pre-season friendly Joan Gamper tournament at Camp Nou against FC Barcelona in August 1983. As the players waited to come out, Forest's eccentric manager Brian Clough walked down the tunnel and stopped in front of a 22-year-old Maradona, saying, 'You might be able to play a bit, but I can still grab you by the balls.' After releasing his grip on the most expensive pair or testicles in world football, Clough walked out on to the pitch. On a heavy, rain-drenched pitch, Clough witnessed a typically virtuoso performance from Maradona. With the ball often getting stuck in the surface water, on several occasions he flicked the ball up, juggled it a couple of times before volleying passes to his team-mates.

Despite the state of the surface, Maradona scored after a dazzling second-half dribble past two players and the goalkeeper during a 2-0 win for the Catalans. Clough told his players when leaving the pitch, 'Hey lads, get his shirt.' Having already swapped with Víctor Muñoz, Hodge missed out as Maradona exchanged with Kenny Swain. Three years later, Hodge was not going to pass up a second chance.

The scrum that ensued after the final whistle was captured at close quarters by one of the cameramen for the official film of the World Cup. Tony Coggans was standing next to Maradona following his celebrations. Hodge searched out Maradona to shake his hand as the Argentina captain was asked to kiss his shirt for the throngs of photographers. Hodge felt that amid the 'bedlam' he had missed his opportunity of swapping shirts with the world's greatest footballer. Hodge then made a point of shaking the hand of referee Bin Nasser.

Beardsley went around shaking his opponents' hands but did not accept Burruchaga's invitation to trade shirts. In between him being hugged by Pasculli and Islas, Waddle approached Maradona and gestured that he would like to swap shirts. Maradona nodded and pointed towards the tunnel, indicating that he would make an exchange outside the dressing room.

Waddle confirmed to me that he had asked Maradona for his shirt: 'Whoever asked him, he was just "yeah, yeah", he was just nodding his head. I don't think he understood the question. He had that many people around him. Steve Hodge was waiting, I'd give up on it, to be honest. I went down the tunnel bit and I thought, *I'm not getting anyone.* We'd got beaten and I just went to the changing room.'

Fenwick, the man who had fought a physical battle with the Argentina captain throughout the match, claimed Maradona asked for his shirt at the end of the game. He told me, 'As soon as the final whistle went, he tried to come over, and he was still a distance away from me, and I just put my hand up "nah". I walked straight off the field.'

Butcher told me, 'I didn't want an Argentina shirt, I value my shirt, England shirts, better.'

As he left the pitch, a bare-chested Hodge was stopped by Jim Rosenthal, who asked him whether any tears would be shed in the dressing room: 'Well, I don't know about tears. We've given our all, we could do no more. On the day, Maradona was different class.' It was an interview that was to change Hodge's life.

Delayed by Rosenthal, Hodge headed down one side of the Azteca ramp towards the changing room and saw Maradona simultaneously coming down the other with his shirt draped over his shoulders. Taking a chance, Hodge tapped him on the shoulder and gesticulated to swap shirts. Maradona nodded before handing him a multimillion pound gift, putting his hands together and bowing towards Hodge in a gesture of thanks.

Hodge later told Gabriel Clarke during the making of the 2016 ITV documentary, *The Hand of God*, that if he had seen Maradona handle his back-pass past Shilton, he would never have swapped shirts with the Argentina captain.

The new owner of Hodge's shirt, Maradona later discovered in the Argentina dressing room that the suspended left-back Oscar

Garré had got hold of Gary Lineker's shirt. Maradona insisted that he must have it. He now claimed that he collected No.10 shirts from opposing teams. After Argentina had played Italy in the group phase, he had swapped with his Napoli team-mate Salvatore Bagni and proudly wore the Azzurri No.10 shirt as he spoke to the press after a later training session. He had also swapped with Uruguay's No.10 Enzo Francescoli in the Round of 16.

After such a career-defining performance, Garré felt he was in no position to argue with his captain. In exchange, Maradona gave the left-back Hodge's No.18, having owned it for just a few minutes.

While Lineker's shirt has been passed down through Maradona's family, Garré no longer knows the whereabouts of Hodge's. Speaking to *Infobae* in 2022, Garré said his children had lost some of his shirts and his house had later been broken into, with many souvenirs stolen: 'I had practically nothing left as a memory.'[32]

Gary Michael Stevens had made a point of changing shirts after each of England's matches and was keen to do so again. He left the England dressing room to knock on the Argentina team's door. He presented his shirt to a man in a tracksuit, who realised he wanted to swap. Taking Stevens's shirt, he disappeared into the throng, re-emerging with the No.19 worn by Óscar Ruggeri. Stevens told me, 'It was manic in there and I got out as quick as I could. When I looked at the shirt back in our changing room, I thought I'd been given a training shirt because of the stitched-on badge and the general poor quality.'

In contrast, Ruggeri still marvels at how much more luxurious the England shirt feels: 'Look at the quality of the fabric, nothing like ours. Look at ours. The thing about this shirt is that we got it from a market.'[33] Both players have retained each other's shirts

---

32 https://www.infobae.com/deportes/2022/04/08/el-inesperado-final-de-la-camiseta-que-steve-hodge-le-entrego-a-maradona-el-dia-que-diego-le-anoto-los-dos-goles-a-inglaterra-en-el-mundial-86/

33 https://www.youtube.com/watch?si=XsZBmhvmChfbO7kR&v=_pieVLPOZFs&feature=youtu.be

to this day, Ruggeri even bringing out Stevens's shirt on an ESPN show in 2021.

Back in the England changing room, Hodge quietly slipped Maradona's shirt into his kit bag before leaving the stadium. Back at the Holiday Inn, his room-mate Peter Reid told me how he found out about it: 'I remember getting in the room, lying on the bed and you go through things don't you? Steve Hodge got the shirt out and said, "What about this?"' Still incandescent over the result of the match, Reid admitted to me that he swore at Hodge, asking him, 'What the hell have you got that for?' Hodge responded by saying he thought Maradona was a great player, an explanation Reid could not accept: 'I wouldn't have it on my mind, get it out of my sight.'

Post-Match

At the final whistle, Butcher sank to his haunches in desolation. He was pictured crying as he walked off the pitch at the end of his second World Cup. At the age of 27, and having just suffered relegation from the First Division with Ipswich Town, he did not know whether he would ever play at this level again.

He described to me his feelings at the end of the game: 'I was just gutted, really gutted. I ran in. I just got off the pitch really quick, because I'd have killed someone on the pitch. I went down the tunnel, it was quite a steep tunnel, and I was dragged off by one of the FIFA officials for a drugs test, which pleased me even more. I was not a happy camper in the drugs room.'

Butcher, Kenny Sansom and Gary Michael Stevens were randomly selected by FIFA's anti-doping team to give samples for a post-match drugs test. Their mood was not improved when, along with Brown and Enrique, one of the Argentina players summoned was their captain.

The FIFA media officer at the time was Guido Tognoni. He recalls having to knock on the Argentina dressing room door to find the three players drawn out to submit a sample for doping control. Maradona was randomly picked out three times during the 1986 World Cup, and this time too, his number was up.

Speaking to him in a combination of Italian and Spanish, Tognoni did not question Maradona about the disputed first goal as, watching on the sidelines, he had not seen it. 'In that moment,'

Tognoni told me, 'I didn't know yet what had happened. Maradona was always extremely friendly. He gave me a big hug, he was a very happy man. He was like a child you know.'

'We're in first,' recalls Butcher on being in the doping control room. 'We're in tears and just sitting there, heads in our hands, and then you hear the noise. They're twirling their shirts around, as they do, and Maradona comes in. He sees us and you can see he's a bit sheepish because it doesn't look great.'

The players shook hands and Butcher wished them good luck for the rest of the tournament. Butcher told me, 'I look over to him and I just tapped my head and tapped my hand. He tapped his head. So I think he's not stupid to do that because if he'd have said his hand, I would have been across that room, having a go at him.' I asked Butcher if he believed him. 'Well I did at the time, because I never saw it. Obviously, the pictures and everything else proved that it was a blatant handball and that he scored from that. He couldn't even be honest after they'd won the game. If I had known that he did handle the ball, I think there might have been a few fireworks in that doping room, that's for sure. I think he might have passed blood instead of urine.'

'I think Terry was a tiny bit irate really,' Stevens told me. 'We were pretty much sat across a dressing room from each other. It was obviously very hot, so we were all in our shorts, socks maybe. What I noted about Maradona, he carried a bit of weight. He didn't seem to have that when we was running about on the park.'

Producing any fluids at this stage was to prove a problem for the dehydrated players. Stevens told me, 'I think I lost about 11lb [5kg] in that game, and that was drinking as much water as I could, the rest was gone. Typically we were given a crate of lager. Terry and I started to drink the lager, because we were out. They had a crate of water. It must have been an hour and a half before we could give a sample. It just got more and more awkward, because we were getting pissed and they were sat there looking at us.

'Drinking fairly quickly while dehydrated wasn't the best idea. We used to have a team doctor who was always telling us to hydrate. "Hydrate boys, salt boys." He used to hand out salt tablets and tell us to drink. I don't think he meant beer and lager but we were out so we were drowning our sorrows to a degree.'

By the time Butcher and Stevens finally produced their drug test samples, the England coach carrying the rest of the squad was already on its way back to the Holiday Inn. 'I got back in the changing room, everybody had gone, so I had a shower,' recalls Butcher. 'I saw there was an Argentina shirt on the floor so I just took that. I don't know whose it was, what number it was. It's never come out of my bag, I don't think. I don't exactly treasure it, put it that way.'

Years later, Butcher told me the shirt is a No.9. He has never found out who wore it but still has it to this day. It was the shirt worn by José Cuciuffo, who marked Beardsley and was the first member of any of Argentina's three World Cup-winning teams to pass away after he was shot in a hunting accident in 2003.

With the rest of the England squad long since departed, the two defenders, Butcher and Stevens, were eventually driven back in a separate car. Butcher recalls, 'We just got a lift back to the hotel and went into the bar.'

Following his drug test, Maradona's belated arrival into the Argentina dressing room, alongside Luis Islas, who was wearing a pair of England shorts, was captured by Tony Coggans's camera, accompanied by Drummond Challis. After asking AFA chairman Julia Grondona if he had a bump on the back of his head as a result of his last collision with Fenwick – 'it's nothing' – he raised his left fist in knowing fashion as the rest of the squad gave him a round of applause.

Maradona then told his team-mates that 'we are everything, we are everything'. Then, from the corner of the room the other players began singing. Maradona joined in, wearing nothing but his shorts, his white captain's armband and a pair of sliders on his feet.

Using his taut Adidas towel as a percussion instrument above his head, Maradona belted out the prophetic words, 'Argentina is going to be the champions, Argentina is going to be the champions, We dedicate it to everyone, even the whores who gave birth to them.'

Later the towel was ditched and, as Cuciuffo drank from a can of Sprite behind him, Maradona led a chorus of the famous Argentinian sporting chant 'Vamos, Vamos Argentina', popularised by fans of Boca Juniors and amended for the national team ahead of the 1978 World Cup.

> *Let's go, let's go Argentina,*
> *We're going, we're going to win,*
> *For this raucous band,*
> *Won't stop, won't stop cheering you*

As the terrace songs continued, the players began vociferously chanting 'Argentina, Argentina, Argentina'. Burruchaga admitted 'that made you tingle'. Olarticoechea sat in the corner of the changing room crying tears of joy.

As they got changed, Maradona turned to Valdano and said, 'During the whole move, I was waiting for the right time to pass you the ball, as you were running alongside me on the other side of the pitch.'

Valdano swore at Maradona in awe of his team-mate's supernatural awareness. 'I can't believe you were looking at me and you still scored that goal? That's downright offensive, mate, that's humiliating, that's not possible.'

Héctor Enrique, who poked the ball to Maradona in his own half and technically provided the assist for the greatest goal in World Cup history, came out of the shower and quipped, 'I'm hearing a lot of praise for him, a lot of praise, but with the pass I gave him, how could he not score?'

In the England changing rooms, the atmosphere had been one of anger. Journalist Michael Calvin remembers: 'It was clear they were going nuts. The first thing that we heard was they want the FA to get the game replayed.'

Hoddle recalls: 'When we trooped back into our dressing room, some harsh words were spoken. I kicked the nearest thing to me, and the air was blue with some of the language. But none of it was directed at Maradona.'

After giving his interviews to the BBC and ITV, Bobby Robson walked into the dressing room and asked his players, 'He handled it, didn't he lads? He did, didn't he?' After receiving confirmation, he shook his head, looked down at the ground and said, 'Then we've just been flipping cheated.' Robson turned around and left to attend the post-match press conference.

The five unused squad members who had watched the game from the stands also headed down to the changing room area after the match. In his 1986 autobiography *Kerry*, Dixon said that 'the dressing room after the game was not the place for sensible analysis and none was attempted'.

Alvin Martin told me, 'People had thrown stuff everywhere; socks, shin pads, boots were being hurled. Shouting, hollering, you could hear it before you got to the dressing room door. When we got in, it was just fury and anger and frustration. A mixture of everything really.'

Gary Andrew Stevens, an unused substitute on the day, admitted his feelings were mixed with the frustration of believing he should have played: 'There were players wanting to go in their changing room and have a bit of a sort out I think. I think there was a lot of group emotion, there were a lot of other people thinking will I ever play at a World Cup finals again? I never played for England again. That was it for me. Personally, I was on the floor.'

Hoddle admitted to having similar feelings: 'When that game was over a powerful depression set in. I felt my last chance to succeed in the World Cup had gone. In the shower after the match, I remember feeling really frustrated. *The younger players in the team may get another chance*, I thought to myself, *but this could be it for me.* It was a sorrowful experience.'

The FA's press officer Glen Kirton told me, 'I spoke to a couple of the officials from the Argentina team, I spoke pretty good Spanish. They were obviously very chuffed, but I think they quite clearly knew they'd got away with one there.'

In an interview with the *New Zealand Herald*, Kenny Sansom revealed that 'Three or four men from the FA came in and we were asking them to get the game replayed, saying it was a disgrace. They were just as gutted as we were though, there was nothing that they could do. When the Argentine kit-man came in with shirts to give us, I thought Ray Wilkins was going to hit him. I'd never heard Ray swear before but he got this chap out the dressing room, shouting, "We don't want your shirts, you're fucking cheats."'[34]

Speaking to *France Football* in 2020, Gary Lineker admitted 'there was a lot of anger in the dressing room after the game. Bobby Robson was very upset, Terry Butcher was fuming, Peter Shilton, naturally, was very angry, because he probably felt slightly humiliated as well.'

Ruggeri said most of the Argentina team were unaware that Maradona had handled the ball for the first goal because Maradona even denied it to his team-mates. Speaking to beIN Sports in 2021, the defender said, 'We asked him, "Did you use your hand?" No one was showing slow motion at that time so we asked him and he said, "No, I scored it with my head."'

In 1986 there was no obligation for any of the players to speak to the media after any World Cup match. Formal mixed zones for journalists to question players as they passed through were not established until four years later in Italy. In Mexico, trusted representatives from the nation's own media channels were often invited into the changing rooms.

---

34 https://www.nzherald.co.nz/sport/football/big-read-the-hand-of-god-30-years-on/JQ5IWW4WCPNGKHDUIZL5KTZFCU/

Maradona was questioned inside the dressing room by a group of Argentinian journalists. On the first goal, he said, 'I swear on my life, I jumped when Shilton did, but I hit it with my head. You can see the goalkeeper's fist, which is what caused the confusion. But I swear it was a header, no doubt about that. There's even a bump on my forehead. I made that goal with Maradona's head but with God's hand.'

These quotes were only run in one Argentinian newspaper, *Crónica*, and are the ones that credit Maradona with uttering the phrase 'Hand of God'. However, Juan Presta, a journalist for *Tiempo Argentina* has a different recollection of the conversation. Speaking to Andrés Burgo for his book *El Partido*, Presta insisted that the phrase that would go down in history was never said by Maradona but by one of the other pressmen.[35]

Néstor Ferrero was an Argentinian journalist working for the Agenzia Nazionale Stampa Associata (ANSA) press agency. After listening to Maradona claim it was a header but knowing for sure that he had punched the ball in, he quipped, 'Then it must have been the Hand of God?' To which Maradona replied, 'It must have been.'

No recording survives of Maradona's exact words, and speaking to Burgo in 2014, Ferrero cannot remember exactly who first used the phrase 'Hand of God' but, either way, when the quotes were relayed to the Spanish-speaking journalists outside the changing rooms, they ran with 'La Mano de Dios' in their editions. A phrase for the ages.

Working for Reuters, Rex Gowar was one of those outside the dressing room and had the words conveyed to him by an Argentinian colleague, which was translated into English as 'it was a little the head of Maradona and a little with the hand of God'. Reuters then ran with the quote, which went around the world and into sporting folklore.

Gowar believes that such was the scrum around Maradona after the game that very few journalists would have actually heard him

---

35 https://elcomercio.pe/blog/posdata/2016/10/una-historia-insolitamente-argentina-con-final-feliz/

mutter any of the words eventually ascribed to him. Unlike today, where recordings are shared, the quotes would have been spread by word of mouth.

England fan Jono Vernon-Powell had watched the game at the opposite end of the Azteca, behind the goal into which Lineker scored. In no hurry to leave after the game, he wandered around the concourse of the giant concrete bowl and came across a door guarded by a security man with a machine gun. Wearing his England shirt and shorts, the 24-year-old Vernon-Powell was mistaken for a player, given the nod and waved through the door. He carried on and went through another couple of doors to find himself in a room where Bobby Robson was answering questions from the media. Vernon-Powell thought he would stay to listen to what the England manager had to say.

As he sat down on a blue chair for the post-match press conference, Bobby Robson faced a room packed with the world's media. Behind him were officials in red jackets and the official 'Mexico '86' logo. On the long table in front of him, there was a red table cloth on top of which was a haphazard collection of microphones, Dictaphones and some of the official sponsors' drinks placed strategically in front of him.

After putting on a set of white headphones into which he heard questions translated from other languages, Robson paused to take a long swig of water from a paper Coca-Cola cup on the desk. An English-speaking journalist asked him, 'Could you please talk about the first goal.' Robson sighed before challenging the world's media to deny that England had been cheated out of the World Cup: 'Well I haven't seen the television, all I can go on is what I felt I saw, which was the ball in the air with Maradona going for it, with Shilton. Shilton being favourite and Maradona handled the ball into the goal. Didn't he? Didn't he?

'Well I think he did, I suppose television will prove it, but that was the way it was to me. That now gives them the edge. That's a bad decision in a very big match. You don't expect decisions like that at World Cup level. Naturally Peter Shilton was very upset because he knew he had been beaten and that does grieve him. He saw it clearly and he was positive he had been beaten illegally.'

A Mexican journalist questioned whether England had tried hard enough to win the game in the first half. Robson reacted angrily: 'You are joking – we tried very hard. It was a very hard game and in that last half an hour we gave everything we had. Argentina played very well, especially in midfield where they compressed us in the first hour. We decided not to disrupt our back four and to play Maradona with our usual zonal system. He can destroy any man-for-man marking. It's marvellous for football that from time to time the world throws up such a player. He has such grace, such poise on the ball and he can beat people in a way that makes him really exciting.

'We didn't contest the midfield as well as we would have liked, and we couldn't then get the right service to the front two. How can you accuse players of having a lack of attacking spirit in the quarter-finals of the World Cup? We never gave up.'

Robson later added, 'No man can mark Maradona. He was everyone's responsibility. Today Maradona also scored one of the most brilliant goals you will ever see. The first goal was dubious but the second was a miracle. It was a fantastic goal. I have the greatest respect for him in terms of his genius. I didn't like the second goal, but I admire it.'

Watching the England manager talk to the world's media, Tognoni noted his admirable dignity in defeat: 'The most impressive thing for me was Bobby Robson speaking at the press conference. This was unbelievable. For him it was probably the most painful defeat he ever suffered in his life. He never complained, he didn't say one bad word about the referee. He really represented British sportsmanship at its best. This was for me unforgettable. He had tears in his eyes but he didn't criticise FIFA, not the referee, not Maradona. He just lived with it, you know.'

Sat next to Robson throughout the press conference, Kirton concurred with Tognoni's assessment: 'One of the nicest human beings I've met in my life. You knew he would strike just the right note, which he did. He didn't rant and make excuses, but he just made it clear that he felt, as the rest of us did, that we'd been cheated.'

In next, Argentina's manager Carlos Bilardo refused to believe that Maradona had handled the ball for the first goal: 'He headed it in. I think it was all right. I saw him jump and head it.'

His next statement was less open to doubt: 'His reputation has been confirmed in Mexico and he is without question the best player in the world right now. His second goal was the most spectacular I have ever seen him score.'

However, remembering that the victory was achieved by 11 players, Bilardo was quick to refute claims that Argentina were a one-man team. Ironically having won wearing shirts missing the laurels of the Argentinian Football Association badge, Bilardo said of Maradona, 'He cannot lay claim to the laurels on his own – beating England was a great team achievement.'

Following the press conference, Vernon-Powell continued his tour of the inner sanctuary of the Azteca, ending up at the bottom entrance of the stadium where the silver DINA coach was waiting to carry the England team away from the 1986 World Cup. As the players emerged and milled about waiting to get on the coach, Vernon-Powell chatted to several of them. A FIFA official came over with an official match ball and asked some of the England players – Shilton, Wilkins, Bailey and Bryan Robson – to sign it with a marker pen. Each player did in turn and then the official handed it to Vernon-Powell, once more mistaken for a player, who also signed it.

Vernon-Powell carried on his conversations with the 'devastated' players. Chris Waddle was sitting at the back of the coach and talked to Vernon-Powell for 10 to 15 minutes out of the open window. 'They thought they should have won the match.' The winger gave the fan the sweatbands he had worn during the game, which Vernon-Powell still has today, stored in a sock draw at his home.

After the England team bus pulled away, Vernon-Powell finally left the stadium and saw the coach carrying the Argentina squad also depart. 'It was absolutely jumping,' he recalls.

No replays of the game were available to the media present in the Azteca Stadium. Journalists wishing to assess the legitimacy of the controversial first goal could claim a video cassette recording of the match, together with a sheet of paper that offered them a minute-by-minute rundown of the major incidents.

Michael Lewis, a journalist for weekly publication *Soccer America*, described the process to me: 'FIFA did provide facilities to watch it in the stadium. Since we can now watch replays of goals over and over again on our phones, it seemed like the stone age then. I had several Americans surrounding me while we watched both goals, particularly the second one. We kept on playing it multiple times to get who Maradona meandered around and where. I eventually timed the goal with my stopwatch. We timed it in ten seconds. It was strange giving up my press credentials to view the cassette tape. Outside of my wallet and passport, that was the most valuable thing I had at the World Cup. They gave it back to me after returning the cassette.'

After the match, which finished at 2pm local time, the England players returned to the Holiday Inn. Bobby Robson called the players together for one last team meeting. He thanked them and said that they had been a great squad – both on and off the pitch – and a credit to their country. He told them they had worked incredibly hard and done their best.

ITV pitch-side reporter Jim Rosenthal told me, 'Because of the way technology was then, Bobby and the rest of them had not actually seen the first goal. Bobby Robson, Peter Shilton and Bryan Robson came to the ITV room in the hotel and we showed them the goal and what had happened. That was a pretty remarkable piece of television that sadly, as far as I can see, doesn't exist anymore. That was when they saw graphically for the first time exactly what had happened. That memory sticks with me.'

Shilton was then interviewed by ITV News journalist Paul Davies in the hotel. When asked how he felt, a visibly agitated captain responded, 'How would you feel?! Not very pleased. It's blatantly obvious that the referee and the linesman didn't do their job properly.

You rely on them in situations like that. Maradona's obviously not going to get the ball. He's taken the chance to punch it. If the referee sees it, he just gives a free kick doesn't he?'

Speaking to the written press, Shilton later expanded on his view of the first goal: 'The video speaks for itself. Maradona punched at it. I immediately looked at the referee and linesman and they were looking at each other. I was stunned when the referee gave the goal. The referee's position throughout the game was suspect in my opinion. I'm aggrieved he didn't do his job properly. When you lose a goal like that, it's a sickener. Apart from Maradona's brilliant second goal and Argentina hitting the post, those were the only chances they had.'

Meanwhile, his room-mate Lineker could not understand how he failed to draw England level in the final minutes of the game: 'John Barnes' cross was coming in, I was under the bar and as it came over I was saying to myself, *This is the equaliser.* Then I had a bang on the head. Next thing, I was in the back of the net but I still believed the ball was there too. How their defender got it before me and still didn't put into his own goal, I'll never know.'

If Lineker had scored, would England have gone on to win? 'Nobody could have ruled out Maradona having another moment of magic,' Martin told me, 'but it would have been a big ask on a pitch like that. Having come back, I think England would have had the momentum. The way that team finished the game that day, I believe they would have felt pretty confident of then pushing forward and taking the initiative in the game.'

'I thought from 2-0 down, we'd have had massive emotion,' Reid told me. 'As good as Diego Maradona was – and he was exceptional – Barnesy was on absolute fire, he was torturing them. I thought we would have had a chance.'

The 29-year-old Hoddle, who would never play in another World Cup match, felt the same: 'I really thought this was going to be our World Cup. I'm sure if we had got into extra time, we would have won through.'

Fenwick is equally certain, telling me, 'I thought if we'd got that equaliser, there was only one winner – England.'

Watching from the commentary box, Tyler concurred: 'Once England got the goal, they ran out of time. If it had gone to extra time, England would have won, I'm absolutely convinced of that. What would have happened? I think England would have won the World Cup. Certainly, they would have beaten Belgium, we always beat Belgium around that time. Then it would have been a 50/50 against our great rivals [West Germany] wouldn't it? It would have been a chapter in that particular story.'

However, Barnes, the man who catalysed the English revival, saw things differently. 'Maradona would have done something,' he told me, 'that was his World Cup. He was fantastic throughout the game, he was unstoppable. I just feel that was Maradona's year. So, yes it would be great to think we could have done something – and we possibly could have – but stopping Maradona, in my opinion, was virtually impossible in 1986.'

Michael Calvin agrees, believing that Maradona had destiny on his side: 'His legend demanded he would have done something else extraordinary – good or bad – to decide the outcome.'

To prove the point, a week later in the World Cup Final, West Germany did come back from two goals down to equalise against Argentina with less than ten minutes of the game remaining. Nonetheless, that was still enough time for Maradona to find something extra, conjuring up a majestic assist for Jorge Burruchaga to score the winning goal.

After the match, Tognoni praised the way Bobby Robson's team reacted to the injustice in the media: 'What was great was the behaviour of the England team, the way they accepted the goal. This was very important for FIFA. It was a decision that hurt and the way they took it was a real example of English fair play.'

Speaking to me years later, Tognoni confirmed that the FA did not make any official protest and admitted that the world governing body was thankful that the tournament moved on: 'I tell you, we were relieved at FIFA that England did not make a big noise. What could we have done? We could only turn down any protest.'

However, some of the English players were not so accepting of Maradona's behaviour when speaking to the tabloids after the game. Fenwick, who might have been sent off on three occasions during the match, alleged that 'he cons referees. I don't just mean the goal he knocked in with his hand. Go near him and down he goes. He's got fantastic pace and skill but spoils it by cheating. With his ability he doesn't need to do it. Pelé and Cruyff were great players, but you never saw them do the sort of things Maradona does.'

Bryan Robson said, 'We have been cheated. It was handball and everyone bar the referee must have seen it. Anyway, I don't see why a referee from Tunisia with not much experience should have been in charge of such a vital World Cup tie.'

Speaking in his column in the *Daily Star*, the captain went on to claim that 'sometimes we are far too gentlemanly and honest for our own good. In fact, we were the only team in the World Cup trying to play by the rules. Why, for instance did we not protest more heatedly over the Maradona handball? The referee looked so uncertain at the time and the Argentine players were all looking sheepishly at him waiting for him to scrub out the goal. Had our players made more of a fuss. I think it is very possible he would have disallowed it.'

Speaking to me years later, Bryan Robson admitted, 'People say he cheated, but it's not really cheating, you get away with what you can get away with in major games and you want to win them. That's part and parcel of the game. I think all top players, when you're playing at that level, that's what you do. You more or less do anything to try and win the game.'

Bobby Robson said, 'I'm not very happy that he punched the ball into the back of the net. But I wish Gary Lineker had done that and got us a second goal and the ref didn't see it. However, I don't think it would cross Gary's mind to do such a thing.'

He was mistaken, however. At the team hotel, Patrick Barclay approached Lineker sitting at a table, who, he remembers, was an oasis of serenity amid the maelstrom. Asked about the Hand of God, Lineker said, 'Maradona handled, but as a striker I have to say I would probably have done the same in his position.'

Speaking to me, Waddle concurred: 'Listen, if Gary Lineker had done it at the other end, I would have said, "How clever was that?" But Gary Lineker didn't do that, so for me it was a horrible way to lose such a big game. I hate VAR, I'll be perfectly honest, I absolutely hate it. But if VAR was around then, it would have saved us. We saw the good side of Maradona and the bad side. I prefer to remember him for the good side because he was such a genius as a footballer to watch.'

Beardsley was honest in his assessment of the game: 'As a team, we didn't play as well as we played in the last two games, it's as simple as that really. Everybody wasn't together for some reason, we just couldn't get it together. It was an unbelievable game really, we probably only realised we could win when we were 2-0 down. It sounds like a silly thing to say but we really were, in many ways, overawed by the Argentinians and especially Maradona, what a player he was.'

Lineker agreed, saying it was 'probably due to the fact that Argentina were a very good side. They had a lot of good players and put us under pressure. I felt as though we played a little too deep, we didn't come out enough at them. It wasn't until we went 2-0 down that we really responded.'[36]

That afternoon, not yet knowing he would win the Golden Boot as leading goalscorer in the World Cup, Lineker looked back on the few weeks that would change his life forever: 'I've enjoyed every minute of it. It's been tremendous to be playing with all the best teams in the world and seeing all the players and it's been a memorable experience and I'm sure it's one that we can learn from and go on from, from here.'

Peter Shilton added. 'We've put England back on the map in the world of soccer and that has got to be an achievement.'

---

36 https://www.youtube.com/watch?si=XsZBmhvmChfbO7kR&v=_
   pieVLPOZFs&feature=youtu.be

Having had time to reflect on the game, Bobby Robson later spoke to Jimmy Hill for BBC Radio. He expressed no regrets over his team selection when questioned why Barnes was not played earlier: 'It was right to select the same side, we just didn't have the same cohesion today as we've had in previous matches.'

Speaking on the BBC television panel, future England manager Terry Venables argued that Barnes's form in Mexico the previous year had merited his inclusion earlier: 'We played when we were two down; it's like the boxer who waits to get hit on the chin before he fights back.'

When challenged by Des Lynam on the fact that many pundits had called for the wingers to be discarded after the first two games at the tournament. Venables retorted, 'I think it's always [right] to know what is best for us at a particular time and against a particular team.'

Ten years later, Venables would put his theories into practice as England manager, alternating between formations in different matches at the 1996 European Championships. 'He [Bobby Robson] changed it from the winger and it brought us results, so you can understand him thinking that is the valid thing ... We do get the feeling we could have done more. At the end of the day, I think Argentina deserved the result, to be fair.'

Robson agreed that the South Americans presented a significant step up from their previous opponents: 'They're a better team, Argentina, than the other two we've played against. You've got to give them that. I think. They compressed us very hard in midfield, there was little space, we couldn't manufacture the ball. You've got to put that down to them because they marked and snuffed you out and got their foot in and so forth, and as a result we couldn't really bring the ball through. The service to the two front players – the service they like – dried up a bit. As a result, we had no front scene for a while, not enough of it anyway, did we, until the end.'

Robson instead focused on the enforced absence of his namesake Bryan: 'They had a Maradona – let me tell you something – we didn't have a Robson. And if we had a Robson, he might have been the difference. That grieves me, the fact that our best player in the country played little World Cup football, and I think that's been a terrible pity for us, and a shame. You know what he is as a captain, we know what he is as a player, we know his grit and determination, we know his goalscoring qualities. Sometimes you just need one player to change the performance. Take Maradona out of Argentina, they don't win the match.'

After the game, the Argentina players went as usual to eat at the Mi Viejo restaurant. Speaking to ESPN, Ruggeri recalled that the players joked with Maradona about the first goal, asking him, 'Come on, man, how are you going to beat a goalkeeper who goes in with his hands?' Maradona wagged his finger and said 'no', still denying he had handled the ball.

The England players were later thrown a reception by their kit suppliers, Umbro. The squad who had committed themselves totally to winning the World Cup for their country were allowed their first alcoholic drink in weeks.

Butcher told me, 'I just remember being in the bar for a good few hours. I think we had a meal eventually. You're numb, your mind's numb. I was desperate to ring my wife, desperate to ring my family but it's very difficult from that distance with the timings and everything else like that.'

The squad sat down for dinner at 7pm and then drowned their sorrows for the remainder of the evening. 'Yes, we went on it – big style,' Reid told me. 'I think we'd had six weeks alcohol-free, if I'm not mistaken. So even the members of the squad who didn't like a drink, because of the way the game went, we all let our hair down. Suffice to say, there were a few sore heads the next morning.'

The players were joined by the management and some of the journalists who had been with them for the whole tournament. Some did not go to bed until well past midnight.

Reid said, 'Looking back, I'm saying to you, "What will be, will be." But, at the time, it was devastating, especially when we knew about the handball. It was something that you needed alcohol to cloud your judgement or your mind.'

According to Martin, 'Part of being a footballer, especially when you're playing in big games like that, is getting over things. Some players get over it quicker than others, some people take longer. I think you all go into your personal way of dealing with disappointment, in your own way. Mine was, get back to the hotel, have a beer with me dad, phone my wife and kids and then think, right okay, let's get back and get on with whatever you've got to get on with. I think we'd have gone on holiday. A few of us would have had two weeks' holiday and then we would have been back into pre-season.'

In Monday's newspapers, the headline writers for the tabloids did not hold back in their condemnation of Argentina's match-winner. 'Cheat' screamed the back page of the *Daily Mirror* adding that 'Shamed Diego admits it'. Harry Harris misquoted Maradona as saying the first goal was scored 'a little with the hand of Diego and a little with the head of Maradona'. Under the headline 'Gotta Hand it to Diego', *The Sun* claimed that 'Dirty Diego Maradona dumped England out of the World Cup with his hand'. Their front page screamed with the headline 'OUTCHA!', a play on words on 'GOTCHA!' their infamous front page on 4 May 1982, the day after the Royal Navy sunk the *General Belgrano* during the Falklands War. The subheading declared that 'The Argies get their own back on us'.

The *Daily Mail*'s back page declared 'Hand it to Diego, England KO'd by the punch that mattered'. In his match report, Jeff Powell pointed the blame for defeat towards the mistakes made by Bobby Robson in his team selection: 'The folly of recalling Terry Fenwick promptly after his suspension in place of Alvin Martin was revealed as early as his ninth minute booking for a rash lunge at Maradona. It is doubtful if Peter Reid was truly fit to take part in such a momentous occasion either.'

The *Daily Telegraph* posted a small leader under photographs of the soon-to-be-married Prince Andrew and Miss Sarah

Ferguson enjoying an air race on the Isle of Wight. 'Argentina ends England's dream'.

The Times said 'England sent tumbling out by Maradona', adding in a side piece that 'Robson pays a heavy price for his timid tactics'. Correspondent David Miller felt that 'as an argument that, but for Maradona's first goal, England might otherwise be in the semi-final, the controversy holds little substance. On the run of the game, there was no doubt that the right team won. England must question not so much Maradona's fortuitous goal as their own tactical approach.'

Italy's *La Gazzetta dello Sport* led with the headline 'Diegoool' under the subheading of 'Maradona enchants the World Cup.' With little sympathy for their fellow Europeans, they went on to say that 'the Napoli ace takes down England and promotes his Argentina. First he invents a goal with his fist, then doubles his score with a fantastic slalom.'

The back page of Argentinian tabloid *Crónica* screamed with the headline 'Maradonazo' and the initials RIP, standing for Reventamos Ingleses Piratas (We Bust the English Pirates) followed by 'Malvinas 2 Ingleses 1'. With pictures of the two Maradona goals they asked under the first 'with the hand? Go complain to Thatcher! The English say there is a hand, we say "he who steals from a thief ..."' Under the picture of the second they said 'and now you see, it's for the Queen who watches it on TV'.

Clarin also revelled in their opponent's misery, claiming 'England's protest was weak because both goals were actually scored with his hand – the first with a victory salute and the second because he sketched it and then signed it, adding the caption "I am the King".' Football periodical *El Gráfico* simply said 'Don't Cry For Me Inglaterra'.

While condemning Maradona for the handball, Sir Alf Ramsey was quick to praise his game-changing ability. Speaking to *The Mirror*, he said, 'The simple fact is that Maradona went in for the ball determined to get some kind of touch. He did, and that separates the good goalscorers from the great ones. I always believed Pelé was the greatest I've ever seen, but now I think Maradona is. Pelé had nearly everything, Maradona has everything. He works harder, he does more and is more skilful than the Brazilian star. The trouble is that he will be remembered for another reason, Maradona bends the rules to suit himself.'

The coach of Argentina when they won the 1978 World Cup, César Luis Menotti, believed the match 'proved that superior technical ability cannot be overcome by strict marking or non-stop running. England resorted to a workmanlike response, the players who are physically fit rather than technically gifted. Footballers who might have given a different kind of answer – such as Wilkins and Barnes – were left on the bench. And, of course, Bryan Robson was never fully fit.

'Argentina imposed their game of precise passes and ball control on an English side which never seemed to be playing football, which, when faced with close tackling, especially by Brown and Ruggeri, left everything to the creativity of Glenn Hoddle, the only English player capable of bringing some order to their game. Argentina won because they played better and were technically superior, showing once again that running and checking is not the answer.'

However, looking back on the game in his *World Cup Diary*, Bobby Robson did not question any of his preparations or team selections during the tournament. 'I examined my decision, my selections, my substitutions, my preparations and everything else that could have contributed to our exit from the World Cup. There was nothing that I would have changed. I still have no doubt at all that we were the best-prepared team in the competition.

'Whatever great players we have, we needed them all fit and in form. You have to give the lads credit. At two goals down, they never lost their determination, never got dispirited and in the last 25 minutes showed tremendous English spirit to be proud of. We went out fighting like blazes.'

Sports Minister Richard Tracey called the result a moral draw. Bookmakers William Hill made the decision to refund punters who had bet on a draw after 90 minutes: 'As far as we are concerned, the result was 1-1,' said spokesperson Graeme Sharp.

The decision would cost them £10,000 as they also paid out to those who had bet on an Argentina victory. 'The refund is very much a one-off gesture to express our anger,' added Sharp. Rivals Ladbrokes and Coral did not follow suit.

The next morning, the England squad departed from the Holiday Inn. Martin told me, 'After the game, we had a choice. We could either stay on to watch the other matches but we all just wanted to get home. We'd had enough by then.'

Manager Bobby Robson stayed on in Mexico, initially travelling to Acapulco for a short break, before returning to Mexico City for the semi-final and final to work as a pundit for ITV.

Watched by a group of local children, Robson shook the hand of each player before they boarded the DINA coach for the short trip back to the airport. The leading goalscorer in the tournament was last up the steps. Robson patted him on the back before looking wistfully away.

The England players walked through the airport carrying their own holdalls. Butcher clutched the boom box they had played on the team bus. The squad got charter flight PA 498 out of Mexico City, stopping in Miami before heading back across the Atlantic. Steven described the mood on the plane: 'I think we all felt fragmented at that point, because we felt hurt as a group of players, that at that level, something like that could happen. After all of the qualifying that we went through, the tough start to the tournament that we endured, the comeback that we delivered, and then to be eliminated by something that was pretty well obvious to 99.9 per cent of people. That was it, and we departed Mexico and then it is all behind us and in the history books.'

Sansom's mother, who had been out in the country for the entire tournament, flew back first class after an unexpected gesture from the FA. Speaking on the 2016 *Hand of God* documentary, Sansom revealed, 'I was very fortunate, my mum she turned up at the airport because she came and watched me and they upgraded her, because she was my mum. She really enjoyed it, she watched every minute of it.'

'My dad was able to fly back with the team on that plane,' Martin tells me. 'That made his journey. He'd seen me play in the World Cup and flew back with us. We're all playing cards, having a drink, waiting to land at Heathrow. We didn't realise, but we got a fantastic reception. It was like a heroes' return.'

The England players landed at Heathrow Airport on the morning of Tuesday, 24 June after a 13-hour flight. After seven weeks on the other side of the Atlantic, they arrived home to what was described as 'a pop star's welcome'.

Teenage girls jostled to get to the country's new sporting hero, the leading marksman at the World Cup, Gary Lineker. A police officer had to push his luggage trolley as he struggled to get through the crowds. One girl wore a T-shirt declaring 'Lineker is ace'.

'The welcome is absolutely marvellous,' said Lineker. 'I am stunned and amazed that so many people got up so early in the morning to meet us.' Martin was delighted that his father got to witness the reception the team received: 'He was a part of all that. From a personal point of view, it was one of the happiest memories I had playing football.'

'It was a very emotional reunion,' said Hoddle, who was met at Heathrow by his wife and six-month old daughter Zara. He initially did not recognise the baby girl handed to him. After not seeing her for almost two months, Hoddle remarked, 'I couldn't believe how much she had changed.' Yet, Hoddle, despite forgiving Maradona, could not escape the feeling of being cheated out of the World Cup. In his 1987 autobiography, *Spurred to Success*, he admitted that 'the Diego Maradona handball incident played on my mind to such an extent that I would sit at home, trying to relax by watching television, and find I simply couldn't concentrate no matter what the programme'.

Twelve years later, Hoddle was managing England as they once more went out of the World Cup to Argentina. That defeat fell heavily on David Beckham, who was controversially sent off during the game. Hoddle's post-match comments, labelling his actions as 'foolish', were manipulated into media headlines that singled out Beckham for blame.

In 1986, Hoddle may have empathised with some of what Beckham experienced in 1998. 'The phone was going non-stop with journalists wanting me to relive that goal. Relive it … I couldn't stop thinking about it. I was even dreaming about it, although it was more of a recurring nightmare than a dream. For the first time in my football career I didn't want to talk about an incident in a game, not even to members of my family. I never felt like that before, normally I love to talk about football. The pressure began to build-up, become almost unbearable. I felt claustrophobic.'

In 1998, Beckham escaped the vilification he received by immediately leaving England, to spend time with his wife in New York. Similarly, Hoddle felt the only way he could protect his mental health was to escape the country, hastily booking a holiday away with his wife in Spain. There, he was able to relax and even found time on the following Sunday to watch the World Cup Final between Argentina and West Germany. He and friends watched the game in a German restaurant. As the West Germans succeeded where England failed in coming back from two goals down, Hoddle suddenly found his interest piqued. 'I wanted Argentina to win.' Moments later, Argentina regained the lead. 'Despite being surrounded by Germans, my mate and I got completely carried away and jumping up shouting, "Yes, get in there!"' With the entire restaurant glaring at them, Hoddle's party made a swift exit.

Five weeks after their defeat to Argentina, UNICEF organised a charity match at the Rose Bowl in Pasadena between a team from the Americas and a Rest of the World XI. The winner of the Golden Boot at the World Cup, Gary Lineker, was not released to travel to California by his new club FC Barcelona. Therefore, the only English representative was Ipswich Town's Terry Butcher, called up as a late replacement when others pulled out just five days before the game.

There, he would once more came face to face with the captain of the Americas team, Diego Maradona.

Travelling from the UK, Butcher hung out with the other British players selected for the team, Scotland's Gordon Strachan and Northern Ireland's Pat Jennings, during their stay in Los Angeles. Maradona, now the most famous footballer in the world, flew in the night before on a private jet directly from a post-World Cup holiday in Tahiti.

The Americas team also included Argentina's Nery Pumpido and José Luis Brown, and was coached by World Cup-winning manager Carlos Bilardo. After a quarter of an hour, Butcher had the satisfaction of heading a Strachan free kick past Pumpido to give the Rest of the World XI the lead. Such was Butcher's confidence that he later attempted to volley the ball past Pumpido from his own half after the goalkeeper rushed out of his goal to clear the ball.

Having not trained with his team-mates, Maradona struggled to dictate the game, showing only sporadic flashes of his touch and vision. Nonetheless, he once more had the better of Butcher in one-on-ones, turning him so adroitly at one point by knocking the ball one side of him and running around the other, that the defender fell in a heap. For the most part, Butcher acquitted himself well alongside West German sweeper Uli Stielike.

Early in the second half, Paolo Rossi, who Butcher recalls concealing packs of cigarettes under his rolled-up shirt sleeves, turned back the clock to his 1982 heyday. He doubled the Rest of the World's lead with a stunning volley on the counter-attack. This meant, even after Paraguayan Roberto Cabañas reduced the deficit with less than ten minutes remaining, it looked like Butcher might finally overcome the Argentines who ended his World Cup dream a month earlier.

Yet two minutes from the end, Maradona instigated a sharp passing movement, playing successive one-twos around the edge of the box, the second bypassing Butcher. As goalkeeper Rinat Dasayev parried Cabañas's shot, Butcher had turned to track a familiar foe into the six-yard box, but, as it had been five weeks earlier in Mexico City, his desperate last-ditch lunge was too late to prevent Maradona's left foot scoring a decisive goal.

The match, played in front of 57,539 spectators, went straight to penalties. Despite missing first, the Americas won the shoot-out. As if pre-scripted, Maradona stepped up to slot home the winning kick and Butcher was left cursing him again.

Butcher recalled that the players were invited to a Hollywood party after the game, where legendary actor, and UNICEF ambassador, Danny Kaye wore brown loafers that curled up at the toe: 'You think of the genie and all that sort of thing. All I can remember thinking, what the hell were they?!'

The Seven Million Pound Shirt

As the virtual hammer slammed down on the auction of the shirt Diego Maradona wore when he scored perhaps the two most famous goals in World Cup history, a group of Argentines came into the reception area of Sotheby's with one visibly in tears.

Marcelo Ordás describes himself as a 'football archaeologist', travelling the world and recovering lost relics from the game.[37] He has put them all together in one of the most stunning and valuable collections of football shirts in the world at his Legends museum at Puerta del Sol in the centre of Madrid.

It all began at the 1990 World Cup. Then aged 17 he was a student in Italy watching the champions attempt to defend their world title.

He was at the Stadio delle Alpi when a struggling Argentina were expected to be put out of their misery by their bitter rivals from Brazil.

A rampant Brazil battered the holders but wasted chance after chance. Taunted by the Brazilian fans around him, Ordás sat, head in his hands, awaiting the inevitable knockout blow. Then Maradona, hampered by a swollen ankle, turned back the clock to

---

37 https://www.theguardian.com/football/2023/nov/05/footballs-memory-keeper-the-man-with-more-than-5000-shirts

1986, dribbling past three defenders and miraculously creating an opportunity that Claudio Caniggia accepted.

Ordás raced forward and climbed up the perimeter fencing that separated the two sets of supporters, roaring at the Brazilian fans who had goaded him. In his euphoria, he fainted. He awoke to find himself in the stadium infirmary, having been taken there by his father and a friend.

His dad was an acquaintance of the head of the Argentinian federation, and shortly afterwards Ordás was invited to visit the Argentina dressing room. There he was met by the sight of the celebrating players, led by Maradona wearing the Brazilian shirt he had swapped with his Napoli team-mate Alemâo.

Ordás was introduced to Caniggia, who was informed that his goal had caused the spectator to faint. After inquiring about Ordás's health, the striker was given a big hug by the teenager, who told him how happy his late winner had made the entire country. Touched by the sentiment, Caniggia handed Ordás his shirt from the game.

Since then, Ordás has travelled the world recovering other match-worn shirts and memorabilia. Early in 2022, he approached Steve Hodge and offered him £400,000 for his Argentina shirt, four times what he had paid for any other shirt in his collection. Hodge told him it was not for sale due to its sentimental value. A month later he put it up for auction at Sotheby's with a reserve of £4 million.

Maradona's daughter Dalma went to the press to claim that the shirt Hodge had been given was the one her father had worn in the first half, not the second when he scored the two celebrated goals. Maradona had told her, 'How am I going to give him the shirt of my life?' She claimed the second-half shirt had been kept in the family. Her mother, Maradona's ex-wife Claudia Villafañe, was spotted wearing it at a match in 2009, and her nephew Benjamin, the son of Sergio Agüero and her sister Giannina, was pictured wearing it as a young boy in 2015.

However, Sotheby's were adamant that Hodge had possession of the actual shirt Maradona wore in the second half. They enlisted the services of Resolution Photomatching, specialists in the provenance of sports memorabilia. They discovered a series of discrepancies between the two shirts, which were, after all, hastily hand-stitched by the Club América seamstresses rather than the result of industrial mass production. The badge on Maradona's first-half shirt had a clear imperfection in the black stitching on the bottom left corner. This seems to the one worn by Vilafañe and kept in the Maradona family.

The badge on the shirt worn by Maradona in the second half did not have the same black stitching but was unique in its own way. The top-left and top-right corners revealed yellow threads, which were matched to the shirt owned by Hodge. The badge was also slightly askew, tilted to the right as compared with the first-half shirt.

Finally, the numbers on the back were in slightly different places. On the second-half shirt, the right edge of the '0' was aligned to the dark stripe of the shirt. On the first-half shirt, the edge came over the lighter blue stripe. Each time, the photomatching analysis proved that the shirt auctioned by Sotheby's was the one in which Maradona had scored his two never-to-be-forgotten goals.

In Argentina, Maradona's shirt was seen as their Excalibur sword, with comparisons made between it and the curved sabre used by José de San Martín, the general credited with liberating the nation from Spanish rule.

Speaking to *Infobae*, Ordás said, 'It's part of our genetics as Argentinians: never giving up on anything until the last minute. We understand, in an analogical way, that this is San Martín's sabre from the 20th century and that it belongs at home.'

Determined to reunite this sporting relic with Argentina, Ordás put together a syndicate of 30 businessmen to meet the reserve price. 'There's an Argentinian here honouring history, and there were also many people who called me to tell me to count on them. It's not a matter of a collector simply wanting to take credit to put it in a closet. We agreed that, if we take this relic, it will be in the best possible place for all Argentinians to see forever.'

One member of the syndicate told *The Sun*: 'Hodge is selling something that belongs to Maradona and the AFA without authorisation. It should be in Argentina in order for all Argentinians to enjoy it – and not for a millionaire to display it in his closet.'

Ordás travelled to London on the day the auction ended, fully expecting to be able to take Maradona's shirt back home with him. He was prepared to spend over £6 million ($7.5 million). Yet, he was outbid. Seventeen seconds before the virtual hammer went down, an anonymous buyer paid over £7.1 million for the shirt. Speaking to Radio Metro afterwards, Ordás admitted, 'I thought we'd won it because there are so many people behind me who joined this crusade. The dream was to bring it home, to bring it to Argentina. It's sad not to be able to bring it home to share with all Argentinians. On the other side, there were people from the Middle East with much greater financial resources, not with the historical and passionate resources we have.'

Later that year, the shirt was loaned to the Qatar Sports Museum, where it was displayed ahead of the 2022 FIFA World Cup. Ordás told *The Guardian*: 'He had it on display in this dreadful place on a wooden mannequin; it was awful, horrible.'

Eight years earlier, Hodge had called his former Nottingham Forest team-mate, Viv Anderson. Hodge told him that he was looking to sell the Maradona shirt to raise some money for his retirement. He said he wanted £150,000. At the time, the most a match-worn shirt had gone for at auction was £157,750. The Italian defender Roberto Rosetti had sold the shirt he had swapped with Pelé at the end of the 1970 World Cup Final, also played at the Estadio Azteca in Mexico City. The shirt was auctioned by Christie's in March 2002. It was the first six-figure sum for a match-worn jersey.

The Maradona shirt had been in Hodge's attic for over 15 years since the 1986 World Cup, along with other memorabilia from his career. The news of the Christie's auction prompted Hodge to believe his shirt was worth at least as much. It made an appearance on Sky's weekly football magazine show *Soccer AM*, brought out on to the set by the show's 'stereotypical resident of Manchester' to the sounds of 'Step On' by The Happy Mondays.

Producer Robbie Knox revealed in 2022 that Hodge had brought the shirt to the studio in a plastic bag. James Long, aka Rocket, tried the shirt on backstage and it was handled during the programme by presenter Tim Lovejoy and various guests. Hodge said, 'I want to keep it, I'd never let go of it.' Helen Chamberlain flippantly asked, 'Do you think Maradona has ever sat on Argentinian TV, showing off his Steve Hodge shirt?'

In June 2002, Hodge took the shirt, now transported in a hardened suitcase, on to *Johnny Vaughan's World Cup Extra* show, alongside fellow guests Jimmy Greaves and Frankie Dettori. Hodge revealed that he had turned down offers for the shirt of £4,000 in 1998 and £70,000 a few months ago.

Encouraged by Vaughan, Dettori asked to try the shirt on over his own live on air. Hodge was visibly reluctant to hand it over. He later admitted, 'When I realised that he was actually going to pull it over his head it was more than the studio lights that were making me sweat! I was worried that he might rip it and I don't think he realised how old it was.' The diminutive Italian jockey, an inch shorter than Maradona, luckily had no trouble slipping on the most valuable football shirt in the world.

Hodge then decided to get it valued and keep it stored in a bank vault. Anderson advised him to get it out of there, telling him it would deteriorate in storage. Unable to find anyone who would insure it, Hodge eventually loaned it to the new National Football Museum in Preston, which moved in 2012 to Manchester. They put it on display there and insured it for Hodge.

In 2014, Hodge asked Anderson if he knew anyone who would be interested in buying the shirt off him. Then in Singapore as part of an event for a company called Play on Pro, Anderson asked around. William Hill, one of the owners of Play on Pro, wanted to know how much Hodge wanted for it. Anderson inquired, and Hodge said £150,000.

The next morning Hill asked Anderson to offer Hodge £125,000. Hodge declined: 'It's part of my pension and, to look after my kids, I want £150,000.' Anderson went back to Hill to see whether he would up his offer. He pulled out: 'Nah, it's too much for me.' Eight years later it would sell for almost 50 times as much.

Anderson tells me he does not believe that his associate would have sold the shirt. 'I think he would have kept it. He's got a lot of British memorabilia, I know he's got a lot of Manchester United memorabilia, so he would have kept it, I would have thought.'

England's captain, Peter Shilton, sold his grey goalkeeper shirt from the same match to a private collector who wishes to remain anonymous. It was featured in the 2022 coffee-table book *Three Lions on a Shirt: The Official History of the England Football Jersey*. In July 2025, the shirt was put up for sale through BUDDS Auctions among a collection of other World Cup memorabilia. I went to see it at the headquarters of the auction house in Northampton. It will be auctioned just before the 2026 FIFA World Cup, to coincide with the 40th anniversary of the Hand of God match.

Shilton's shirt would have held no special value had he merely been the goalkeeper Maradona went past on the way to scoring the Goal of the Century. Instead, the image of him jumping forlornly against Maradona for the Hand of God goal is forever seared on our consciousness. The shirt worn in that unique moment of sporting history had a reserve placed upon it of between £200,000 and £300,000.

What Happened Next for the Boys of '86

Aged 36, Peter Shilton was the fifth-oldest player at the 1986 World Cup. Yet, inspired by Pat Jennings who played against Brazil on his 41st birthday, Shilton was in no mood to step down ahead of the next World Cup in Italy. He continued to be one of his country's most important players, with his performance away to Poland in a vital World Cup qualifier in October 1989 critical in enabling England to reach the tournament. He was still regarded as the world's finest goalkeeper by the end of the 1990 World Cup, after which he retired, having earned a then-world record 125 international caps.

To this day, no goalkeeper has ever kept more clean sheets in World Cup finals matches than Shilton (ten). Three of those helped England surpass their 1986 showing by finishing fourth at the 1990 World Cup. Yet, in retirement, his failure to beat Maradona to the ball in the 51st minute of the 1986 quarter-finals has come to define him, becoming more important to his legacy than a 31-year career laced with significant achievements.

Even in a football world renowned for the merciless mocking between team-mates over misfortunes, the Hand of God was one incident never joked about on future England camps. Peter Reid told me, 'It's one of them where you didn't mention it. I never, ever brought it up with him, and I've seen him on numerous occasions and socially. It's a no-go area.'

Gary Michael Stevens would also continue to be first choice for England until the 1990 World Cup. Yet there, after a poor team performance against the Republic of Ireland, he was replaced when Paul Parker, nominally a central defender, came in to play right wing-back as Bobby Robson deployed a sweeper system for the first time in eight years as England manager. Stevens nevertheless returned to play in the Third Place Play-Off, with Parker moving to centre-back. He continued to start games for another two years, even earning a place in the Euro '92 squad after Lee Dixon was ruled out, only to suffer a pre-tournament injury himself that ended his international career.

Since losing his son Jack at the age of four to leukaemia in 2021, Stevens has become a vocal campaigner for greater stem cell donation in Australia. Together with wife Louise, the Stevens' work led to a change in the law, making it easier for potential donors to volunteer. The Forever Four charity was set up in Jack's honour to continue to raise awareness of the new process and offer support for families affected by blood cancer.

For his part in the 1986 World Cup quarter-final, Stevens has been immortalised in a four-piece Argentinian stamp commemorating Maradona's Goal of the Century. The England right-back appears in the top-right of the set in a 75 centavo stamp of his own, which he has framed at his house in Perth, Australia. 'I used to collect stamps when I was a kid,' he told me. 'To now know I'm on an international stamp – an Argentinian stamp – that's almost my claim to fame. I don't know anyone else, apart from the Queen, who's on a stamp. I dine out on that story!'

Having played every minute of every England game in 1986, the match against Argentina would be the final World Cup appearance for Kenny Sansom. 'The World Cup that, in my opinion, we could have easily gone on to win. That should have been our year, our glory.'

The Arsenal full-back started a remarkable 37 consecutive matches for his country between 1984 and 1987, but in the 38th a debut was given to the Nottingham Forest left-back Stuart Pearce.

Sansom returned to play every game at the 1988 European Championships but there, his Steve Hodge-like loft into his own penalty area precipitated the confusion from which Ray Houghton scored the winning goal in the opening match against the Republic of Ireland. Approaching the age of 30, he was not selected again by Robson following the tournament. He then put his faith in Pearce for the World Cup qualifiers. No one represented England more times during the 1980s than Kenny Sansom.

After being overlooked for the Argentina match, Bobby Robson selected Alvin Martin to play alongside Terry Butcher in England's first post-World Cup match, against Sweden in Stockholm. Missing World Cup goalscorers Gary Lineker and Peter Beardsley, England lost 1-0, and Martin was never selected to represent his country again.

He told me he has kept his match shirts and a suit with a Three Lions badge on the breast pocket, which he wore to a dinner in London that the squad was invited to by the FA. They are items he still treasures to this day: 'My overriding feeling is that I was part of a World Cup in 1986 that everybody remembers. Every World Cup is massive. It's hard to explain how big they are. The 1986 one will always be remembered for right and wrong reasons, now it's part of history. I was part of something that happened that will always be remembered. I played a game in the World Cup. Many players go to World Cups and don't play a game. My dad had seen me play at the stadium in a World Cup game.'

Terry Fenwick was injured for the Sweden game and never started another game for England after the Argentina match. Despite playing in three sides managed by future England manager Terry Venables, Fenwick only made a single appearance as substitute for his nation after the 1986 World Cup, playing 16 minutes in an underwhelming 0-0 draw away to Israel in 1988. The return of Mark Wright and the emergence of Arsenal's Tony Adams pushed Fenwick out of the squad by the time England went to the European Championships that summer.

Speaking to Talksport after Maradona died in 2020, he admitted the defeat left him feeling 'bitter and twisted' for many years. He told me he feels as though the public and media held him responsible for the defeat. 'I think so, because of the way I let him get past me. I went through a few tough years where I was to blame for that goal. I've kicked myself a few times. I wondered whether it would have been easier if I'd gone man-to-man with him from the first kick of the ball. I thought one of my biggest talents was I read the game, I read it very well. More often than not, I'd get in front of players, I'd intercept that ball, I didn't have to be making that big tackle all of the time.'

Fenwick has lived in Trinidad for the past quarter of a century, setting up the Football Factory Foundation for young children in the country after coaching San Juan Jabloteh to four national league titles. That managerial experience has given him fresh insight into how England approached the game: 'When you are playing in a back four unit and you're not just marking a player but you're looking after space as well as that, it can be quite difficult. Which is how he scored the great goal that he scored.'

Also missing from that tournament in 1988 was Terry Butcher, but his absence was enforced due to a broken leg sustained playing for his new club Glasgow Rangers. Often unfairly maligned during his international career as slow and immobile, Butcher's importance was magnified as England conceded seven goals during three calamitous defeats at the European Championships.

Re-established in the side for the 1990 World Cup qualifiers alongside a new defensive partner, Nottingham Forest's Des Walker, the pair were the cornerstone of a defence that remarkably qualified for the tournament without conceding a single goal.

At the World Cup, Butcher was handed the captain's armband when Bryan Robson had to once more leave the tournament early due to injury. Yet, concerns over the England defence's ability at the highest level led to Bobby Robson introducing Mark Wright as a third centre-back in between Butcher and Walker. Four years after first hoping they would play together at a major tournament, Robson finally had both Wright and Butcher in the same team.

England, abetted by huge slices of luck against Belgium and Cameroon, excelled, finally reaching their first World Cup semi-final on foreign soil. Butcher captained England on his 90th and final appearance, against West Germany, during which time he had been the beating heart of the national team's defence in three successive World Cups.

Only a penalty shoot-out denied Butcher the opportunity of leading England out against Argentina in the 1990 World Cup Final alongside the man who had lied to him about the handball in Mexico City.

Eighteen years later, Butcher was the assistant manager of Scotland facing an Argentina team coached by Diego Maradona. The build-up was dominated by the question of whether the two would shake hands. Maradona was unperturbed: 'I'm not going to lose any sleep over it. If he doesn't shake my hand, I'm still going to be alive tomorrow.' Asked after the game if Butcher had congratulated him on Argentina's 1-0 win, a smiling Maradona replied, 'I greeted the Scotland manager [George Burley] after the game. Who is Butcher?'

Aged 22, Trevor Steven was the youngest player starting on the pitch when England faced Argentina. Having come in for Chris Waddle against Poland, the two would continue to battle for the right-wing position for the next few years. Waddle began in that position at the 1988 European Championships but Steven again replaced him as a starter in the other two games. The emergence of Arsenal's David Rocastle added a third right-winger into the equation and he seemed to have edged Steven out of the squad ahead of the 1990 World Cup until an untimely knee injury allowed Steven another opportunity.

Despite playing just twice in two seasons, Bobby Robson ultimately plumped for Steven's greater experience and versatility, dropping a fit-again Rocastle in his final cut. With Waddle now the undisputed first choice, it took the threat of another quarter-final elimination for Robson to call Steven off the bench as a substitute for captain Butcher. As an emergency right-back to cover Wright, who had suffered a head wound, Steven defended heroically as England turned the game around to win after extra time. He played the same role with England trailing to West Germany in the semi-finals. After Waddle skied the decisive penalty in the ensuing shoot-out, Steven started the Third Place Play-Off against Italy ahead of him, his sixth World Cup finals match.

Late injuries ensured that Steven also made the squad for the 1992 European Championships, and this time he started the first two games, only to be replaced for the third group match against hosts Sweden by the more dynamic Tony Daley. England lost, and Steven never played for them again, his international career ending at the age of 28.

While living in Dubai, three decades after the 1986 World Cup, Steven took his teenage daughter, Ava, to play in a women's league match one evening. On the far side of an open field, surrounded by his entourage, was Diego Maradona, watching his girlfriend, Rocío Oliva, play for the opposition team, who were wearing Argentina colours.

Steven had the family dog with him and contemplated going around to introduce himself. 'I did walk around, but I walked on past him as he was watching his girlfriend. It was just a moment, it was bizarre. On a field in the Middle East, my daughter playing against his girlfriend, but I didn't say hello, that's typical me!'

After playing every minute for England at his third major tournament, it appeared the time was right for Glenn Hoddle to finally take centre stage for his country. He continued to start in central midfield even after the eventual return of captain Bryan Robson from injury. The pair played together in a stunning 4-2 win away to Spain at the Estadio Santiago Bernabéu in February 1987.

However, during the 1986 World Cup, Hoddle had made the decision to leave Tottenham Hotspur, informing David Pleat of his intention to play abroad. Convinced by the incoming Spurs manager to stay for one more year, Hoddle eventually signed for AS Monaco the following summer.

Despite starting the first England game of the 1987/88 season away to West Germany, he was replaced during a chastening 3-1 defeat by debutant Neil Webb, the man who went down in history as the 1,000th man to represent the England senior team. Webb soon replaced Hoddle as Bobby Robson's preferred starter in central midfield alongside Bryan Robson, the manager favouring the Nottingham Forest midfielder's box-to-box athleticism.

Hoddle was only recalled to the starting line-up following the crisis that resulted after England's European Championship defeat to the Republic of Ireland. With Hoddle and Robson starting together, England lost again, 3-1 to a rampant Dutch team featuring Ruud Gullit and Marco van Basten, the men challenging Maradona's supremacy in Serie A.

Already out of the tournament, Hoddle started the final group match against the Soviet Union in a five-man midfield, but within three minutes he was caught in possession by Sergei Aleinikov, who scored the opening goal in another 3-1 defeat. Hoddle's international career ended that day. In spite of shining with AS Monaco for another two seasons, he was never selected by Bobby Robson again.

Apart from Shilton, Peter Reid was the only England player above 30 years of age who started against Argentina. Surgery on the trapped nerve he played with during the World Cup meant he missed the majority of the following season, returning to start only two more England games, against Brazil and West Germany in 1987.

He was included in the squad for the 1988 European Championships but did not even make it on to the substitutes' bench. His place as the midfield enforcer from Merseyside was taken by Liverpool's Steve McMahon, who went to the 1990 World Cup wearing the same No.16 shirt.

Like Shilton on the Hand of God goal, Reid's glittering career will always be overshadowed by the single moment in which he failed to stop Maradona going past him for the second goal. He admitted to me, 'Listen, I won things as a player, I was PFA Player of the Year, LMA Manager of the Year, and all I get is Diego – everywhere I go. I wish I had a pound for every time it's mentioned because it would beat the £7.1 million that Steve Hodge got for the shirt. So, yeah, that's a cross I have to bear.' Reid keeps his match shirt from the Argentina match on display at his home. It is framed and has been signed by the rest of the squad.

Steve Hodge had been one of the revelations of the tournament for England and, at the age of 23, seemed set for a long future in the national team. However, in extremis, Bobby Robson had found a better option on the left wing, with John Barnes's late cameo ensuring he would be the man who eventually replaced Hodge in the starting line-up.

Robson kept faith in Hodge for most of the next season, with Barnes starting only two games. The next summer, Barnes signed for Liverpool and his ability to consistently perform at the highest level became undeniable. He started every game he was fit to play in for the rest of Robson's tenure.

Hodge was omitted from the squad to go to the 1988 European Championships but fought his way back into the reckoning after re-signing for Brian Clough's Nottingham Forest. He earned a place in the 1990 World Cup squad but injury prevented him from playing a single minute at the tournament. His final appearance for England came at the age of 28 in 1991.

Barnes would never recreate the impact he made in those final 16 minutes at the Azteca Stadium at another major international tournament. Caught between being the winger who made those two chances for Lineker and the marauding free spirit who became by far the best player in the English league, Barnes could never live up to other people's expectations of him while wearing the Three Lions on his chest.

After finishing as the top goalscorer in England in all competitions, ahead of Lineker, at the end of the 1989/90 season,

Barnes went to the 1990 World Cup spoken of as someone capable of making a similar impact to Maradona in Mexico. However, just as he became liberated from the rigours of the 4-4-2 system, Barnes injured his groin against Belgium and was unable to complete the tournament. It was Waddle who played as if freed from the shackles, and a new star, the more bombastic Paul Gascoigne, who assumed the lead role as England's creative playmaker.

The 25-year-old Waddle, winning his 20th cap against Argentina, felt that the 1986 World Cup was just the start for him at international level: 'For me, it was my first World Cup, I only got capped in 1985. I didn't have a lot of caps going into the World Cup. To go to Mexico was probably ahead of schedule, I'll be perfectly honest.'

Four years later, Waddle would shine at Italia '90, emancipated by the move to a sweeper system and now playing, as Maradona had predicted, in Europe, having joined Olympique Marseille in 1989. In the 1990 quarter-final, England were largely outplayed by Cameroon, only going through this time due to two Gary Lineker penalties.

Looking back on the 1986 tournament, Waddle told me that he believed the only difference between the two World Cup teams he played in was luck: 'Obviously I did some things right [in 1986]. It was any footballer's dream to represent your country in a World Cup, and we had a great squad, by the way. Everyone talks about 1990 being brilliant, 86 was as good as 90, I'll tell you that now. If it hadn't have been for the brilliance of Maradona – and you've got to be perfectly honest – the cheating of Maradona, we probably could have gone to the semis or the final again.'

After being named as one of the substitutes for the match in Mexico City, the 24-year-old Gary Andrew Stevens was never selected to play for England again. Had Peter Reid not declared himself fit to play against Argentina, Stevens may have been the one closest to Maradona throughout the 1986 World Cup quarter-final. It is the sliding-doors moment of his career.

Speaking to the *Three Lions* podcast in 2019, Stevens wistfully said, 'I can't help looking back and thinking, if I had been given that job – because at the time there was no doubt about it, I was super, super-fit – it just might have made me … But it could have absolutely wrecked me, football-wise and psychologically.'[38]

Few emerged with more credit from the 1986 World Cup than Peter Beardsley. After edging out Trevor Francis in the final cut as a back-up for Gary Lineker, Beardsley excelled alongside him and established the partnership through which both players would become world-renowned.

Beardsley would miss just a handful of the next 50 England games over the next four years. After joining Liverpool from Newcastle the following summer, his exhilarating club form alongside John Barnes made the pair the English league's most consistent performers. The deep-lying Beardsley was seen for years as the perfect foil for Lineker, providing the direct assist for seven of his goals.

Yet, while Lineker scored 25 goals for England in that period, Beardsley found the net just five times and never again at a major tournament. Speaking on the *Aldo Meets* podcast in 2024, Beardsley joked about Lineker, 'He was perfect for me because even if I didn't make any goals for him, everybody thought that I did, so it kept me in the team!'[39]

When Bobby Robson moved to the sweeper system during the 1990 World Cup, it was Beardsley who was dropped to make way for the extra defender in a more fluid system. After a groin injury ended Barnes's tournament, Beardsley came back in to start the World Cup semi-final against West Germany, once more alongside Lineker.

Thereafter, new England manager Graham Taylor saw him as part of the past rather than the future, starting him just twice during his stewardship despite the fact that Beardsley was becoming a more prolific goalscorer at, first, Everton, then Newcastle United. In 1994,

---

38   https://threelionspodcast.com/gary-stevens-in-conversation
39   https://www.youtube.com/watch?si=XsZBmhvmChfbO7kR&v=_
     pieVLPOZFs&feature=youtu.be

Terry Venables recalled Beardsley after an absence of three years to reprise his role as a second striker behind the man who had replaced Lineker in the goalscoring role, Alan Shearer.

Yet, in the end, the now 35-year-old Beardsley was not included in the England squad for the 1996 European Championships as Venables opted for the similar skills of Teddy Sheringham, just five years his junior, in the same deep-lying position.

Nonetheless, Beardsley's appearance against China PR in Beijing means he was the last of the 1986 World Cup squad to represent his country, a month shy of a decade after the Argentina match in Mexico City.

No England player's life was changed more by the 1986 World Cup than their centre-forward. Gary Lineker finished as the outright top goalscorer in the World Cup. He was to remain as his country's first-choice striker for the next six years.

His goals in Mexico even earned him a place on the *World Cup Grandstand* panel a week later for the 1986 final between Argentina and West Germany. Sitting alongside Des Lynam, the man he would eventually replace as BBC Sport's main football presenter, the softly spoken Lineker displayed glimpses of the modest manner and deadpan wit that would make him the most recognisable presence in English sport to this day.

Television was for the future. In 1986, Lineker was at the height of his powers. The move to FC Barcelona was finalised, and he scored 21 league goals in his first season, including a hat-trick at Camp Nou against arch-rivals Real Madrid, displaying once more his propensity for performing on the biggest of occasions.

He remained untouchable as England's first-choice striker until his retirement from international football in 1992, scoring another 36 goals. Four of those came at the next World Cup in Italy, which made him the country's all-time record goalscorer at the finals with ten goals in just 12 matches.

Harry Kane, who matched Lineker as a Golden Boot winner in 2018 with six goals (albeit three of them penalties) may yet surpass him at his third World Cup in 2026, having currently scored eight times in 12 games. Behind Kane, Wayne Rooney and Bobby Charlton, Lineker remains the fourth-highest goalscorer of all time for the England men's team.

Three days after scoring twice against England, Diego Maradona proved it was no fluke by doing it again against Belgium in the semi-finals. When the two teams went in at half-time with the scores tied, Argentina's head coach Carlos Bilardo told his players to pretend they were playing England again.

Maradona said, 'We went out saying, "They're English, they're English."' It worked. Maradona again scored two second-half goals to win the game. The first, once more in the 51st minute, an opportunistic flick of a ball for which the goalkeeper was favourite to win, followed by another mesmerising dribble through a packed defence.

With Michel Platini's France surprisingly eliminated by West Germany in the other semi-final earlier that day, the world was denied the ultimate final showdown between the two outstanding players of a generation. The stage was instead set for Maradona to lift the World Cup at the same venue in which Pelé, 16 years earlier, had cemented his international legacy. Man-marked by Lothar Matthäus, Maradona was not allowed to hit the heights of performance he had reached in the earlier games but still shone brightly enough to make the match-winning goal for Jorge Burruchaga with an outstanding first-time pass.

Maradona insisted he was a fitter and better player by the time of the 1990 World Cup in Italy. Playing in his adopted home at the age of 29, a more experienced Maradona was hampered by a persistent ankle injury and Argentina stuttered through the championship. Nonetheless, through a combination of doggedness and good fortune, they reached a second successive World Cup Final against West Germany. Diego Maradona thus became the first man in history to lead a nation in the final of two World Cups.

Had Argentina won in Rome, as captain of the team, Maradona would have achieved something unprecedented in the sport. Yet, the match ended in defeat and acrimony and Maradona never got as close to the trophy again.

It would also be the last time Argentina reached the final for 24 years, despite having, on paper, much better teams in the interim than the ones Maradona played in. Like England over the same period, the quarter-final stage was the step they could not surmount.

The glow of the 1986 World Cup triumph thus grew brighter with each passing failure. The status of Maradona as a world champion was something that even the great Lionel Messi, for all his club achievements, could not attain while Maradona lived.

In November 2020, just 25 days after his 60th birthday, Diego Maradona died. The complications and controversies of his later life were put aside as the world remembered a talent so great it overcame abject poverty and brutal marking to reach the pinnacle of sporting achievement.

Nowhere was that ability demonstrated better than on Sunday, 22 June 1986, the day that Diego Maradona transcended the mortal plain and, in the unique set of circumstances surrounding this particular game of football, became a symbol of something to everyone – a cheat, a genius, an avenger, a saviour. No other match in history has represented one man more than this one.

From all the games he commentated on during a 58-year career in football, Barry Davies said to me, 'I think it does stand out. Maybe the historical relationship of the two countries was a factor in it, but Maradona was so much the best player in the world. It was really a very special, special match.'

Michael Calvin told me, 'I do think it was predestined that Maradona would win. The occasion almost gave you an insight into where his life would probably end up going. Like most of the journalists, we were fascinated by Maradona, as much for his faults as for his genius. There was almost a life foretold I think.'

Speaking to *France Football*, Gary Lineker agreed: 'There is a degree of truth in saying that this was the game of his life, in so many ways, I suppose. The game that defined his life, except that he ended up winning that game, and it doesn't show the downside of his existence. But what you get in that game is the cheekiness, the impish nature of the first goal, and the absolute genius of the second.'

Whatever you might think of Diego Armando Maradona – if you choose to judge him by his achievements or addictions, his infamy or his infidelity, his football or his foibles – the truth is he has indelibly etched his name in the sporting psyche due to his actions in the course of 230 seconds on a football pitch in Mexico City. For that reason alone, the 1986 World Cup quarter-final between Argentina and England will live forever.

As Maradona said himself in 2016, 'People told their children about it and those children will tell their children. Because 30 years have already gone by. Thirty years. And they keep on telling the story.'

With Special Thanks To ...

Players

Clive Allen, Viv Anderson, Gary Bailey, John Barnes, Terry Butcher, Stan Collymore, Micky Hazard, Alvin Martin, Peter Reid, Bryan Robson, Vinny Samways, Lianne Sanderson, Kenny Sansom, Trevor Steven, Gary Andrew Stevens, Gary Michael Stevens, Chris Waddle, Chris Woods

Commentators/Journalists

Ian Abrahams, Philippe Auclair, Patrick Barclay, Alison Bender, Carrie Brown, Michael Calvin. Barry Davies, Rex Gowar, Samindra Kunti, Michael Lewis, Paul McCarthy, Gary Newbon, Christian Radnedge, Keir Radnedge, Jim Rosenthal, Chris Slegg, Anton Toloui, Martin Tyler, Barry Wilner

Filmmakers/Photographers

Drummond Challis, Eddie Keogh, Steve Powell, Peter Robinson, Juha Tamminen, Bob Thomas

Referees

Ali Bin Nasser, Abraham Klein, Alan Snoddy

Supporters

Paddy Buckley, Joe O'Connell, Jono Vernon-Powell, Mark Woodroffe

Others

Pablo Ardiles, Daren Burney, Dave Cockram, Lisa Gibson, Jon Holmes, Glen Kirton, Giovanni Marti, Will Shand, Guido Tognoni, Darragh Toolan, Rick Wakeman, Evan Wilner

Bibliography

BBC Sport
British Film Institute Mediatheque
British Library
British Newspaper Archive
BUDDS (formerly Graham Budd Auctions)
Channel Four
ITV Sport

Against the Odds: An Autobiography – Bobby Robson & Bob Harris (Hutchinson, 1990)
Born to be a Footballer: My Autobiography – Liam Brady (Eriu, 2023)
El Diego: The Autobiography – Diego Maradona (Vintage Publishing, 2005)
El Partido – Andrès Burgo (Tusquets Editores, 2016)
First Among Unequals – Viv Anderson (Fullback Media Ltd, 2010)
In the Eye of the Whistle: The Refereeing at the 1986 World Cup – David J Ross (Onereal, 1988)
Kerry : The Autobiography – Kerry Dixon (Queen Anne Press, 1986)
Lineker: Golden Boot – Rob Hughes (Collins Willow, 1987)
Love Affairs and Marriage: My Life in Football – Howard Kendall (De Coubertin Books, 2013)
Mexico On Fifty Dollars a Ticket – Mick Worrall (Tyneside Free Press, 1986)
Motty: Forty Years in the Commentary Box – John Motson (Virgin Books, 2010)
Ossie's Dream – Osvaldo Ardiles (Corgi Books, 2009)
Peter Shilton: The Autobiography – Peter Shilton (Orion, 2004)

Playmaker: My Life and the Love of Football – Glenn Hoddle (Harper Collins, 2021)

Robbo: My Autobiography – Bryan Robson (Hodder & Stoughton Ltd, 2006)

So Near and Yet So Far: Bobby Robson's World Cup Diary (Collins Willow, 1986)

Spurred to Success – Glenn Hoddle with Harry Harris (Queen Anne Press, 1987)

The Man with Maradona's Shirt – Steve Hodge (Orion, 2010)

The Match – The Story of Italy v Brazil 1982 – Piero Trellini (Pitch Publishing, 2023)

The Story of the World Cup – Brian Glanville (Faber & Faber, 1993)

Three Lions on a Shirt: The Official History of the England Football Jersey – Simon Shakeshaft (Vision Sports Publishing, 2002)

To Cap it All – Kenny Sansom (John Blake Publishing Ltd, 2008)

Top Mark! An Autobiography – Mark Hateley and Ken Gallacher (Mainstream Publishing, 1993)

Touched By God: How We Won the Mexico '86 World Cup – Diego Maradona and Daniel Arcucci (Penguin Random House, 2016)